The Kavieng Massacre

The Kavieng Massacre

A War Crime Revealed

Raden Dunbar

First published in 2007 by
Sally Milner Publishing Pty Ltd
734 Woodville Road
Binda NSW 2583
AUSTRALIA

© Raden Dunbar 2007

Design and typesetting by Simon Paterson, Bookhouse, Sydney
Editing: Anne Savage
Printed in China

National Library of Australia
Cataloguing-in-Publication data:

Dunbar, Raden.
    The Kavieng massacre : a war crime revealed.

    Bibliography.
    Includes index.
    ISBN 978 1 8635 1368 5.

    1. World War, 1939-1945 - Atrocities - Papua New Guinea -
    New Ireland Island. 2. Massacres - Papua New Guinea - New
    Ireland Island. 3. New Ireland Island (Papua New Guinea) -
    History. I. Title.

940.5405

All rights reserved. No part of this publication may be reproduced, stored in a retrieval system, or transmitted in any form or by any means, electronic, mechanical, photocopying, recording or otherwise, without prior permission of the copyright owners and publishers.

10 9 8 7 6 5 4 3 2 1

Contents

Introduction and acknowledgements   vii
Prologue   xi

PART I: THE SETTING, THE BACKGROUND AND THE CRIME

1   Kavieng, December 1941: a rather wonderful tropical paradise   3
2   The future is bright   13
3   Not a place for anyone to be moving to   23
4   The raids were executed with violence and precision   29
5   Escape   34
6   Into captivity   47
7   The Kavieng internment camps   59
8   The American offensive   66
9   War returns to Kavieng, February 1944   71
10   Captain Tamura's instruction   77
11   A change of plan: the great bombardment of Kavieng, 20 March 1944   83
12   'Kill the Europeans!'   97
13   The vision of Hell   102

PART II: THE CONCEALMENT

14   The fabulous lie   111

PART III: THE CRIME REVEALED

15	A very difficult investigation	125
16	I am a naval officer and will speak the truth!	132
17	A neat, diminutive, wiry young man of unusual intelligence and curiosity	143
18	I am indeed sorry to have to inform you…	154
19	Extremely unlikely that Europeans would have been on the ship	161
20	For official purposes his death has been presumed	174
21	We know you did it! How did you do it?	182
22	The prisoners of Sugamo	192
23	The trial	204
24	Punishments to fit the crime	218
25	And then what happened?	227

Appendix A: Lists of the Kavieng victims — 240

1. List compiled from Australian sources
2. Commonwealth War Graves Commission list

Appendix B: The civilian and missionary victims of the sinking of the *Montevideo Maru* — 253

1. New Guinea Civilians Previously Reported Missing Now Reported Lost at Sea
2. New Guinea Missionaries Previously Reported Missing Now Reported Lost at Sea

Endnotes	263
Abbreviations	285
References	286
Index	292

Introduction and acknowledgements

This is the first attempt in over sixty years to produce a comprehensive and historically accurate reconstruction of events surrounding the 1944 murder by Japanese sailors of a large group of Australian male civilians and German Catholic priests at Kavieng, on New Ireland in the then Australian-mandated territory of New Guinea. It has involved painstakingly bringing together many hundreds of pieces of fragmentary evidence from a variety of original and secondary source materials, and has taken much time and effort to develop into a form which narrates the correct details and sequence of long-ago events in Australia, New Guinea, Japan and Hong Kong. There were many important gaps in the official records; and original archival and other material often turned out to be incorrect, sometimes raising more questions than providing answers. Many of the people who could possibly have provided the answers turned out to be already deceased, or un-contactable.

This endeavour started in 1994 as a search to discover the true fate of my maternal uncle, J.K.V. Griffin, who was a planter employed by Burns Philp & Co. Ltd. on New Ireland at the time of the Japanese invasion in January 1942. Over the years the scope inevitably broadened to include many of the stories of the key actors in this tragedy, at least as many as I could gather information about within the constraints I faced. Detailed background information about some of these people, especially the seven German priests, turned out to be especially difficult to obtain and, in the end, I reached dead ends in my enquiries. I am truly sorry that this has been the case for some of the victims.

For help given to me over so many years to overcome the many obstacles to developing this story I would particularly like to thank four people. Firstly my maternal aunt, Ruth Griffin, for leaving to me so many of the original family documentary records about J.K.V. Griffin following her death in 1993.

I would like to thank the Australian military historian and author Tom Hall, who has worked indefatigably to unearth the truth about Australian servicemen and civilians who disappeared during the Pacific war, and who in 1994 set me on the right path with my enquiries.

Considerable assistance was provided by Albert Klestadt, the persistent Australian Army war crimes investigator in Tokyo in 1946 and 1947, whom I first had the pleasure of meeting in Melbourne in 2000 following my surprise discovery that he was still alive and well, nearly sixty years after the events he was so closely associated with. Despite his advanced age, Albert remained a supporter and adviser until beset by serious illness in 2005, followed by his death in Melbourne at 92 on Good Friday, 14 April 2006. His 1959 book *The Sea Was Kind*, which describes his 1942 escape to Australia from the Japanese-held Philippines, is still considered a classic account of a long and dangerous open-water voyage by small sailing craft.

I would especially like to thank Jim Ridges, a local historian residing in Kavieng, to whom I was introduced by Margaret Reeson in 2000. He freely provided me with a large amount of valuable information, and made numerous corrections to geographical and historical details in draft manuscripts. Jim has singularly kept alive the memory of people of all races who disappeared in the eastern islands of New Guinea between 1942 and 1945, and was the person behind the memorial plaque and roll of honour unveiled in Kavieng in July 2002 to commemorate civilians from New Ireland who died during those years of Japanese occupation.

Many other people have assisted in developing this story, so many it has been like a large team effort, although few members of the team have known of each other until now. I had the good fortune to meet in Brisbane with Moya Carter, daughter of the Kavieng victim Claude Chadderton, and her daughters Kate and Claudia. These fine ladies provided valuable information, images, and support. With help again from Margaret Reeson, I was able to talk with and obtain crucial information from Gwen Diercke, the widow of Vivian Ives, another of the victims of Kavieng.

My cousin Geraldine Condron generously provided various images relating to J.K.V. Griffin from her private collection. Margaret Reeson, author of *A Very Long War*, and former Moderator of the Uniting Church in Australia in NSW, gave valuable assistance to my attempts to track down families of the Kavieng victims and other people.

A number of professional archivists have provided help over the years. In particular I would like to thank Andrew Griffin (no immediate relative of J.K.V. Griffin) of the National Archives of Australia in Melbourne; staff of the National Archives of Australia in Canberra; Julie Gleaves, archivist for the Westpac Banking Corporation in Sydney; Joan Humphries, archivist for Burns Philp and Co. Ltd. in Sydney; and especially the staff of the Australian War Memorial Research Section and Photographic Records Section in Canberra. I also acknowledge help received from staff of the Commonwealth War Graves Commission in London.

I would like to thank Craig Smith, my colleague in Washington, DC, for helping obtain good images from the US Naval Historical Center. I also thank Tieke Brown of the National Library of Australia for helping locate important original NLA texts and journals, and Robin Brown for conducting research on my behalf at the NLA.

I would like to also acknowledge the panel of readers who reviewed the first working draft of the manuscript in 2005 and provided useful feedback and insight. These include Beth Pearce, Lynne King, Geraldine Condron and Tony Osman in Australia; Paul Brown, Michael Holliday and Wayne Bougas in Jakarta; and Jeff Bost in Port Moresby.

I wish to extend my apologies for any inadvertent errors or omissions in the text, particularly to families of the victims of Kavieng whom I was unable to locate despite my considerable efforts; and to families of the Japanese naval officers and men mentioned in the story but un-contactable by me, many of whom indirectly became victims of Kavieng as well.

I wish to acknowledge the unequivocal support given to this project by Ian Webster, Libby Renney and Penny Doust of Sally Milner Publishing, copy editor Anne Savage and designer Anna Warren, who had the unenviable task of carrying the book through production. I trust that the product will honour all their hard work and care.

Finally, I would like to acknowledge those authors and researchers who, through their published works, inspired me to persevere with this project. Their names appear in the References section, and include the Australian historians Sir Paul Hasluck, Professor Joan Beaumont, Lynette Ramsay Silver and Margaret Reeson; the Australian ex-POW, artist and author Ray Parkin; the American historians John Dower and Edwin Hoyt; and many Japanese authors, particularly Shohei Ooka and Michio Takeyama.

The story of the terrible tragedy of Kavieng describes how a group of entirely innocent Australian and other civilians became the helpless victims of the grand wartime political and military strategies of American, Australian and Japanese politicians, generals and admirals. Those strategies and the hubris, secret deceptions and cover-ups which characterised them, were of no use at all to the Kavieng victims. I hope the story makes a useful contribution to our understanding of how these things can happen, and perhaps help in a cautionary way to prevent similar events from occurring in the future.

Raden Dunbar
Bandung, Indonesia
January 2007

Note on spelling of Japanese names

In original source materials used for preparing the manuscript the names of Japanese navy and army personnel are sometimes spelled inconsistently. Every attempt has been made to obtain the correct spellings and use them consistently.

Prologue

'Such things do not constitute a good reason for raking over the dead ashes of the past.'

For Australia in the middle of 1946 the Pacific war had been over for almost a year and the Federal Government was facing an imminent election, the first of the postwar era. Benjamin Chifley, the Prime Minister of Australia and leader of the governing Labor Party, hoped to stand for re-election on Labor's successful wartime record. After all, it was popularly believed that Labor had won the war for Australia under the leadership of Chifley's famous predecessor John Curtin, who had died in office near war's end, exhausted from selfless effort leading Australia to victory.

It was also popularly believed that the federal Opposition, the United Australia Party led by Robert Menzies and its minor partner the Country Party, had been responsible for numerous diplomatic and military disasters before and during the Second World War. When war had broken out in Europe in 1939, the Anglophile Menzies was Prime Minister and had quickly despatched considerable Australian military assistance for Great Britain, to operations in faraway North Africa, Greece, Crete and the Middle East. Menzies had been widely blamed by the Australian Labor Party for the military losses that followed, the deaths, injury and imprisonment of thousands of Australian servicemen. By August 1941 the UAP and Country Party alliance had been destabilised by the criticism, Menzies lost the prime ministership, and in October 1941 the UAP and Country Party surrendered government to the Labor Party led by John Curtin.

From 1941 on, the Labor Party would never allow the Australian public to forget that Menzies and the conservatives had been responsible for mishandling Australia's security. Every opportunity would be taken by Labor to press this point, leading to the 'Brisbane Line' controversy in 1942 and 1943 which delivered a massive political blow to the Opposition. In a campaign led by the controversial Sydney politician and government minister Eddie Ward[1], Labor claimed it had discovered that Menzies, at the outset of the war, had secret plans drawn up to abandon much of northern Australia in the event of an invasion of continental Australia.[2] This completely unfounded accusation, made entirely for scaremongering political expediency, stuck firmly in the minds of Australians and became a myth so powerful it helped keep Menzies out of office for eight years.

But shortly after assuming power in October 1941 and taking over responsibility for Australia's war effort, John Curtin's Labor government would face its own set of military disasters, much closer to home. Following the start of Japan's Pacific war in December 1941, during the early months of 1942 the Japanese quickly overran every area in South-East Asia and the Pacific supposedly defended by Australian forces, in particular the Mandated Territory of New Guinea, which had been under Australian control for twenty years and was home to thousands of Australians. The Japanese thrust southwards into New Guinea was a catastrophe for these Australians, and would turn out to be the only time during the war that Australian territory was actually occupied by an enemy, with substantial loss of Australian lives and property. When after war's end in August 1945 the extent of those losses began to be publicly revealed, Ben Chifley's government faced a potential political embarrassment which could easily damage Labor's carefully managed image as Australia's wartime saviour.

Wounded for so long by the Brisbane Line accusation, from 1945 the Opposition United Australia and Country Parties, once again under the leadership of Robert Menzies, began quietly accumulating evidence of Labor's wartime failures. This effort was led by a NSW Country Party politician, H.L. Anthony[3], who had been conducting detailed research, all with eager assistance from New Guinea community organisations and ex-servicemen's groups representing the victims, groups which had long been clamouring for the truth to come out. The political purpose of this Opposition effort was to produce solid evidence of Labor's own failures to safeguard Australian lives and property, evidence which could support demands for a formal parliamentary enquiry. It was intended that this enquiry would not just be limited to what had happened in New Guinea, but that it would also cover the Brisbane Line issue and any other accusations made by Labor against the earlier Menzies' wartime government.

Now in mid-1946, with a federal election approaching which had to be held by September, and after months of heated parliamentary exchanges in Canberra between Government and Opposition, the sensitive issue of a parliamentary enquiry into wartime failures erupted in the House of Representatives. On the night of Thursday 27 June 1946, and in the middle of an otherwise innocuous parliamentary debate over budget appropriations, a few inappropriate remarks by Eddie Ward caused emotions to finally and completely boil over. Hours of accusation and counter-accusation followed well into the night, with the Opposition repeatedly demanding an enquiry and the Government steadfastly refusing to bow to the pressure. At one o'clock in the early morning of Friday 28 June they were still at it, with all key actors including the Prime Minister and Leader of the Opposition still present in the House, and Eddie Ward still trading insults, particularly over his Brisbane Line accusations.

At ten minutes past one the Prime Minister, Ben Chifley, rose to speak. The very last thing he wanted to have at this point was an enquiry, particularly one which might dwell heavily on what had happened between 1942 and 1945 when the Japanese had invaded and occupied Australian territory in New Guinea, all during the wartime watch of the Australian Labor Party. He had had a number of hours to prepare for this moment, and his speech as recorded in *Hansard* was a masterful performance:

> CHIFLEY: Some of the remarks that have been made in this chamber today are not to the credit of the Parliament. I have listened to some of the statements made during this and previous debates and, in my opinion, they do not reflect credit on the Opposition.
> INTERJECTION FROM THE OPPOSITION: Or on the Government!
> CHIFLEY: At times, each of us may have offended in some way, but I have always tried to treat the Parliament, which is the instrument of democracy, with respect. I certainly thought that an appropriation bill would not have led to the demonstrations that have occurred in this chamber tonight. Although I greatly deplore what has taken place, I

wish to make it clear that I see no purpose in raking over the dead ashes of the past. That opinion is held by men occupying higher positions in the world than I hold. If I could be shown that men have been guilty of corruption, dishonesty, or treason, I could understand a request for enquiries to be made. I do not impute those crimes to any member of a previous government or of the present Government, or to any of the military leaders of this country. Some of them might have been guilty of stupidity, or a lack of foresight, but in my opinion such things do not constitute a good reason for raking over the dead ashes of the past. If the British Empire were to do that, it would want to know all about what happened at Dunkirk, Malaya, the Middle East and elsewhere. There would be endless enquiries into the actions of all sorts of people, many of whom have rendered honourable service, and their names would be besmirched because of the actions made against them. I do not propose to be party to any enquiry into what might only have been military mistakes. The Government will not support any motion for such inquiries because there could be no end to the things that might be inquired into. The British Empire and its allies suffered many disasters in the war in which they were recently engaged, and endless enquiries could be instituted to find out what really happened. I do not believe that any of those mistakes were due to treason or corruption, although probably there were instances of lack of capacity, and of failures to realize the potentialities of the war position. After all, human beings are fallible. I shall not order a survey of what has happened in the past, or be a party to the making of charges against people who, although they made mistakes believed at the time that they acted for the best. So far as I am concerned, there will be no inquiry at all.[4]

In the two parliamentary divisions that immediately followed, the Opposition demand for an enquiry was defeated along party lines. Alone in the Labor Party, Eddie Ward as Minister for Transport and Minister for External Territories had to the end pretended to demand an enquiry, but when it came to the vote he twice sided with the Government to defeat the proposition. The matter now finally laid to rest, at 1.36 am parliamentary debate about the matter ceased forever and the House adjourned.[5]

What sort of wartime events was Ben Chifley so concerned about raking over? Going into an imminent election, which he won, what was

Prologue

so embarrassing about events in New Guinea between 1942 and 1945 that they had to be concealed?

This book does rake over some of the ashes of World War II in New Guinea, and attempts to explain what happened to a group of 25 Australian expatriate men and seven German priests who found themselves interned by the Japanese at Kavieng, on New Ireland in New Guinea, in September 1942 and who subsequently disappeared without trace. In January 1942 Kavieng had been the first Australian territory to have ever been siezed and occupied by a hostile invader. At the time Ben Chifley rose to speak in the Australian Parliament in June 1946, a wide-ranging and largely secret enquiry by the Department of External Territories and the Australian army into the fate of these missing civilians had been underway since August 1945. Presumably Eddie Ward, as Minister for External Territories for much of the Pacific war and subsequently, would have known all about this enquiry.

But even after the Australian government had completely resolved and settled the mystery of Kavieng by March 1948, still during the life of the Chifley government, only the barest details would ever be released to the Australian public, or even to the families of the men who had disappeared.

PART I
The setting, the background, and the crime

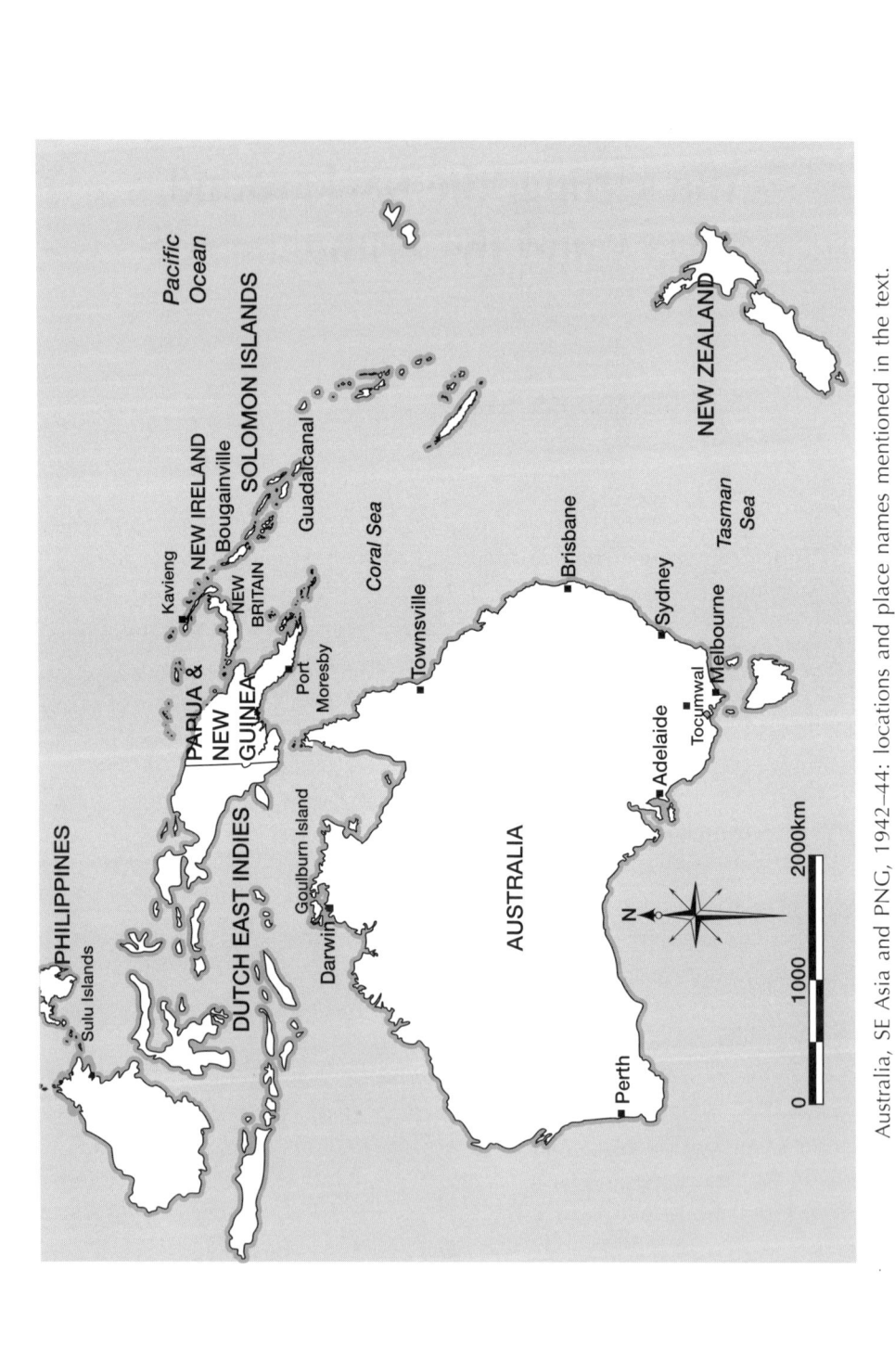

Australia, SE Asia and PNG, 1942–44: locations and place names mentioned in the text.

chapter 1

Kavieng, December 1941: a rather wonderful tropical paradise

The tropical South Pacific setting for this story is the small, obscure, and spectacularly beautiful harbour township of Kavieng located at the extreme northern tip of the four hundred kilometres long, narrow mountainous island called New Ireland, first sighted and named by English mariners during the great era of Pacific exploration in the eighteenth century.[1] The first Englishman to arrive in these waters, in 1700, was the British buccaneer and explorer William Dampier on his famous voyage through the south seas in the battered British admiralty barque HMS *Roebuck*. Dampier sailed around what was to be later called New Ireland and its neighbour New Britain, and assuming they were a continuous island, named the whole New Britain. Apart from his legendary career as a pirate, navigator, and explorer, Dampier had a gift for writing, and the published journals of his voyages in the South Seas were wildly popular in England, inspiring Daniel Defoe to invent the wonderful stories of Robinson Crusoe. Dampier's long-ago presence in the waters of eastern New Guinea is permanently memorialised in the Dampier Strait, immediately to the west of New Britain.

In 1767 the next British explorer arrived on the scene and, upon closer investigation, was able to determine that Dampier's New Britain was in fact two separate, large islands. Commander Phillip Carteret was attempting an east-to-west circumnavigation of the globe in the very slow and poor-handling HMS *Swallow*, having left England in August 1766 and finally entering the Pacific through the Magellan Straits at the tip of South America in April 1767. Four months later Carteret arrived at New Britain and in September 1767 discovered the wide channel immediately to the east of modern-day New Britain, which Dampier had thought was a gulf. Carteret named it St George's Channel after the waterway between Britain and Ireland, and then named and claimed all of New Ireland for the English crown. *Swallow* then headed for home, finally returning to England in March 1769 via Makassar and Batavia in the Dutch East Indies, Table Bay at the tip of South Africa, and Ascension Island in the mid-Atlantic. This had been one of the slowest circumnavigations ever undertaken, but among many achievements Carteret had been able to correctly identify New Britain and New Ireland as separate entities.[2]

New Ireland is aligned roughly north-west to south-east, and lies adjacent to and to the north of the much larger island of New Britain. Together in the tropical South-west Pacific, New Ireland and New Britain and their outlying islands form the bulk of the Bismarck Archipelago, and together with the smaller Admiralty Islands in the north encompass the Bismarck Sea. Further to the west lies the much bigger island usually called Papua[3], immediately to the north of the vast island-continent of Australia. New Ireland and New Britain are in the Pacific 'Ring of Fire', prone to occasional large volcanic eruptions and earthquakes.

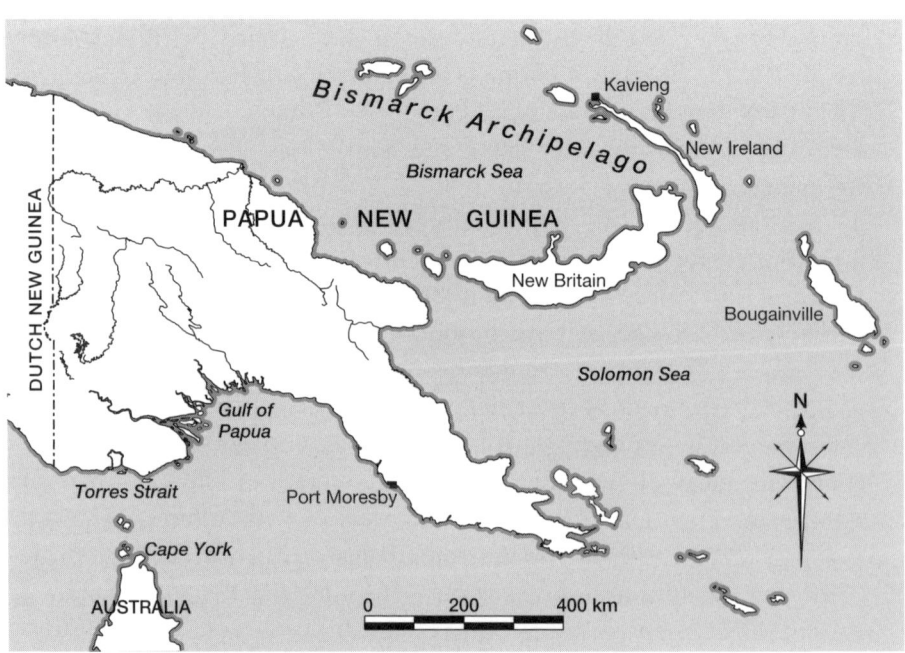

Papua and New Guinea, including New Ireland and New Britain

Before the Pacific war of 1941–45, the islands of the Bismarck Archipelago and the large north-eastern section of the island of Papua formed the Australian-administered Mandated Territory of New Guinea. In 1941 the administrative and commercial centre of New Guinea was the large harbour town of Rabaul, sited at the northernmost tip of New Britain. The smaller south-eastern section of the island of Papua formed the Territory of Papua, under separate Australian administration since 1906, with Port Moresby serving as its commercial and administrative centre. In 1941 the entire western half of Papua was under Dutch control and administratively part of the then Dutch East Indies.

Originally annexed by the German Empire in 1884, in 1921 the territory of New Guinea had been formally mandated to Australian care by the League of Nations as one condition of the larger post-World War I political settlement negotiated in May and June 1919 at Versailles in Paris. This international treaty divided the old German colonial empire among the victorious allies, and its onerous conditions had been imposed upon Germany as the price for having been defeated in that terrible conflict between 1914 and 1918. Perhaps anticipating this, long before the Treaty of Versailles was negotiated Australia had in fact already assumed de facto control of New Guinea. In 1914, following the outbreak of war in Europe, an Australian Naval and Military Expeditionary Force had been sent to sieze the territory from Germany and occupy it for the duration of hostilities.

For the twenty years from 1921 to the outbreak of the Pacific war in December 1941 general administration of the two vast and undeveloped territories of Papua and New Guinea was conducted from Canberra by a small and relatively unimportant bureaucracy, the Department of External Territories, under the political control of a Minister for External Territories who was an elected Member of the Commonwealth Parliament. Detailed administration in the islands was conducted by a network of government administrative officials, magistrates, policemen, patrol officers, medical workers, and educators. Although the citizens, extensive lands, economy, and laws of Papua and of New Guinea were effectively parts of Australia, the distant territories had only marginal significance for most Australians, and were of little interest to them.

Since 1921 thousands of Australians had settled in Papua and New Guinea to administer the law, conduct missionary and education activities among the indigenous people, and establish businesses, especially mines and plantations. Many of the new Australian settlers were encouraged

The Kavieng Massacre

A typical neatly kept pre-war copra plantation on New Ireland. AUSTRALIAN WAR MEMORIAL NEGATIVE NUMBER AWM P00001.395

The Australian Plenipotentiaries at the Peace Conference at Versailles, Paris, in 1919. At this conference W.M. Hughes, Prime Minister of Australia (seated centre front), managed to secure the Territory of New Guinea for Australia, against the wishes of Japan and the United States. AUSTRALIAN WAR MEMORIAL NEGATIVE NUMBER AWM A02615 to purchase expropriated German property for agricultural enterprises, usually coconut plantations for production of copra, then an important industrial raw material used for making coconut oil, a basic ingredient of soap, detergent, shampoo, margarine, candle wax, and industrial chemicals and explosives.

On New Ireland, Kavieng became a settlement for Europeans because of its perfect all-weather deepwater harbour, in an era when steamships were still the most common form of transport for passengers and cargo. Protected by a string of small islands in the Steffen Straits, a narrow stretch of sea separating the mainland from the outlying New Hanover Island, Kavieng harbour was capable of berthing very large vessels and by 1941 was a busy little seaport with four wharves and regularly scheduled passenger and cargo services. With the advent of air transport during the 1930s Kavieng also offered a safe harbour for seaplanes, and with an adjacent expanse of 10 kilometres of flat, open country to the south-east of the town, a perfect location for the construction of airfields. The first airfield had been developed by the territories administration just 500 metres to the east of Kavieng town in 1940 and 1941.

In 1941 about 50 000 indigenous Melanesians and persons of mixed race populated New Ireland. For over half a century they had come under the influence of first German, and then Australian settlers, and in the colonial spirit of the times most had been 'civilised' under the rule of European law. Many had received basic European education, and many had been converted to Christianity by missionaries of the Catholic and Methodist faiths. As they had done for centuries the Melanesians lived an idyllic life, in balance with nature and surrounded by an abundance of the natural resources on which their comparatively easy lives depended. Although some had become regularly employed in the labour-intensive copra industry as copra cutters and plantation labourers, most, to the despair of their colonial masters and the missionaries, shunned 'regular work'.

The indigenous and mixed race population on New Ireland was supplemented by about 200 Australian men, women, individuals and families. Most of these Australians were the owners, managers, and overseers of copra plantations, the 'planters' as they were known. Many of the planters were ex-soldiers of the First World War who had acquired expropriated German plantations and property during soldier-settler schemes organised by the Department of External Territories in the 1920s and 1930s. The Treaty of Versailles had caused the wholesale eviction of German planters and their families from New Guinea, and the Australian Prime Minister of the time, William Morris Hughes, had promised 'New Guinea for the returned serviceman'.[4] The ex-soldiers who became settlers were survivors of an especially brutal conflict, in which little Australia had lost 60 000 killed and 156 000 wounded, gassed or taken prisoner during campaigns in the Middle East, the Mediterranean and Europe. They had been collectively given the affectionate nickname 'diggers' because of their constant trench digging activities during a war which was largely fought at close range from earthworks and dugouts. In New Guinea adventurous ex-diggers were offered easy purchase terms when large numbers of expropriated German plantations were sold by the government after 1925[5], so scores had arrived with their families from all parts of Australia to take up the challenges of becoming copra producers.

A typical copra plantation covered a large area of between 200 and 500 acres.[6] Restoring an overgrown expropriated German copra plantation or clearing and planting a new plantation was back breaking work, only for determined and physically strong men to take on. The planters who succeeded were a tough breed, practical men who could survive and prosper in a difficult environment. Scores of their plantations were soon established along the coastal fringes of New Ireland and on smaller outlying islands, each usually having a large bungalow for the planter's family, copra storage and other sheds, an orchard and vegetable garden, and perhaps a small wharf. On the east coast they were linked by the only well-made road on the island; plantations on the west coast and other islands could only be easily reached by boat. In the 1920s and 1930s, world demand for copra steadily increased, and if prices were good a plantation could turn out to be a lucrative investment. It was entirely possible for enterprising planters to become wealthy and respected by the standards of the time, occupy the best positions in the social order, and generally enjoy a markedly superior standard of living. The government officials, copra traders, and other expatriate 'islanders' employed in the shipping, storage, supply, banking, and repair services in Kavieng, upon which the copra industry depended, also enjoyed similar high status.

The small Australian expatriate community of planters, traders, and administrators on New Ireland was close, and the families well known to each other. They had, in general, only comparatively recently forsaken their lives in faraway New South Wales, Victoria, and Queensland to

Kavieng, December 1941

A 1914 photograph of the waterfront at Kavieng, the year the Australian Naval and Military Expeditionary Force arrived to take control of New Ireland from Germany.
AUSTRALIAN WAR MEMORIAL NEGATIVE NUMBER AWM H15061

settle in this new, exotic place. They had readily taken to the islander way of life, balmy climate, spacious bungalow homes and domestic servants, and in Kavieng had surrounded themselves with all the comfortable attributes of a small and respectable Australian colony. There was the Kavieng Sports and Social Club, Tsang Tsang's pub; golf, tennis, cricket, fishing and sailing; church on Sundays; a well-attended branch of the Australian Returned Servicemens' League; and picnics on the nearby picture-postcard islands. The regular Burns Philp passenger ships, including the modern MV *Macdhui*, kept them in touch with Australia bringing mail, newspapers, supplies, and visitors from 'down south'. Despite the occasional downturns of the copra trade, and spells in the Kavieng hospital with exotic tropical diseases[7], life for the Australians was generally pleasant, fulfilling, and usually profitable, and by 1941 they thought of themselves as permanent residents of their own, rather wonderful tropical paradise.

Apart from the Australians there were other Europeans living on New Ireland and the surrounding islands. Some were adventurers from all over the world who had settled during the German era, married locally and started families. But most were unmarried, devout Christian missionaries of German extraction who had remained following the

Australian takeover of the territory after 1921. In 1941 dozens of these mainly elderly men and women lived and worked on New Ireland and the smaller adjacent islands. Mainly Catholic priests and nuns of the venerable Mission of the Sacred Heart, they proselytised among the native people from well-established mission stations and managed various useful social services including schools, hospitals, and a leprosarium.

Also long-established in Kavieng was an Overseas Chinese trading community of about one hundred people who had originally settled there with the arrival of the first Europeans in the late nineteenth century.[8] The Chinese lived in their own separate Chinatown in the northern section of the town, and Chinese merchants owned many of the businesses supplying the Melanesian population with consumer goods, and the Europeans with their entertainment. Outside Kavieng there were smaller Overseas Chinese settlements at other locations on New Ireland, particularly far to the south at Namatanai, the island's second largest port and township.

By 1941 commerce throughout Papua and New Guinea was dominated by two large Sydney-based trading companies, Burns Philp & Co. and W.R. Carpenter & Co., which after 1921 had rapidly developed as the principal shipping, trading, and agricultural enterprises in the territories. Both had branch offices and warehouses in Port Moresby, Rabaul and Kavieng, extensive copra plantation holdings, and regularly-timetabled shipping between these three major ports and the outlying islands.[9] In Kavieng the companies built large warehouses in the port area where the copra was accumulated to await shipment to overseas markets. From the time New Ireland had been a German possession the primary market for copra had been Europe, the product shipped there by cargo steamers as quickly as it was produced. One of these steamers was the German *Bremerhaven*, owned by Norddeutscher Lloyd, which still maintained a regular schedule between ex-colony and motherland until the outbreak of war in Europe in 1939 curtailed its Pacific voyages, and also severely interrupted the copra trade. During 1939 and 1940 world copra prices took a tumble, and the copra warehouses at Kavieng became crammed with product awaiting shipment.

Until 1941 another regular visitor to Kavieng was the Japanese cargo and passenger vessel *Carolina Maru* which during the 1930s had added Kavieng to its regularly-scheduled circuit between Japan and the Japanese-controlled Caroline Islands[10], bringing consumer products to the local market and returning to Japan loaded with copra, timber, and trochus

Kavieng, December 1941

The road from Kavieng down the east coast to Namatanai, the only land link between the north and south of New Ireland at the outbreak of the Pacific war. AUSTRALIAN WAR MEMORIAL NEGATIVE NUMBER AWM H15073

shell. Commencing in 1941, and observed with suspicious interest by the Australian community, the *Carolina Maru* began making more frequent calls, now bringing almost no cargo but instead disembarking groups of what the Japanese referred to as 'student-tourists'. These young people freely roamed the highways and byways of the town photographing places of interest including harbour installations, prominent buildings, and particularly the new airfield.

During negotiations in Versailles in 1919 over the future ownership of New Guinea Japan had staked a strong claim to have the territory mandated to its control, a claim strongly backed by another major power, the United States. But Australia, perceived by Japan and the United States to be a very minor participant in the negotiations, had walked away with this prized possession. To put things right, long before 1941 Japan's military government in Tokyo had begun a meticulous secret survey of New Guinea and other areas of strategic interest and economic value throughout the European colonies in Asia and the Pacific ocean. Japan was rapidly emerging as a major industrial nation with a vast appetite for industrial raw materials and energy, which could not be satisfied from within its own borders. Using representatives of the big Japanese trading companies, local Japanese and helpful residents, ships crews and visiting Japanese 'tourists', very detailed military intelligence was developed about hundreds of places which could be invaded and introduced into Japan's secretly proposed colonial empire, the grandly-named Greater East Asia Co-Prosperity Sphere. When the time came this vast array of useful information would enable the invading Japanese armies to quickly overrun a large part of the earth's surface with minimal loss to themselves.

Until early 1942 Kavieng was a distant tropical outpost of Australia, a tiny town and port lying far from the main thoroughfares of trade and civilisation and comfortable in its unimportance and isolation. Unfortunately for its indigenous, European, and Chinese residents it had already been secretly selected by Japan to become a major military base, and the whole of New Guinea to become an important economic possession. Kavieng's beautiful deepwater harbour and the new airfield, so important to the town's prosperity in peacetime, would soon become its twin curses. For a few short years after January 1942 the fateful decision by the Japanese to occupy Kavieng would suddenly elevate it to become a prominent landmark, objective, and target in the intense military struggle which would soon play out.

From the point of view of the oncoming Japanese, control of New Ireland was part of a grand plan to create a perimeter of defended island bases across the Pacific enclosing the eastern part of their Co-Prosperity Sphere. As well as seizing Port Moresby and Rabaul by force, occupation of Kavieng for a naval and air base was to be an important step for Japanese dominance of Papua and New Guinea, especially New Britain, New Ireland, and the Admiralty and Solomon Islands. Strategically located at the junction of the Bismarck and Coral Seas and the Pacific Ocean, the little port offered excellent base and communications facilities for an invading force. The protected harbour was an ideal anchorage for naval vessels of almost any size and for the squadrons of naval float planes which would be extensively used for long-range reconnaissance and attacks on shipping. The flatlands surrounding the airfield could be developed as a network of airfields for land-based military aircraft. As the commercial center of the lucrative copra industry Kavieng also offered a fully-developed economic prize.

Never properly appreciated by Australia before 1941, the early seizure of this isolated town was a key step in overall Japanese strategy, and meticulous preparations for its conquest had already been made.

chapter 2

The future is bright

In December 1941, just at the time when Japan's secret military plans for the seizure of Kavieng were about to be revealed in spectacular fashion, big Jack Griffin became one of the Australian copra planters of New Ireland.

His long journey from a sheep station in outback Australia to a copra plantation on an island near Kavieng in New Guinea was full of twists and turns. But in all kinds of ways his story is typical of the stories of so many Australians who found success as expatriates in New Guinea before the Pacific war, who ended up, much to their pleasant surprise, discovering just how comfortable they could be doing something completely unexpected and adventurous with their lives. If the Australian expatriates in New Guinea before the war could have been, famously, categorised as either missionaries, mercenaries, or misfits, then Jack Griffin was an unusual young man who might not have quite fitted the mould of a conventional Australian, but who found that life in New Guinea fitted him perfectly.

'Little Jackie' was raised by Ethel and George Griffin as the youngest of a family of five children, far from the big cities in the Tocumwal area of the western Riverina district in southern New South Wales, where his father managed large sheep stations for the venerable F.B.S. Falkiner, owner of the fabled Haddon Rig Station and Tuppal Station merino studs, and the founder of a pastoral dynasty.[1]

George Griffin was originally employed by the Falkiner family as a book-keeper, rising to become station manager at Tuppal Station. In 1902 he married Ethel Barker, nineteen years his junior, daughter of an Irish-Anglican minister, and also employed by the Falkiners, as governess

George Griffin and his five young children, about 1913 or 1914. 'Little Jackie' is seated on his father's lap. Eldest son Gerald is standing, and eldest daughter Ruth is seated to George's right. Alison is seated on the ground, and Marjorie to the extreme right on the bench. George was about 53 when this shot was taken.

for all the children at Tuppal, which meant she was their teacher, nurse and nanny. In quick succession they had five children, Gerald, Ruth, Alison (nicknamed Pat), Marjorie and John, 'Little Jackie'. George and Ethel were hard-working practical people with strong beliefs and values drawn from the conservative ethics of Victorian England, true believers in God, King and Country. The children were imbued with their same strong values: the importance of God, family, industriousness, thrift, and persistence in the face of adversity.

Throughout his childhood and early teens Jack lived entirely on Tuppal Station, a vast 60 000 hectare sheep run on the plains between Tocumwal and Deniliquin, through which flowed the Tuppal Creek, a tributary of the mighty Murray River. Around the time of Jack's birth, about 200 000 sheep were being shorn each year in the great 72-stand shearing shed at Tuppal, producing over 3000 bales of wool, which was all painstakingly carried by barge down the Murray River to Adelaide and shipped off to the woollen mills of England by fast clipper.

Staffed by large numbers of overseers, stockmen, seasonal shearers, station hands, grooms, gardeners and household staff, Tuppal was a self-sufficient community producing its own meat, fruit, vegetables, poultry, milk and butter. Clustered around the big manager's homestead were numerous cottages, the shearer's quarters and farm buildings, so many the place was like a small village. Tuppal also employed an aging Chinese man to tend the vegetable gardens, a person so singularly out of place he was taken in by the Griffins as one of the family.

Like most isolated rural children at the time, Jack was tutored at home with his brothers and sisters by his parents, learning all the practical and useful things children learnt who were lucky to be reared and educated on remote sheep stations in outback Australia. From his mother he learnt arithmetic, reading and writing; and from his father and the farm workers how to raise vegetables and grow fruit; raise poultry and produce eggs; milk cows, rear animals and ride horses. He also learnt about nature and the seasons, and how to look after and entertain himself through expressing his abundance of creative talent, in an age when families created their own entertainment. Following his gifted mother Ethel and encouraged by her drawing, music and singing lessons, Jack became a talented pianist and skilled artist, watercolourist and print-maker. The big homestead at Tuppal Station was filled with music and art enthusiastically provided by Jack and his mother for the benefit of anyone who was interested.

More than anything else, Jack was a reader. He read anything he could obtain, and was lucky that his parents had collected a good library of books in the Tuppal homestead. The most popular boy's books in the early twentieth century were the fabulous adventure stories of the English and American writers Robert Louis Stevenson, Rudyard Kipling, Daniel Defoe, Jack London and Mark Twain, and the great science fiction writer H.G. Wells, and illustrated editions of their stories set Jack Griffin's imagination afire. He was particularly drawn to *Treasure Island* and *The Life and Adventures of Robinson Crusoe*, and the adventures they told of in faraway Pacific islands.[2]

But Jack was not a bookish recluse. He relished the vigorous, physical aspects of farm life and the vastness, freedom and adventure of the sheep station he was so lucky to be raised on. A strapping lad who grew to be over six feet tall, he became a resourceful bushman, hardened by years of upbringing in the outback. He knew how to kill and skin a sheep, make fences, cook a meal, erect buildings, mend windmills, and to fix cuts and burns and bruises without a doctor. Despite a leg injury incurred during his early youth he enjoyed physical exercise and regularly indulged in the recreations of that time in rural Australia, horseriding,

Magpies. Undated linocut by Jack Griffin.

Bookplate. Undated linocut by Jack Griffin.

tennis, fishing and swimming in the muddy rivers and billabongs. Tuppal Station was a place of learning, adventure and freedom for Jack, and his experiences there marked him for life.

But when he turned sixteen, things started to go wrong for him. Old George Griffin had decided that the teenager's future would be best taken care of if this young man of many talents was to work as, of all things, a bank clerk! Jack's two older sisters Marjorie and Alison were already working for banks, and their father had declared that bank work was a safe bet. By this time George had himself retired from sheep grazing and had bought a small farm at Rooty Hill on the far western outskirts of the big city of Sydney, with a plan to raise poultry for retirement income, with Jack as his part-time helper. In early 1927 George arranged for Jack to join the Bank of New South Wales at the nearby Penrith branch on probation as a junior clerk. F.B.S. Falkiner, also retired and now living at Bellevue Hill in Sydney, agreed to pull a few strings and to to act as Jack's guarantor. Now pushed into following his father's original vocation, Jack commenced learning the trade of book-keeping, at the lowest rung of a banker's career.[3]

He knew he was not ever really cut out for this, following the routine of a bank branch year in and year out, the cashbooks and the journals, for ever, even if he had a secure job in insecure times. His real interests lay elsewhere in art, literature, music, history, and satisfying his abundant curiosity about the wider world. As well, the older he grew the more rebellious he became towards his stuffy old parents. Slowly but surely he began to seek a way of becoming independent of Ethel and George, and escape from Rooty Hill.

So it was natural that when a series of opportunities presented for him to break away and do things completely new and adventurous he was more than ready to take them. In 1929, still a teenager, he transferred to the Bowral branch of the bank, far enough away in the highlands south of Sydney to remove him from Rooty Hill but still close enough for weekend visits if need be. In 1932 he took an even bigger step, moving back to the Riverina to take up a position in the Bank of NSW branch at the tiny township of Grong Grong, near the big town of Narrandera. Now back in the wide open spaces of his childhood and youth, he was to experience true independence for the first time in his life, and a yearning for even farther horizons. He also became heavily involved in the social life of the little town, particularly in amateur theatre and music where his skills as an artist and pianist flourished.

Staff of the Bank of NSW, Rabaul, mid-1930s. Jack Griffin is in there somewhere. All branch staff were male.

At about this time, Jack decided to become known as 'Peter' Griffin, at least to new friends outside the immediate family circle. Two possible reasons have come to light regarding this mildly eccentric name change, which was never legally formalised. In 1897 H.G. Wells had published the popular science fiction masterpiece *The Invisible Man*, a story about a mad scientist called John Griffin—'a younger student, almost an albino, six feet high, and broad, with a pink and white face and red eyes—who won the medal for chemistry'—who discovers how to make himself invisible, and commits various evil crimes while in that state. In 1933 the first Hollywood film version of the story was released, with Claude Rains playing 'Jack Griffin' in Universal Studios' production. The immense popularity of the film and notoriety of the name 'Jack Griffin' was probably too much for our Jack. But it may also have suited him at this time to symbolically break with the past and express his independence by encouraging others to call him Peter.

In 1935 an opportunity came for Jack to embark on a really serious adventure to faraway places with strange-sounding names, an adventure in the same league as a Robert Louis Stevenson story. This was a transfer far, far away to the Bank of NSW branch at Rabaul on the exotic island of New Britain in the eastern islands of the Australian Mandated

Bank of NSW staff bungalow at Rabaul, a typical New Guinea bungalow home of the 1930s.

Territory of New Guinea. After travelling by passenger steamer all the way from Sydney, he disembarked thousands of kilometres from outback Australia into a startlingly different world, a world so vivid and enchanting and mysterious he immediately became fascinated by it. He would see plenty of it in the first few years as he worked as a roving book-keeper and auditor for the bank's customers all over New Britain and New Ireland, travelling to isolated plantations in boats of all sizes, and on foot and horseback on wild and winding mountain tracks to mines and timber camps. If there was a job in banking made exactly to fit Jack's attributes and talents, this was it! Here in the tropical south-west Pacific, surrounded by new interests, Jack found his place in the world. His work and travels were satisfying, and he enjoyed a thriving social and sporting life in a community of like-minded adventurous Australians who had also been drawn to the challenges and pleasures of this little outpost of Australia. And no one seemed to care that Peter Griffin was in fact known as Jack to his family back in Australia. In fact, because of his height and impressive physical stature, he was now also to be given the ironic Australian nickname 'Tiny' by his new friends in the islands.

In December 1938 Jack wrote to his sister Alison in Sydney, and included in this letter are some requests for her to spend part of his bank balance to send newspapers, books, and materials for his latest craze, photography.

> What happened to the Herald's? I haven't received any for a long time. If you like, just take out the literary pages and send them along. Please send me 'In the steps of Moses the Conqueror' by Louis Golding, and 'The Windsor Tapestry' by Compton Mackenzie. If I send some negatives could you get them enlarged for me? This camera I have only takes small pictures and they are really intended for enlargement. I have some beauties now and if you find out about enlargements (from Kodak) I will send them down and you can have your pick.[4]

Jack also made some observations about his older brother, and his parents.

> Seems strange to hear of Gerald 'settling down' as they call it. Always strikes me as being remarkably dull, that kind of life. Like having eggs and bacon for breakfast every day of your life; still, I suppose they're happy in their own way. Mother and Father still progressing? Funny, I can't seem to raise a spark of filial affection these days—something radically wrong with my make-up. Perhaps it will come with time.

During his travels for the Bank of NSW at Rabaul, Jack Griffin was a regular visitor to New Ireland, and particularly to Kavieng town. He liked everything about Kavieng, and took a great interest in the goings-on there, being especially drawn to the Chinese. To Jack, who had first learnt about China from the family gardener at Tuppal Station, the Oriental Chinese were a truly exotic bunch. In a December 1938 letter to his sister Alison he wrote of his fascination for the 'smells, strange sounds and mysterious lights behind closed doors' of Chinatown in Kavieng. He described attending a fundraising concert for Chinese refugees from the Japanese war in China[5], and how:

> the Chinese just sat about at little tables and jabbered at each other, and not one of them took the slightest notice of anything on the stage. Of course, the concert was all in Chinese and we laughed at all the wrong moments too, I expect. The Kongs here are a very queer lot, just the coolie class but some of them are very wealthy. They blame England for the war in China…poor England, I'm afraid, has bigger burdens to bear nearer home.[6]

The future is bright

Two shots of Jack Griffin taken by Sydney's ubiquitous street photographers, probably around 1939–40.

In 1939, after four years auditing the books of plantations, farm and mines for the bank, another opportunity came his way. A local customer of the bank, a large company with which he had worked closely, offered him employment. The new position was with the Australian shipping, trading and plantation company Burns Philp & Co., which by 1939 had acquired scores of plantations located across the length and breadth of New Guinea, many purchased from the original soldier-settler owners. Faced with the problem of managing so many businesses scattered over such a big area, the company needed trustworthy and loyal field supervisors who were prepared to spend long periods away from home, visiting company properties to ensure that everything was being carried out properly and profitably. Apart from being a travelling auditor Jack was also given a promise that he could commence actual plantation work, initially as a part-time overseer on a copra plantation near Rabaul.

In October 1939, at the age of 29, he left the bank and commenced this new job, one even more suited to his temperament and background.[7]

Soon afterwards he moved into a new home at Burns Philp's Wat Wat Plantation in the mountains above Kokopo, on the other side of Blanche Bay and about 20 kilometres from Rabaul. Writing in March 1940 to Alison he described his surroundings. 'At last I'm in my own home about three miles from the sea and about 1,000 feet up—imagine the view—the house is right on the edge of a steep cliff about 300 feet—quite an ideal place to get rid of bottles and bodies etc.' He had with him his art books, a much-used German camera, literature, drawing and painting materials, a piano and, for company, a German Shepherd dog imported from Australia.

> I'm with BP's and providing everything goes according to schedule the future is bright. I talked this job over with the BP's head here and as soon as I get practical plantation experience am in the running for the local plantation Auditors job. Thanks for fixing everything up for me about the dog. It is an Alsatian and he was 2 months arriving and had a very rough spin on the way—doubt if he will ever be much of a dog.
>
> Please send a pair of sun glasses, Crookes lenses and strong frames. Also a pair of military working boots size 11—medium weight—sewn soles, wide toes and brass nails (so won't rust). Also a good cookery book. Please let me know how much everything is.
>
> Jack[8]

By late 1941, just before the outbreak of the Pacific war, Jack had worked for Burns Philp all over the islands of eastern New Guinea. He had rapidly risen to become Assistant Plantation Inspector of all Burns Philp plantations on New Britain and New Ireland, and was regarded as an experienced, trustworthy employee. Peter 'Tiny' Griffin had become well known to the islanders, especially among the Burns Philp community as he moved around from company plantation to plantation, often walking great distances and almost always accompanied on these long walks by his amiable German Shepherd. He was to stay at practically every company plantation while he conducted audits and inspections, and was always a welcome guest.[9] Content and fulfilled, he felt quite sure that his future with the company, and in his new life, was as bright as it could possibly be.

chapter 3

Not a place for anyone to be moving to

The Australian government had long contemplated a possible threat by Japan to its Mandated Territories of New Guinea but when threat suddenly became reality in late 1941 it was caught under-prepared for the alarming developments on its doorstep. From 1939 to 1941 Australia had been militarily preoccupied with assisting Great Britain in the distant war with Germany and Italy in Europe, the Mediterranean and North Africa, and had gone to great lengths to render assistance to the 'Mother Country'. As well, although concerned about the brutal war the Japanese had started in China in 1937, Australia was seriously influenced in its thinking about Japan by the apparent over-confidence of its two great allies, Britain and the United States. These were the two powers upon whom Australia would be almost completely dependent for protection if Japan became a direct threat. They were the only major allies with substantial military assets in the region, and from them Australia repeatedly sought reassurance. Unfortunately for Australia, the quite fallacious estimates of US and British planners was that Japanese forces could not possibly match their combined military might if it came to a fight in the Asia-Pacific area, and that any warlike actions by Japan would be quickly checked by the large British garrisons in India, Singapore and Malaya, and by American forces in the Philippines and particularly from the large US navy and army bases in Hawaii.[1]

Lulled into an uneasy sense of security, development of serious contingency measures by the Australian government for protection of its northernmost territory in New Guinea proceeded only tentatively. In mid-September 1939, just as war was breaking out in Europe, a local civilian militia force called the New Guinea Volunteer Rifles had been formed in Port Moresby, with companies and platoons also located at Rabaul and Kokopo on New Britain. An NGVR Rifle Platoon was also planned for Kavieng but was never raised, although some years earlier enthusiastic local officials and planters had formed their own little unit, the Kavieng Volunteer Rifles, the members mainly being ex-World War I diggers and their sons. Throughout 1941, as signs of possible hostilities with Japan became clearer, plans were laid in Canberra for possible evacuation of Australian citizens, and some military units were sent to the territory as a precaution. For protection of key airfields and ports in the eastern islands the Australian army deployed in mid-1941 the 1000 men of 2/22 Infantry Battalion to Rabaul (called 'Lark Force'); some 250 commandos of 1 Independent Company to New Ireland, Bougainville[2], the Admiralty Islands and the Solomon Islands; and minor elements of the Royal Australian Air Force to New Britain.

Then suddenly, far away across the Pacific on 8 December 1941, Japanese bombers from aircraft carriers of Vice-Admiral Chuichi Nagumo's First Air Fleet, led by Air Group Commander Mitsuo Fuchida, attacked the great US naval base at Pearl Harbor in Hawaii. This attack was immediately followed by furious Japanese military activity in Asia and the south Pacific. The militarist and ultranationalist government of Japan, backed by the Emperor Hirohito and led by General Hideki Tojo, had launched their long-planned campaign of colonial expansion. Having earlier hijacked the political institutions of Japan, and then overrun parts of East Asia in the 1930s, this stridently racist government now intended to eject the Europeans, Americans and Australians in the Asia-Pacific area, and take over their colonies and economic resources. The catastrophes about to explode would see a vast area of the earth's surface rapidly overrun by the Imperial Japanese Army and Imperial Japanese Navy.

When in December 1941 war with Japan suddenly came, Australia, like its great allies, was surprised by the force and unexpected speed of the Japanese advance. With the vast bulk of the Australian army, navy and air force still helping Britain in North Africa, as things turned out Australia was unable to immediately protect its territories and citizens in most of New Guinea. The government belatedly attempted rushed evacuations from islands most exposed to danger, and quickly mobilised what were soon to be exposed as the entirely insufficient military resources deployed. In Canberra the hope was that British and

The Kavieng Volunteer Rifles on parade, Anzac Day at Kavieng, 1935. The men are, from left to right: Dusty Miller, Claude Chadderton (rear), Alf Lussick, Ernest Stanfield, unidentified; in command at front, Jerry MacDonald; unidentified, Frank Saunders, and extreme right in the front row, Harry Murray.

US forces would hasten to the rescue and rout the supposedly inferior Japanese forces. In an atmosphere of great alarm and with very little time apparently available, not everyone could be moved from danger, especially from New Britain and New Ireland. Evacuation plans were only for removal to safety of European women and children, not for Australian men. This deliberately discriminatory policy was rigorously applied by the local officials charged with organising the evacuations, and, at least initially, was strongly supported by many of the Australian expatriate men. Not knowing they would shortly be facing a massive Japanese invasion force, on New Ireland the planters and ex-diggers of the Kavieng Volunteer Rifles believed they had a special personal duty to remain and protect their homes and livelihoods. And if the worst possible thing happened and they simply had to leave, the men felt sure they would be plucked to safety by ships and aircraft sent by a protective and concerned Australian government.

Jack Griffin was also about to become entangled in this time of calamity but, just before all the disasters unfolded, and having been rejected for enlistment in the Australian army on medical grounds because of his old injury, he was offered a new position within the company by Burns Philp, the opportunity to manage a plantation. It was the chance he had been looking for, and he talked about it in another letter to Alison.

Dear Pat,

Have just returned from a three weeks trip out to Witu Islands, about a day's steamer from Rabaul doing a plantation audit. That job I wrote to you about has at last come to light, and most interesting it is too. I expect to be leaving next week for another jaunt, and when I return from that will be leaving again almost at once for a three months trip. I have given up all thoughts of going to join up (at present at least); the medicals here won't pass me on account of my leg, and I won't take the risk of going south with the offchance of them not taking me, and anyway I'd have to resign my work here to do that. At the moment I have the urge to go away very strongly, who wouldn't, but there it is.

Just at the moment the copra market is very shaky and the firms up here have ceased buying as all the storage space is used up, and there doesn't appear any likelihood of ships coming to take the copra away. If these conditions keep up it will mean a serious setback to New Guinea, as no ships, no copra, no money is the way of things.

Cheers, Jack[3]

Like hundreds of other Australians, Jack Griffin was not to be moved from New Guinea to the safety of Australia. Instead, extraordinarily, his new job with Burns Philp would move him even closer to the Japanese threat. In December 1941, as a single male without dependants, he was despatched by the company from Rabaul to travel by steamer 200 kilometres to the north to take up temporary management of a company plantation on Lemus Island, among the coral islands of the Nusa Channel and about 15 kilometres west of Kavieng. The permanent manager at Lemus had left with his family to travel south on 'extended leave', and Jack's job was to look after the business for at least three months, possibly much longer. Lemus produced copra, and was a self-sufficient operation with its own large bungalow, household and plantation staff, copra and poultry sheds, vegetable garden, orchard and sturdy wharf. The nearest civilisation was Kavieng, and the only means of communication with Kavieng was by taking a three-hour trip in the plantation's small motorised sailing pinnace, a timber vessel crewed by Melanesian boatmen.

In some ways Lemus Plantation was a small tropical version of Tuppal Station, remote from civilisation and entirely dependent for its success on the resourcefulness and energy of its manager. If circumstances had been different, managing the plantation would have been a heaven-sent opportunity for the self-sufficient, practical and ambitious Jack Griffin. To survive and thrive, he would need to draw deeply on all those useful experiences he had been exposed to and things he had learnt so long ago in his formative years in the Riverina. Who knows, he might have ended up settling at Lemus, finding a wife (his family thought that this was overdue, even though Jack's father had been 42 before he married), raising children, profitably producing copra, and drawing, painting and playing the piano for his family to his heart's content, happily ever after.

But Jack was an adventurer by nature, and adventurers always hazard risks. Sometimes their risky lives lead to fortune and fame, but very often end in personal disaster. By a terrible stroke of bad luck Jack was now located in a part of the south-west Pacific squarely in the face of extreme danger, in a group of remote islands from which, when the time came, it would be almost impossible to escape. The little port of Kavieng was soon to be located at the centre of one of the most protracted and

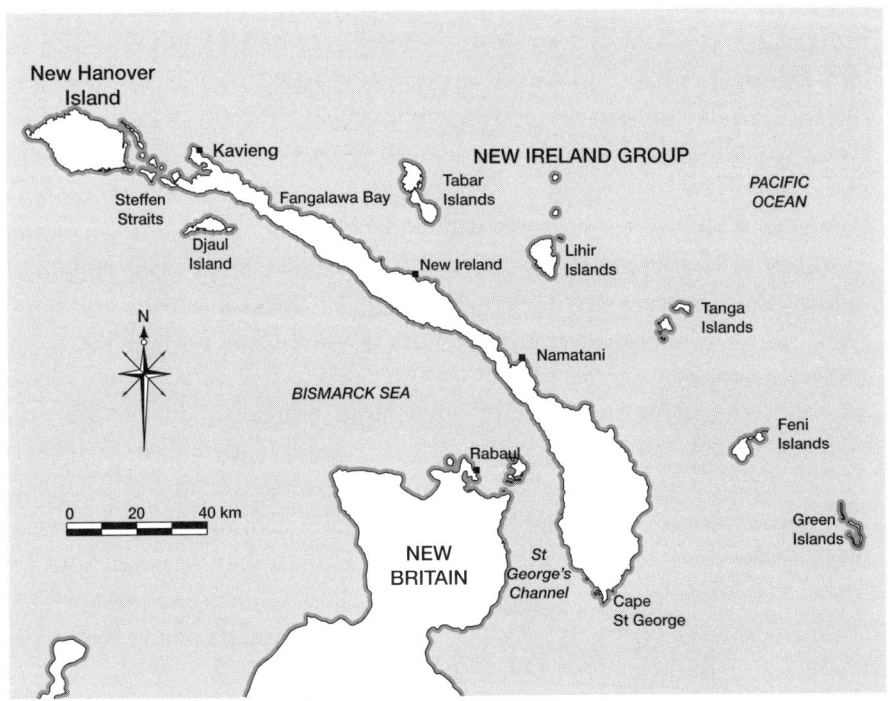

New Ireland, including outlying islands, and New Britain.

violent military struggles of all time. Over the next few years Kavieng's remaining European inhabitants would surrender control over their lives to important strangers, Japanese and American generals and admirals, men they had never even heard of. Kavieng was certainly not a place for anyone, not even the most shrewd and calculating of risk-takers, to be moving to in December 1941.

As it transpired, the thinly spread Australian forces deployed to the island extremities of New Guinea would be no match for the invaders and anyway would be secretly abandoned as 'hostages to fortune' by a hapless Australian government.[4] Each small army unit was to be quickly overrun by much larger, better-coordinated and more experienced Japanese forces. In the eastern islands of New Guinea, 1 Independent Company at Kavieng and 2/22 Battalion at Rabaul would be forced to scatter into the jungle within hours of coming face to face with the enemy. After their surrender, of over a thousand 2/22 Battalion soldiers taken prisoner, about 160 were immediately murdered in early February 1942 at Tol Plantation, and another 35 at Waitavalo Plantation. These early mass murders of nearly 200 Australians would turn out to be the first in a long series of such atrocities perpetrated in New Guinea.[5]

Elsewhere, Australian battalions hastily dispatched to Ambon[6], Timor[7] and Java in the Dutch East Indies were also quickly defeated, and in mid-February 1942 the entire Australian Eighth Army Division was surrendered in Singapore, along with the large British garrison, when about 70 000 Allied servicemen were marched into captivity. Within three months of the start of the Pacific war, over 22 000 Australian service men and women and about 1000 civilians had quickly become prisoners of the Japanese. By any standards, this was an unprecedented catastrophe, and although the country was not to know it for some time, even greater disasters were to befall these Australian civilian internees and prisoners of war.[8]

chapter 4

The raids were executed with violence and precision

Jack Griffin's arrival in the Kavieng area in December 1941 coincided with the hurried departure from New Ireland of an important section of the small Australian community, the last of the women and children. Although through the last months of 1941 there had been a steady trickle of voluntary evacuations to the south, many families still remained intact. The events at Pearl Harbor spurred the Australian Government to sudden action. On 12 December 1941 a decision was communicated through the Department of External Territories in Canberra to compulsorily evacuate all European women and children from New Guinea to Australia. The only exceptions permitted were female missionaries and nurses who could remain if they so elected. On 18 December the District Officer at Kavieng and the most senior government official on New Ireland, Jerry MacDonald, received an instruction from Rabaul to this effect, and worked long and hard to organise two evacuation routes. One route would be for Australian women and children situated in the northern part of New Ireland, the second for those situated in the south.

Those living in Kavieng and on plantations in the north were given short notice to leave Kavieng on the MV *Navanora*, a large locally-owned motor schooner, which would immediately convey them to Rabaul for later trans-shipment to Australia. On the evening of 19 December 1941 the *Navanora* cast off from Kavieng wharf with about twenty mothers and children on board, and set course for Rabaul, which they reached after a very rough passage caused by unseasonably bad weather. From here the women and children were shipped to Townsville in northern Australia, then on by rail to points further south.

Families in southern New Ireland were instructed to gather at Namatanai on the east coast, the only major township where there was an Assistant District Officer, Alan 'Bill' Kyle, to arrange an evacuation. After a number of false starts caused by the bad weather, about forty women and children were eventually evacuated on 27 December from Ulapatur on the west coast. They were conveyed to Rabaul on two schooners, the *Paulus* and the *Theresa*, which had been sent by the German Catholic mission at Vunapope on New Britain. From Rabaul they were flown to Port Moresby, and then to Cairns.[1]

Along with the Melanesian, Chinese and mixed race populations, there were now left behind on New Ireland about fifty mainly Australian male civilians, mostly planters on the east and west coasts and adjacent islands; the traders and government officials in Kavieng; small groups of missionaries, priests and nuns who had refused to leave their mission stations; the approximately 150 Australian soldiers of 1 Independent Company deployed near the airfield and harbour in Kavieng; and one Australian nurse, Sister Dorothy Maye, who had volunteered to help maintain medical services at the Kavieng hospital. Also left to see to their own survival were the Overseas Chinese and people of mixed race on New Ireland, none of whom had been included in the evacuation plan, and the tens of thousands of Melanesians living across the islands.

These were the innocents about to be dragged into a great Japanese military adventure, and within a short time the first of a series of entirely unwarranted catastrophes would be visited upon them. Vice-Admiral Nagumo's four aircraft carriers *Akagi*, *Zuikaku*, *Shokaku* and *Soryu* would very soon be cruising in waters immediately north of New Ireland, and Commander Mitsuo Fuchida, who had led the raids on Pearl Harbor, would soon be leading destructive air raids on the two biggest towns in eastern New Guinea: first Kavieng and then Rabaul.

Not long after the evacuations, and within just a month of Jack Griffin's arrival at Lemus Island Plantation, the Japanese invasion of New Ireland commenced. This was heralded early in the morning of 21 January 1942 by the first in a series of air raids on the Kavieng township, airfield and wharves. The raids were executed with violence and precision by pilots flying off the carriers *Akagi* and *Soryu*, and caused considerable destruction and some civilian and military casualties.[2] The big Burns Philp and Carpenter's warehouses crammed with highly inflammable

The raids were executed with violence and precision

Japanese troops occupy Kavieng, 23 January 1942. AUSTRALIAN WAR MEMORIAL NEGATIVE NUMBER AWM 127910

copra were set alight and the copra fires burned for days thereafter. The population was thrown into panic, and an exodus commenced from the town. By that evening the District Officer had managed to organise an evacuation convoy of trucks and cars to carry the first group of Australian civilians away from immediate danger, and this joined a steady stream of Chinese and indigenous refugees heading down the eastern coastal road to temporary safety in the south-eastern hinterlands.[3]

Claude Chadderton, some time in the 1930s. He was by then the owner of three copra plantations on New Ireland.

The air raids and the movement of evacuees away from Kavieng were to continue for the next 24 hours until, during the very early hours of 23 January, the first wave of 5000 sailors and marines of the Maizuru Special Naval Landing Force stormed ashore and proceeded to spread out through the town and beyond. This was the very first enemy invasion of Australian territory in the country's history, and was followed within hours by the Japanese invasion of Rabaul.

The desperate defence made at Kavieng airfield by commandos of 1 Independent Company against this overwhelming force could only be short-lived. After hurriedly attempting to demolish the airfield facilities and destroy the airstrip, the surviving soldiers retreated into the jungle, about 140 of them later regrouping and evacuating from Kaut Harbour, about 20 kilometres from Kavieng down on the west coast, on the Independent Company's small chartered coastal vessel, the MV *Induna Star*. This ship was subsequently bombed at sea near Rabaul by a Japanese float-plane and badly damaged. *Induna Star* was taken in tow to Rabaul by a Japanese destroyer, where the survivors were initially concentrated in a prison camp with about 200 Australian male civilian internees, who had also been abandoned after the December evacuation of women and children, and about 800 survivors of 2/22 Battalion, now prisoners of war.[4]

By the end of January 1942 control of much of New Ireland had been assumed by the Japanese, who then commenced a build-up of naval, land and air forces which during the next year grew to over 13 000 military personnel and over 1000 civilian contractors. At Kavieng, now pronounced Kabien in Japanese (which also means 'beautiful-garden'), construction of a second airfield was quickly commenced on the coast near Panapai, and a seaplane base was established on the foreshore. At Rabaul, now Rabauru, a huge garrison comprising an army base, air force base and a naval base at Simpson Harbour was rapidly developed. Rabaul became the most formidable Japanese military installation in the South-west Pacific, and the total number of service personnel based there grew to almost 100 000.

The resoundingly successful conquests of Kavieng and Rabaul had taken just over 24 hours, and these Japanese bases were soon to be used to obtain similar victories further to the south-east in the Solomon Islands archipelago, and to the west on the island of Papua.

chapter 5

Escape

Through the early months of 1942 numerous attempts were made by European civilians, soldiers and sailors to escape to the safety of Australia by small boat from many different points throughout South-East Asia and the Pacific islands. Unsurprisingly, most of these attempts ended in failure. The combination of vast ocean distances, dangerous seas and wild weather, poorly equipped and provisioned vessels, problems with navigation and communication, and the constant danger of detection by Japanese naval and air units swarming through the area, meant that chances of success were never good. The comparative few of these 'boat people' who eventually succeeded with these risky voyages usually did so because they were better prepared; experienced with small boats and open water navigation; were persistent and resourceful; and, most important of all, were extraordinarily lucky.[1]

The Australian and other European civilians still scattered over New Ireland gradually formed into two groups. There were those with either the means or the determination to quickly attempt to escape by boat completely, preferably to Australia; and there were those who believed they had no other choice than to stay on the island and become 'hostages to fortune'.

Among the civilians who tried escaping by small boat, at least five attempts were made; only three were completely or partly successful. The earliest occurred at the time of the air raids on the night of 21 January when Frank Saunders, a wealthy Kavieng shipowner, hurriedly arranged for a convoy of five motorised schooners, including the *Navanora*, *Neptuna*, *Shamrock* and *Zenda*, to convey a group of seventeen Australian men and a large quantity of stores towards Rabaul, and hopefully on to

Australia.² This escape party was a mixture of Saunders' own employees, planters and government employees including Bill Box, Harry Doyle, John Goad, Col Mackellar, Roy Macpherson, Cedric Pines, Dudley Roberts and Bill Wilkin.³ Passing through the Albatross Passage not far into the voyage the *Shamrock*'s engine broke down and the convoy halted while repairs were slowly made. The following day the Japanese invasion fleet overtook the little armada and the Australians were captured and returned to Kavieng, where they were locked up in the gaol. Some weeks later most were transferred to Rabaul and internment with the many Australians already in the big internment camp there.⁴

A partly successful escape from the area was made by K.W. Chambers, a civilian teleradio technician and coastwatcher on Emirau Island, about 100 kilometres north of Kavieng. On 21 January Chambers had heard and witnessed the nearby Japanese carrier fleet launch numerous aircraft in the direction of Kavieng and Rabaul, and had successfully sent a message of warning to Rabaul, but could not raise the alarm for Kavieng. The following night he set out in a pinnace for what he thought might be the safety of Kavieng, with his radio equipment and two Seventh Day Adventist missionaries on board. As the little craft approached the town at 2 am on 23 January, Chambers could see the fires and explosions of the copra storage sheds going up in smoke. They decided to bypass Kavieng altogether and, continuing their sea journey by night and hiding by day down the west coast of New Ireland, at length crossed to New Britain, where their boat was detected by a Japanese destroyer. The little group of escapees hurriedly put ashore, scrambled inland and then watched as the pinnace was destroyed. The missionaries decided to walk to the Seventh Day Adventist mission at Put Put, near Rabaul, while Chambers joined other New Britain escapees, pressing on to eventually reach safety.⁵

Another partly successful escape was made from Mussau Island in the St Matthias group, about 100 kilometres to the north-west of Kavieng, in the small vessel *Malalang*. This party comprised a Seventh Day Adventist missionary, Pastor Arthur Atkins; his friend Trevor Collett, sawmill manager at the mission; and Charles Cook, manager of a plantation on nearby Emirau Island. They also managed to sail undetected almost 400 kilometres directly south, and had successfully passed through the long and dangerous St Georges Channel between New Britain and New Ireland when they too were finally forced ashore on New Britain to the south of Rabaul. Pastor Atkins felt he was unable to continue⁶,

First World War studio portrait of Sapper Alan Fairlie 'Bill' Kyle, 4th Divisional Signal Company, taken in 1916. During the Second World War he was a resident and Assistant District Officer at Namatanai, New Ireland, and became a naval coastwatcher, ranked as lieutenant. Another resident and patrol officer of Namatanai, Sub-Lieutenant Gregory Wade Benham, became a coastwatcher at the same time. Both were executed on 1 September 1942 on Nago Island. AUSTRALIAN WAR MEMORIAL NEGATIVE NUMBER AWM P03419.001

so he and Collett[7] made their way inland to give themselves up. Cook continued on alone in the boat, and made his escape.[8]

Far down the east coast of New Ireland, the Assistant District Officer at Namatanai, Bill Kyle, and his Patrol Officer Greg Benham, who had just received official appointments as naval officers in the Australian navy coastwatcher unit[9], collected a group of eight local planters, a missionary, and six soldiers of 1 Independent Company who had been stationed at Namatanai, and headed down the coast towards Cape Metlik, which they reached by the end of January. Here Kyle and Benham radioed Port Moresby for assistance and, on being instructed to remain on New Ireland to continue secretly observing the Japanese as coastwatchers, sent the civilians and soldiers on to safety in the Solomon Islands in a small expropriated vessel, the *Gnair*. Because of the Japanese presence the escapees avoided the nearby Buka and Bougainville islands, and eventually reached Tulagi on 8 February, from where they made their way to Australia.[10]

Two decorated, resourceful ex-soldiers together organised the largest successful escape. The energetic Harry Murray was a World War I Gallipoli veteran, had won the Military Cross and Distinguished Conduct Medal serving as a lieutenant with the 2nd Infantry Battalion AIF, and until their destruction in the air raids had owned a general store and a number of agencies in Kavieng. His partner Jerry MacDonald, the District Officer and most senior government official on New Ireland, had been awarded the Distinguished Service Order and Military Cross as a major in the 20th Infantry Battalion AIF. This small escape group, eventually comprising nine civilians and eight soldiers of 2/22 Battalion who had escaped from Rabaul, developed from MacDonald's road convoy out of Kavieng and gradually wended its way to the south-east, moving under cover from plantation to plantation by land and sea, criss-crossing between the eastern and western coasts of the island. In the course of their long, incident-filled journey to the southern tip of New Ireland, Murray and McDonald were to meet many of the Australian men remaining on the island, but were able to convince only a handful to join their escape party. Eventually, on 30 April 1942, at Boang Island off the far southern coast, they forcefully expropriated a small motor vessel, the *Quang Wha*, and almost three months after setting out from Kavieng departed New Ireland on the dangerous voyage to Papua far to the south-west. After an open sea crossing of 800 kilometres undetected by the Japanese they made landfall near Buna on 5 May 1942, and subsequently sailed on to Port Moresby where MacDonald was able to prepare an official report on the fall of New Ireland and provide the names of Australians and others believed to be still alive there.[11] The escapees were repatriated to Australia on the Dutch ship *Van Hertz*.[12]

By early February 1942 there were still thirty to forty Australian civilians left behind on New Ireland. These were mainly planters, some gathered together for mutual protection at some of the bigger plantations on the east and west coasts. The remaining, mostly German male and female missionaries, now numbering about 25, were gathered at missions on the east coast and on nearby islands. A German priest, Father Karl Martin, was at Ulaputur on the west coast; and an Irish priest, Father Michael Murphy, was on Tabar Island off the east coast. The McDonald-Murray escape party was making its secret journey down the west coast. At the far southern tip were the coastwatchers Bill Kyle and Greg Benham at Cape St George; and to the east of Kavieng in the Tabar Islands group were two planters-turned-coastwatchers, Con Page[13] and Jack Talmage.[14]

In the end, Jack Griffin would not escape from New Ireland. The day after the air raids and on the evening of the invasion, and unaware that the attacks had occurred, he had made the sea crossing to Kavieng from Lemus Island using the plantation pinnace to deliver poultry and eggs to the Kavieng Club. To his surprise he entered a mysteriously deserted and burning township; as night fell he searched the town for signs of life. At police sergeant Bill Livingstone's house he eventually teamed up with seven other Australians who had remained behind to await developments. Apart from Livingstone, Harry Murray was there, with Major Wilson of 1 Independent Company. Murray Edwards, the Assistant District Officer in Kavieng, had driven up from Kaut Harbour, unaware that an emergency evacuation had been organised the day before by his boss Jerry MacDonald.[15]

Also at the house were Phil Levy, the local Burns Philp manager, who explained to Jack what had happened, and two other planters, Dusty Miller and Lon Davies. Phil Levy, 50, originally from Adelaide, was married but his wife Mabel had already evacuated to Australia. The stocky Dusty Miller, 57, an unmarried ex-soldier originally from Eltham in Victoria, had also just come across to Kavieng in his schooner from his plantation on Tsaliui Island, near New Hanover Island to the north. Miller was a well-known copra trader who had acquired his plantation in the 1920s, and also owned boats for copra-carrying, and a boatyard.

Escape

Harry Murray, the energetic organiser, photographed at a 1930s Kavieng sports day.

Torokina, South Bougainville Island, 25 April 1945. Presentation of the American Silver Star medal by Major General Mitchell, Commanding 1st US Marine Wing, to Captain H.J. Murray MC DCM of the AIF, attached to the Allied Intelligence Bureau, for conspicuous gallantry. AUSTRALIAN WAR MEMORIAL NEGATIVE NUMBER AWM 030500/31

Lon Davies, 35, had come in from W.R. Carpenter's plantation on Ungan Island, quite near Lemus and close to Kavieng. Davies was also unmarried, and originally from Roseville in Sydney.

The eight joined in a boisterous farewell party during which a large quantity of scrounged liquor and food stores from the Burns Philp and Carpenter's warehouses were consumed in a gathering that went on well into the night. When the Japanese invasion commenced shortly after midnight the group rapidly broke up and scattered further inland just ahead of the invaders, most heading south-west for nearby Kaut Harbour to link up with the remnants of 1 Independent Company.[16]

It was now impossible for Jack Griffin to return by boat to Lemus Island. Leaving his Burns Philp colleague Phil Levy and Lon Davies to try the west coast escape route to Kaut with the others, and Miller to try an escape on his schooner, in Kavieng Jack managed to commandeer an abandoned car and quickly drove off through the night down the east coast road to Burns Philp's big Kimadan Plantation, 170 kilometres to the south, halfway down the island, which he knew well from his numerous pre-war visits. Here he found Burns Philp's area manager Leon Williams, and a group of nine Australian planters who had moved for mutual support to Kimadan from nearby east coast plantations, and to listen for news on the plantation's big radio receiver.

Leon Williams, 38, was another young, single Burns Philp manager, responsible for company affairs in central New Ireland.[17] The group of planters gathered with him at Kimadan included six elderly ex-soldiers who had moved to New Ireland years before to establish plantations and raise families, but whose wives and children had now left the island. John Bell, 62, originally from Queensland, owned Soubu and Penipol Plantations, adjoining estates on the mid east coast. He was married to Ethel, and had four sons, but none of his family was now present, the last having evacuated to Australia in December from Ulapatur.[18] Claude Chadderton, 51, had settled on New Ireland in the 1920s, owned Lamerika and Darlam Plantations on the mid east coast, and Kapsu Plantation, further north up the coast road. Also married, he had sent his wife May back to Sydney in 1941 where she had joined their daughter Moya, a medical student at Sydney University.[19] Bill Garnett, aged 59 and from Melbourne, whose wife's name was also May, owned Kamiraba Plantation, next door to the Chaddertons. Les Gordon, 51, another Queenslander, was married to Dorothea and owned Bulu-Logon Plantation. Albert Moseley, 60, also originally from Queensland, and married to Annie, was manager of Belik Plantation, further to the south. Ed Woodhouse, 48, another Queenslander and married to Jessie, was manager of Katu Plantation.

The others gathered at Kimadan included Bob Furlong, 40, husband of Agnes, originally from Sydney and now manager of Lamussong Plantation, about 15 kilometres from Kimadan; Len Pinnock, 54, married to Louise and also from Sydney, manager of Ulul-Nono Plantation much further to the north and quite close to Kavieng; and Boyd Whitehead, 44, from Victoria, married to Eileen and father of two children, and manager of Karu Plantation.[20]

All these men were friends and neighbours, their families well known to each other. They had elected not to join the escape group organised at Namatanai by Bill Kyle and Greg Benham, and had settled in at Kimadan with ample supplies of food and other stores. Like others who were to remain on the island they were hoping that, one way or another, the war would soon be over and life would return to normal.

Most of them had invested many hard years of their lives cultivating their plantations and developing loyal Melanesian employees who they were not going to abandon. Anyway, if the situation really threatened their lives, they felt sure that official attempts would be made to rescue them.

At about the same time these events were occurring at Kimadan Plantation, on the west coast the MacDonald-Murray escape party reached W.R. Carpenter's Panaras Plantation where they joined the manager, Forbes Cobb[21]; Phil Levy and Lon Davies who had arrived from Kavieng; and two planters from the east coast, Len Woolcott and Stan Ashby, who had crossed the island to Panaras following the fall of Kavieng.[22] Woolcott, aged 42, unmarried, and originally from Sydney, was the manager of Fileba Plantation on the north-east coast of New Ireland. Like their Australian counterparts gathered at Kimadan Plantation on the east coast, Cobb, Levy, Davies, Woolcott and Ashby settled in at the comfortable Panaras bungalow with plenty of stores and a radio receiver to await what was to unfold. Despite Harry Murray's attempts to persuade them to move on, they were content to stay where they were. In fact, some were now openly hostile towards MacDonald, who as the most senior remaining Australian official on the island became the butt of criticism and complaint. Here at Panaras he was blamed for the apparent abandonment of the planters by their government, and criticised for now suggesting that they join him for his risky escape attempt.

A few days later the remnants of the MacDonald-Murray escape party reached Burns Philp's Kolube Plantation further down the west coast, where they were welcomed by the manager, Ray Heming. Heming, 56, was originally from Sydney but had lived for years on New Ireland. His wife Minnie and his son and daughter were no longer on the island. He too was sceptical of the need to escape, but provided Murray and MacDonald with whatever assistance they needed.

Back on the east coast, after a few days at Kimadan Plantation it became apparent to Jack Griffin that the Japanese would soon overrun the area so, after unsuccessfully attempting to persuade his ten companions to join him on an overland journey to the greater safety of the more inaccessible west coast, he set off alone to walk along native paths over the high Lelet Plateau and down to another large Burns Philp plantation at Kalili Harbour, which he had also visited many times before the war. Here at Kalili he was welcomed by his colleagues Leigh

26 June 1918 at Picardie, Somme River, France. Group portrait of officers of the 20th Battalion. The young Major Jerry MacDonald DSO MC is seated in the front row, fourth from the right, next to the Battalion CO, Lieutenant Colonel F.W.D. Forbes DSO. AUSTRALIAN WAR MEMORIAL NEGATIVE NUMBER AWM E02594

Lightbody, the plantation manager, and Jim Naughton, the plantation overseer and mechanic; and Frank Consterdine, a plantation manager for W.R. Carpenter & Co.

Lightbody, 49, originally from Warragul in rural Victoria, was an unmarried ex-soldier who had moved to New Ireland in the 1920s. Naughton, 31, was also unmarried, and like Jack Griffin originally from the Riverina in New South Wales, where his mother lived in Wagga Wagga. Frank Consterdine, 48, from Sydney, was manager of W.R. Carpenter's Koka Plantation further up the west coast.[23] His wife Mabel had been sent to Australia in 1941.

Jack's premonition that the east coast was dangerous quickly proved to be correct. On 25 January 1944, Japanese troops arrived at the Lemakot Mission, about 30 kilometres south of Kavieng, which had been providing shelter for five badly wounded Australian soldiers, Sister Dorothy Maye, and Catholic priests and nuns. Three of the soldiers soon died of their wounds, two others were taken by the Japanese to

Kavieng hospital but died soon afterwards, and Sister Maye sent away to captivity in Rabaul.[24] The Japanese then developed an army base in the bush behind Lemakot, eventually for an infantry regiment. Later, and much further down the east coast at Namatanai, civil administrators and an army brigade eventually established their authority.[25]

Some weeks after Jack's arrival at Kalili Plantation, the MacDonald-Murray escape party entered Kalili Harbour in a broken-down cutter after laborious travel down the west coast. While searching the Kalili area for a new engine, shaft and propeller for the boat, Harry Murray and Jerry MacDonald exhorted Lightbody, Naughton, Consterdine and Griffin to join their group and find an ocean escape route to the south-west and eventually, to Australia.

Jack Griffin was now faced with a choice of two equally unpalatable courses of action. He could either risk his life in an unpredictable and potentially dangerous sea voyage, or remain in familiar territory with his feet on dry land to take his chances with the invaders.

To Leigh Lightbody, Murray and MacDonald's escape plans seemed foolhardy and probably unnecessary. The self-assured Lightbody was much older than Jack, had experienced World War I as a sergeant in the 13th Field Ambulance AIF, and had lived for years in the islands. He was firmly of the opinion that, once things settled down, the Japanese, wishing to re-establish the copra industry, would want the planters to continue their work. Already the Japanese had begun circulating pamphlets advising to this effect. Despite the persuasive efforts of Murray and MacDonald, Lightbody steadfastly refused to join in the escape attempt and, indeed, was openly hostile towards MacDonald, who was again blamed for the predicament the planters were now facing. By contrast, Naughton and Consterdine were excited by the prospect of getting away and were strongly tempted to take the risk and join in.

While MacDonald and Murray were busy patching up their little boat, Jack had plenty of time to make up his mind. By 14 March 1942 he had made what would later transpire to be the most momentous decision of his life. He would remain where he was, concurring with Lightbody that this course of action probably presented the lesser risk. That day he wrote again to his sister Alison in Sydney, using the plantation office machine to neatly type what would become the last letter he would ever send home. Being suitably vague about his whereabouts, just in case the letter fell into the wrong hands, he wrote to Pat that day:

> New Guinea, 14/3/42.
>
> Dear Pat,
>
> I'm writing this, and sending it to Rooty Hill , as for the life of me I can't remember what the name of your firm is, with the hopes it gets through.
>
> I've written to the Bank at Brisbane, as I understand the Officers from Rabaul got away, to, write and advise you the state of my affairs, and to pay you the sum of twenty five pounds from my current account.
>
> The future at present is very obscure, but I may get a chance to get through.
>
> Enclosed Will, for you.
> All the best, and call in to B.P.Head Office (ask for Mr.Gauld) sometime for news as to what I'm doing , as it will be going along verbal.
>
> cheers
> Jack

Jack Griffin's last letter to his family, written in March 1942 while he was hiding from the Japanese at Kalili Plantation.[26]

This letter and the enclosed will were given to Harry Murray to join the little pile of mail collected from other planters he had met on the way to Kalili. Murray carefully stowed them in his personal kit for delivery should he eventually make it back to Australia.

So when on the following night, 15 March 1942, the escape party set out in its repaired cutter from Kalili for what was to be almost another two months' precarious journey, Jack Griffin and Leigh Lightbody remained behind. Just two days later, after rough voyaging not much further down the coast to Kokola Plantation, Jim Naughton and Frank Consterdine had had enough. They had been badly seasick and had no confidence the boat could carry them to safety. At Kokola they turned back for Kalili, walking along the coast to rejoin Lightbody and Griffin and await developments.

Months later, Jack Griffin's last letter from New Ireland was delivered personally in Sydney by Harry Murray to Alison Griffin, would then become a most active representative in Australia for her brother during the long vigil which would now unfold.[27]

Murray would later return to New Ireland to work as a coastwatcher for the Australian Navy, mainly attached to the US Marines, and would later be decorated by the Americans with the Silver Star medal.[28] After the war he was prominent among those investigating wartime disappearances of civilians in the eastern islands of New Guinea. His wife Mary recorded the story of her husband's adventures in two 1960s books.

chapter 6

Into captivity

As it turned out for the planters, Leigh Lightbody's faith in Japanese good intentions proved, for a while at least, to be sound. Unlike other early incidents in the Pacific war when large numbers of civilian internees of all ages and sexes were arbitrarily killed or imprisoned, on New Ireland the occupying forces wanted the Australian planters who had chosen to stay to immediately return to work; after a delay, they also permitted the missionaries to continue their duties. As the practical organisers and managers of the valuable copra industry the planters formed an important part of a local economy the Japanese wished to preserve. If the Europeans agreed to abide by the new order and continued to make themselves useful by maintaining local industry they were not to be troubled.

To regulate civil affairs over the newly conquered territory the Imperial Japanese Navy had on the day of the invasion issued a proclamation which, although claiming ownership of all property in the name of the Emperor Hirohito, and while listing detailed restrictions on the movements, labour, trade, gatherings, religious activities and daily business of all inhabitants, had also exhorted everyone including Europeans to return to their homes and places of work, and guaranteed safety in exchange for their obedience and loyalty to the Emperor. This was followed by a second proclamation, issued by the garrison commander in Kavieng on 12 February 1942, containing further detailed instructions and orders regarding appropriate displays of loyalty and subjugation to the Japanese emperor, the expected use of the Japanese language, and currency exchange rate information.[1]

So with their safety seemingly assured the remaining planters and traders were one by one identified, registered, and instructed to return to their normal duties. Under this arrangement the Japanese placed restrictions on the freedom of movement of the Australians, and retained supervisory authority over them. Local Japanese civilian administrators and overseers were involved in this supervision, backed up by the military if necessary.

The remaining Australians identified by the Japanese included two planters located on the west coast of New Ireland. They were Ray Heming at Burns Philp's Kolube Plantation, who had helped the MacDonald-Murray escape party; and Vivian Ives, 47, manager of Burns Philp's Kurumut Plantation far to the south. Ives was an Englishman, an ex-soldier who had twice won the Military Cross serving with the British and Indian armies. His young wife Gwendoline had been moved out of danger to Australia, and was now living in her hometown of Melbourne with their little daughter.

Two more planters were identified on islands off the east coast of New Ireland. Walter Heydon, 58, an unmarried ex-soldier originally from New South Wales, was at Put Plantation on Malendok Island in the Tanga Island Group. Henry Topal, 49, was living with his son David, 12, at Tereri Plantation on Tabar Island. Topal was another ex-soldier, and had lived briefly on New Ireland in 1917 when he was a member of the Australian Naval and Military Expeditionary force which had been sent to occupy German possessions during World War I. It was said that the Topals had arrived in New Ireland only two weeks before the Japanese invasion, possibly from New Britain, sent at the last minute to manage Tereri.

More planters were identified on the north-east coast, close to and in Kavieng. Charlie Ostrom, an elderly Finnish-Russian and long-time resident, owned and lived at Lakurafanga Plantation with his son Max, 20. In Kavieng town was Bill Attwood, 30, the garage owner who had tried to escape with Frank Saunders at the time of the invasion, and was now reluctantly working for the Japanese fixing motor vehicles. Phil Levy and Lon Davies, each of whom had been in Kavieng when the Japanese landed, and had escaped as far as Panaras Plantation with the MacDonald-Murray escape party, were also there, but in hiding.[2]

It appears that Jack Griffin was never able to return to the Burns Philp plantation on Lemus Island, either to resume work or recover his personal possessions. It seems certain that from March until July

Claude Chadderton following his enlistment in the Australian Army in 1918.

1942 he remained far to the south on the west coast of New Ireland, initially at Burns Philp's Kalili plantation with Leigh Lightbody, and then further south at Kurumut Plantation with Vivian Ives. We then know that in July the Japanese in that area ordered him and Vivian Ives to Bopire Plantation, just north of Namatanai on the east coast. In July 1942 Bopire was being used by the Japanese as a staging camp for civilian internees, and the following month Griffin, Ives and other Australians were sent north, even closer to Kavieng.[3]

The period of uneasy calm and relative freedom since the invasion in January was ended with this sudden round-up of the Australians in June and July 1942. The Pacific war had suddenly begun to go very badly for Japan. Although not obvious at the time, the US-led Allies had been presented with some decisive military advantages by the many mistakes made by the Japanese during their short three-month rampage after Pearl Harbor. Two of their biggest mistakes would prove to have enormously harmful consequences for them, and sow the seeds of their eventual defeat.

Despite the raid being promoted as a great victory to the Japanese public, at Pearl Harbor the previous December the Japanese navy had in fact failed to complete the task of destroying the US Pacific Fleet, especially America's most potent weapons in the Pacific, the three large aircraft carriers *Enterprise*, *Lexington* and *Saratoga*, and their pilots, aircraft and escorts. Fortuitously for America, two of these carrier groups had been absent from Pearl Harbor on the day of the attack, exercising in the Pacific Ocean in a location far to the south-west of Hawaii; and the *Saratoga* was docked at a US mainland port for repairs. Vice-Admiral Nagumo did not know any of this, and could easily have carried out a second, more devastating attack, but the invisible threat of the US carriers weighed heavily on his mind. Despite polite exhortations from his subordinates to continue with a second large raid, the surprisingly timid Nagumo had prematurely called off further action, and fled with his fleet back to Japan and a huge hero's welcome. Nagumo's superior, Admiral Isoroku Yamamoto, Commander of the Combined Japanese Navy, knew that the Nagumo's failure to complete the destruction at Pearl Harbor and then quickly engage and destroy the American carriers would now force an inevitable but unwanted showdown at a later stage. To Yamamoto, Pearl Harbor had not been a victory at all, but his private opinion could not be widely shared in the atmosphere of triumphalism and invincibility pervading Japan in the early months of the Pacific war.[4]

As well, long before the outbreak of the war, US and British signals intelligence codebreakers operating from Hawaii and Hong Kong had managed to progressively break into many of the Japanese naval and diplomatic radio and telegraphic communications codes. After December 1941, these codebreaking activities were rapidly intensified, and so carefully protected that the Japanese were completely unaware that their plans and actions would become largely known in advance by the

Into captivity

Allied high command. In 1943 Admiral Yamamoto would himself be assassinated by the Americans as a direct result of secret intercepts. It has often been observed that the success of the teams of US, British, Australian and Dutch codebreakers between 1941 and 1945 were probably the greatest military achievement of the Pacific war. Conversely, the failure to believe this security breach was even possible, and to detect it was happening, was one of Japan's most extraordinary mistakes.[5]

So, unknown to the over-confident Japanese leaders, the US and its allies were slowly beginning to accumulate considerable secret information about Japan's navy and army intentions in the Pacific, and had preserved the men, ships and aircraft with which to commence an immediate and powerful counter-attack.

Three spectacular events involving the US Pacific carrier fleet would now unfold. The first was an air raid on Tokyo by American B-25 Mitchell bombers, launched in April 1942 from the aircraft carrier *Hornet*, which had secretly cruised to within range of the Japanese islands. The 'Doolittle raid', as it became known (it was led by Lieutenant Colonel Jimmy Doolittle), inflicted very little physical damage, but had a startling impact on the minds of the militarists in Tokyo. However, the raid indirectly killed great numbers of Chinese. Fifteen of the sixteen B-25s used ran out of fuel and crashed in bad weather in Japanese-occupied coastal areas of China, and the surviving American crews were rescued by Chinese civilians. Infuriated, the Japanese army of occupation immediately embarked on a vicious campaign of indiscriminate reprisals against communities suspected of helping the Americans. Very early in the war, without America fully understanding what was happening, Japan demonstrated its violent reaction to US attack by punishing innocent men, women and children from a third nation.[6]

The second event, in May 1942 in the Coral Sea to the east of New Guinea, was the first direct confrontation between the US carriers and their Japanese counterparts. It was initiated by the Americans using secret information provided by Allied codebreakers listening to Japanese naval signals, and was designed to prevent the seizure of Port Moresby, one of the last of the major South-west Pacific ports still to be captured by Japan. Historically, this was to be the first naval battle fought entirely by carrier aircraft, and the outcome was a stalemate in terms of ships and planes lost on both sides. However the invasion of Port Moresby was immediately postponed, then abandoned; and importantly, Japanese naval planners became single-mindedly obsessed

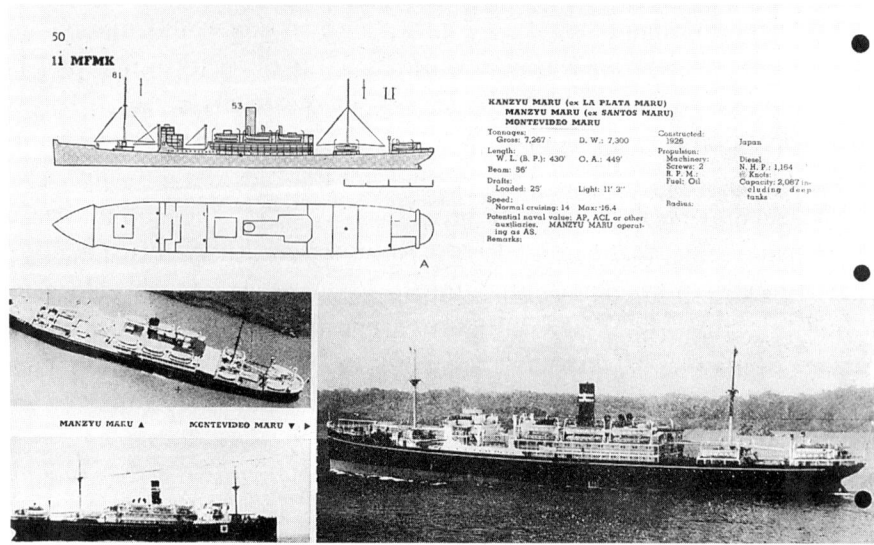

The Japanese transport ship *Montevideo Maru*, which left New Britain on 22 June 1942 unmarked, carrying Australian prisoners of war and civilians from Rabaul. All were lost when the ship was torpedoed on 1 July 1942. AUSTRALIAN WAR MEMORIAL NEGATIVE NUMBER AWM 106138

with dealing with the threat posed to their territories and supply lines by the US Pacific carrier fleet. In late May 1942, Admiral Yamamoto gathered together a huge naval force with aircraft carriers, again under the command of Vice-Admiral Nagumo, to lure the US carrier fleet into a trap at Midway Island, in the central Pacific, and destroy it totally, once and for all.[7]

Occurring just seven months after Pearl Harbor, the outcome of the battle for Midway Island in early June 1942, where a comparably small American fleet defeated a vastly superior Japanese opposing force, again with the instrumental help of secret signals intelligence and luck, was a huge blow to Japan. What was meant to have been a carefully planned trap laid for the Americans had suddenly become a trap for the Japanese, who lost four aircraft carriers, including *Akagi*, *Shokaku* and *Soryu* (which had participated in the invasion of New Guinea just over five months earlier); the heavy cruiser *Mikuma*; over 300 naval aircraft; and a large number of irreplaceable navy pilots. The military government in Tokyo ensured that the Japanese public knew nothing of this disaster by boasting that Midway had been yet another great victory, a deception supported by the naval officers who had participated, even though they fully understood the unpalatable truth. It has often been observed that the Coral Sea and then Midway were the turning points of the Pacific war, when the Japanese completely lost the initiative they had hitherto held so confidently, and were abruptly turned from unstoppable conquerors to dogged defenders of what would turn out to be their un-defendable empire.[8]

Finally, to cap off this great US-led offensive in 1942, on 7 August the US 1st Marine Division landed on the Japanese-held island of Guadalcanal in the southern Solomon Islands, the first large-scale American land, sea and air campaign of the Pacific war.

At exactly the same time the US offensive was gaining momentum, Australia commenced its first direct military confrontation with Japanese forces. Early in July 1942, 800 kilometres to the south-west of New Ireland on Papua, the Australian army launched the first of a series of land campaigns intended to eventually reclaim the Mandated Territory of New Guinea from the invaders. The initial objective for Australia was to block enemy land forces from seizing Port Moresby, which the persistent Japanese were now attempting with an overland approach, having failed two months earlier to achieve a successful landing from the Coral Sea. A particularly ambitious attempt was being made directly from the north over the rugged Owen Stanley Ranges, using the difficult Kokoda track as the route of approach. In a series of bitter jungle engagements fought throughout July and August 1942, Australian forces steadfastly pushed the Japanese forces back over the mountains, eventually all the way back to their fortified bases on the north coast.

The immediate consequence of this progressively worsening situation for Japanese occupation forces throughout the Pacific in mid-1942 was a much more defensive mentality. Thus commenced preparations to grimly defend the islands which so recently had come under their control. Part of this defensiveness was a general tightening of security within the occupied territories, and a hardening of attitudes towards those they had conquered. For their unfortunate prisoners and captive populations, from mid-1942 a new pattern of Japanese behaviour began to manifest. Each military setback would be soon followed by a worsening of the treatment meted out to those under their control.

On New Britain, in June 1942 it was decided to move most of the Australian POWs and civilian internees, including those brought from New Ireland earlier in the year, from the big internment camp at Rabaul to points further north, in Asia. Early in the morning of 1 July over 1000 of these unfortunates would be drowned in one of Australia's greatest wartime catastrophes, when the Japanese ship provided to transport them to work as slave labourers on Hainan Island in southern China was sunk in the middle of the night by an American submarine. Due to standing Japanese policy the *Montevideo Maru*, like many other Japanese POW and hospital ships at the time, did not advertise the nature of its cargo. It was among the first of many Japanese ships which were inadvertently attacked by the Allies between 1942 and 1945, when they should have been protected under international rules. The *Montevideo Maru* was identified in the middle of the night of 30 June 1942 as an enemy ship by the US submarine *Sturgeon*, west of the island of Luzon in the Philippines Sea, and torpedoed shortly afterwards. The only survivors were a small number of the Japanese crew.[9]

On New Ireland, the suspected existence of Australian coastwatchers operating surreptitiously on the island, the presence of priests able to influence opinion among the Melanesian population and negative reports about the Chinese and some planters made by various informers all contributed to arousing Japanese suspicions about all the 'foreigners'. While Australia's Kokoda campaign was beginning to make progress far to the west, the Japanese authorities began to more closely supervise the activities of the planters and missionaries on New Ireland, gradually moving them in small groups to live at guarded plantations and mission stations. From now on the Australians would be held under house arrest, and their personal freedom strictly limited.[10]

Searches for anyone suspect of harbouring anti-Japanese sentiments or committing anti-Japanese acts were also intensified. The Japanese military police, the fearsome Kenpeitai[11], were turned loose on the population to terrorise everyone on New Ireland into submission, cooperation and informing. The Kenpeitai prided themselves on their ability to obtain confessions from persons suspected of disloyal acts. Their principal method was the use of the most brutal tortures, and they were extraordinarily creative in devising ways of making suspects suffer so greatly that they were likely to admit to anything. Thus commenced a long sequence of arrests, internments, disappearances, beatings, tortures and executions which continued until the end of the war. The Kenpeitai selected the small Nago Island, just off the coast south-west of Kavieng and a favorite pre-war picnic destination, as their principal execution ground, while many Chinese accused of 'anti-Japanese activities' were tortured and killed at a number of other locations on the island.[12]

The Melanesian population was terrorised by the Kenpeitai into reporting 'spies' and 'traitors', and many were forced to become collaborators and secret agents for the Japanese. Their task was to move around and report on any subversive activity, which led to much tension and mutual suspicion, with most natives constantly living in fear of being reported as spies. The Kenpeitai were so successful at intimidation and 'discipline' that the terrified Melanesians quickly became subservient, obedient, and many learned to speak Japanese.[13] In these circumstances it was impossible for free Europeans to remain undetected and unreported.

In June 1942 the Australian planters-turned-coastwatchers Con Page and Jack Talmage were captured in the Tabar Islands and took them to Kavieng gaol. The following month they were seen, blindfolded and bound, being escorted to a wharf and taken by barge to Nago Island, where they were executed as spies, it was said by beheading. In early July the coastwatchers Bill Kyle and Greg Benham were finally arrested in the far south, after being tracked for five months. Although the Australian navy had tried to rescue Kyle and Benham their secret locations were repeatedly betrayed by native informers.[14] The two were triumphantly brought to Kavieng for Kenpeitai interrogation, and on 1 September 1942 were also taken to Nago Island and executed. Later in November the German priest Father Karl Martin and his Irish colleague Father Michael Murphy were also arrested for anti-Japanese activities and beheaded, again on Nago.[15]

Although their exact movements after mid-1942 are not clear, the elderly German nuns, considered harmless, lived under enemy observation at various missions and plantations, including Namatanai and Lemakot, until March 1944, when the mission was destroyed by Allied bombs. Afterwards the five surviving sisters lived in caves at Baia Plantation until August 1944. They were then ordered into an internment camp at Lakuramau Mission, where two died and the last three survivors remained until the end of the war.[16] In mid-1942 a number of the younger German priests also attracted Japanese interest, and seven in particular were singled out for special attention. All members of the venerable Mission of the Most Sacred Heart of Jesus[17], they were Father Heinrich Kohlstette MSC of the big Komalu Catholic Mission on the west coast; Father Josef Krutzenbichler MSC of Tanga Islands Catholic Mission off the east coast; Father Paul Kutscher MSC of Lamussong Catholic Mission on the east coast; Father Karl Schluetter MSC of

Lihir Catholic Mission on Lihir Island, also off the east coast; Father Franz Utsch MSC of the Lavongai Catholic Mission on New Hanover Island; and Father Josef Lakaff MSC and Brother Heinrich Zunkley MSC, both of the Kavieng Catholic Mission.

Commencing just after the US invasion of Guadalcanal in early August 1942, and following Australian successes in the Kokoda campaign, and initial Japanese indecision about where to intern them, by early September approximately 25 detained Australian civilians and the seven detained German missionaries were concentrated into two permanent civilian internment camps near Kavieng. The Australians were imprisoned in a camp created in a cluster of three houses[18] in the bush at Kulangit village in the northern part of Kavieng town, near Chinatown.[19] At Burns Philp's big Panapai Plantation, about 6 kilometres south of Kavieng, the seven missionaries were imprisoned in the large plantation bungalow. The Panapai camp was west of the newly constructed Japanese 'Number 2' airfield, a location which would make the camp particularly exposed later in the war. The Japanese had now officially categorised the Australians as 'European Enemy Aliens' and the German missionaries as 'Neutral Aliens', despite Japan and Germany having signed a pact of alliance.[20]

At the time of internment, eight of the Australian men at the Kulangit camp were aged in their forties, eight were in their fifties, and three, John Bell, Albert Moseley and Charlie Ostrom, were over sixty. This was a very elderly group to be facing the harsh life of a Japanese internment camp. Only a handful of the internees was under forty. Leon Williams from Kimadan Plantation was 38, Lon Davies was 35, Jack Griffin had just turned 32, Jim Naughton from Kalili was 31, and Max Ostrom of Lakurafanga Plantation was just 20. Also in the camp was David Topal, the youthful son of Henry Topal.

Most of the interned Australians were copra planters, and most knew each other well from pre-war associations in the close-knit New Ireland expatriate community. The only non-planters in the group were Bill Attwood, the mechanic and garage owner from Kavieng; and Phil Levy, the pre-war Burns Philp manager from Kavieng. About fifteen of the men were married, and had been separated from wives and children during voluntary departures and the evacuations of the previous year.

Significantly, thirteen of the internees were ex-soldiers from World War I, most with very long service records. Some had been at Gallipoli, nearly all had fought in France, and most had experienced the violence of modern warfare while serving far from their homes and families. As young men they had seen a great deal of shocking death and injury, and had learnt that one major key to survival was to stick together as mates, selflessly and equally sharing the best and worst, and to never, ever give in to the Turks or Germans or to their inner enemies, depression, homesickness and hopelessness.

Prominent in this group of ex-diggers was Albert Moseley of Belik Plantation, who had won the Military Cross as a lieutenant with the 14th Australian Light Horse Regiment. Another ex-Lighthorseman was Edmund Woodhouse from Katu Plantation, who had been a lieutenant in the 2nd Australian Light Horse Regiment. Les Gordon had been with the 28th and 51st Infantry Battalions, eventually as a staff sergeant; Walter Heydon had been a private in the 13th Infantry Battalion; and Dusty Miller had served in the 4th Infantry Battalion and later as a corporal in the Australian Pay Corps. After making seven attempts to enlist, Claude Chadderton was finally accepted into the Australian army in June 1918, too late to see overseas service, but later became involved with the Kavieng Volunteer Rifles. It seems that John Bell may also have served in the Australian army between 1914 and 1918. Vivian Ives of Kurumut Plantation, an Englishman, had been a captain who had seen service with the British and Indian armies in the Middle East and had twice won the Military Cross. Two of the younger internees, Lon Davies and Boyd Whitehead, are believed to have had military training as members of the New Guinea Volunteer Rifles.[21]

There was no shortage of firm leadership, mateship and good camp organisation with so many old soldiers present in the Kulangit internment camp. Most importantly, three of the ex-diggers had been members of the Australian Army Medical Corps. Bill Garnett had been a second lieutenant with the 10th Field Ambulance, and later became a member of the New Guinea Volunteer Rifles[22], and Leigh Lightbody served as a sergeant with the 13th Field Ambulance. Henry Topal had from 1914 been a private in the Australian Army Medical Corps, and had in fact been in Kavieng in September 1917 as an acting corporal in the AAMC unit attached to the Australian Naval and Military Expeditionary Force.[23] With their practical experience dealing with serious battlefield injuries, illness and hygiene, and their later hands-on experiences with tropical diseases in the islands, the medics Garnett, Lightbody and Topal would become vital to the survival of the internees over the coming years.

Despite the very difficult living conditions they were to experience, the group was to remain almost intact for the next twenty months. The only known deaths during the period of internment were those of Leigh Lightbody, Jack's Burns Philp colleague from Kalili Plantation, who contracted dysentery, died on 29 March 1943, and was buried outside the camp at Lemakot Mission two days later[24]; and of Dusty Miller, the planter and trader from Tsaliui Island, who reportedly died at the Kavieng hospital in early 1944.

Much later, in November 1943, when it became too dangerous for the seven German priests to continue to be held at the Panapai Plantation camp near the Japanese airfields, they were moved into the Kulangit camp with the Australians.

Lists of the names and backgrounds of the Kavieng internees appear at the end of this book in Appendix A.

chapter 7

The Kavieng internment camps

Not much is definitely known about the lives of the internees from September 1942, but much can be guessed. No physical evidence relating to this period exists. There are no personal effects, photographs, drawings, documents or diaries; no clothing or luggage.

The Japanese navy, which was directly responsible for all the Kavieng internees, appears to have kept no records of their names and activities, nor supplied this information at any time to the International Committee of the Red Cross, even though the ICRC managed a POW and internee identification and records operation in Japan throughout the war under the auspices of the neutral Swedish government. The Japanese also ran an organisation in Tokyo called the Prisoner of War Information Bureau[1] which, although it gave the appearance of maintaining and providing humanitarian information about captured Allied POWs and internees, was little more than a vehicle for Japanese propaganda and a repository for hundreds of thousands of hopeful letters and packages sent to prisoners by their families, but rarely passed on to them.

In addition, this small band of mainly middle-aged and elderly male civilian prisoners was of little numerical significance in the overall scheme of things on New Ireland where at the height of the occupation there were over 13 000 Japanese sailors, soldiers and civilian contractors; and over 50 000 Melanesians. The personal affairs of the internees were not important enough to merit close observation and reporting, particularly as the war situation worsened for Japan and every one of the island's occupiers became more and more concerned about their own security and survival.

Everything we know and can deduce about the internment period is fragmentary, obtained from postwar interviews with members of the former occupying forces, members of the Melanesian community and other local residents, the few elderly nuns who had survived, and four witnesses who had passed through Kavieng in 1942 and 1943. The information gathered from locals was quickly found to be of uneven reliability, and important facts like names and dates only vaguely remembered. Information gathered from the Japanese was, at least for an initial period, believed to be much more plausible.

The internment camps at Kulangit and Panapai were guarded by a detachment of a warrant officer and a number of sailors of the Kavieng-based 83rd Naval Garrison Unit (83 NGU), part of the 14th Naval Base Force (14 NBF), the supreme military authority in the Kavieng area, itself in turn subordinated to the Japanese South-East Area Naval Fleet headquarters in Rabaul. From the time of their internment in 1942 until December 1943 the Australians at Kulangit were supervised by Warrant Officer Tomezo Funayama[2], Petty Officer Tomoichi Iwaoka, and between two and five sailors from the anti-aircraft platoon of 83 NGU. During this period Petty Officer Iwaoka frequently visited the camp delivering rations and other supplies and became well acquainted with the Australians.[3] From December 1943 until March 1944 supervision of the camp was said to have been assumed by a platoon of the security detachment of 83 NGU led by Ensign Shose Suzuki.[4]

In 1942 the command structure of the Imperial Japanese Navy was rigidly hierarchical and authoritarian, with officers and men at each level subservient to those above, and dominant over those below. Absolute, unequivocal and unquestioning obedience to authority was a strictly enforced rule of naval culture (as it was in the army and air force). The position of individuals in the hierarchy determined their personal allotment of authority, and lower in the ranks the rule was enforced by brutal and arbitrary administration of corporal and other punishments by those above to those below. The commissioned officers at the upper reaches of this system, the admirals, captains, commanders, lieutenant commanders and lieutenants, received the lion's share of power and perks; the non-commissioned officers, and especially the sailors at the very bottom, received progressively less. The lot of vast numbers of sailors at the base of this pyramid of authority was little better than that of beaten, obsequious slaves.

Placed below this hierarchy in the occupied territories were the 'natives' who had been released from their 'servitude' to European colonial powers and were now to be 'enlightened and liberated' under Japanese rule; and still further below them were the vanquished foreigners who had been captured, the European internees and prisoners of war in the camps, and the Overseas Chinese. As the war progressed and living conditions worsened for the Japanese, things became ever more insufferable for those below them.[5]

There was also a malevolent side to the outlook of the occupiers in Kavieng which would be seen more and more as the war progressed, causing them to be indifferent to the sufferings of those from other races and nationalities. During their harsh training as members of the Imperial Japanese Navy they had been acculturised to be unafraid of death, and to willingly offer their lives for Emperor Hirohito when ordered to do so, proudly and unflinchingly. It was utterly disgraceful, an unbearable loss of face, to fail the obligation. At least outwardly, Japanese sailors were proud of this culture of self-sacrifice, and contemptuous of a respect for human life, which they characterised as a pathetic Western weakness. Each officer and sailor of the 14th Naval Base Force and 83rd Naval Garrison Unit had been indoctrinated to believe that living as close as possible to death, and loving and glorifying dying, gave them a huge advantage in battle over their opponents. They knew that they could only ever be revered and decorated for brave deeds on the battlefield after they had died. The Orders of the Golden Kite, the Rising Sun and the Dual Rays of the Rising Sun were only awarded posthumously, and many medals would be awarded when the time for Japan's mass self-sacrifice came later in the war.[6]

The Japanese and their internees were also located within a wider economy which, although called a 'Co-Prosperity Sphere', was an economic disaster. On New Ireland the occupation had severely interrupted the normal production and distribution of food and other essentials, while simultaneously introducing greater demand. The sizeable navy and army garrisons on New Ireland, eventually numbering 13 000 hungry (and sex-starved[7]) young men, had suddenly increased the island's population by about 25 per cent, without any provision being made for a commensurate increase in supply. As the war progressed and the Allied blockade intensified, the food shortage became particularly acute, and supplies of medicines, clothing and other essentials were rapidly depleted.

As they were in Japanese civilian enemy alien internment camps everywhere in the Asia-Pacific region, living conditions for the Kavieng inmates were a test of survival. The Japanese presence made it extremely difficult for the internees to obtain supplies from any local residents who were still willing to help them, although food and medicine was acquired from time to time in this way.[8] Most of the time the internees had to depend on their ingenuity and resourcefulness to obtain supplies of food, medicine and other necessities through persistent negotiation with their unpredictable and often capricious captors. The golden rule in these negotiations was that if prisoners were prepared to make themselves useful to the Japanese and were willing to cooperate, they were more likely to stay alive. Usefulness and cooperation meant obediently supplying their skills and labour in exchange for the basic necessities of life. And, like farm animals which had become unproductive, if prisoners were deemed useless or non-cooperative, their lives could be terminated through neglect, or by direct action.[9]

The Australian internees at Kavieng obtained rations in exchange for performing menial labour, and the men were often seen in groups around Kavieng, digging, loading, repairing and carrying. If they possessed very useful technical skills they could live reasonably well. The two qualified mechanics in the group, Bill Attwood and Jim Naughton, were permitted to work in Attwood's old Kavieng garage off and on for much of their internment, fixing and servicing civilian trucks and cars expropriated by the Japanese, often living in the Kavieng Hotel to be closer to work.

The constant endeavour to obtain food was supplemented by the internees' own well-organised efforts at poultry raising, egg production, and fruit and vegetable growing using gardens, orchards and groves they cultivated near the Kulangit camp. The planters were practical men skilled at producing food from the land, and their agricultural, horticultural and poultry-raising activities were enthusiastically encouraged by the Japanese guards in exchange for a vastly disproportionate share of production. The great usefulness of the internees as skilled food providers for their captors appears to have been one key reason for their survival during eighteen months of captivity. As well, daily work in the vegetable gardens and poultry pens gave the men a sense of usefulness and accomplishment.[10]

It was also necessary to organise camp life to apportion rations fairly, minimise conflict, deal with ever-present sickness and disease, and maintain the highest standards of hygiene and sanitation that the cramped circumstances and a tropical climate would allow. Again, the rural and military backgrounds of the men would have provided invaluable skills for meeting such organisational challenges.[11]

Importantly, the civilian internees at Kavieng would have needed to maintain a sense of optimism and hope in a situation that could easily descend into hopelessness, completely isolated from knowledge of the progress of the war and the chance of rescue. There were no reliable sources of news and information, no mail deliveries, and radios of any sort were utterly prohibited. Internees became adept at interpreting the meaning of war news provided by their captors, which was always biased and exaggerated in favor of Japan. The married men had no way of knowing the whereabouts or welfare of their wives and children, some sent back to Australia long ago in 1941, and others farewelled at Kavieng wharf and Ulapatur in December of that year. The planters also worried about the condition of their properties and their employees.

The daily struggle against depression, isolation and homesickness was something the men dealt with together. It was to meet this challenge of maintaining morale and lifting spirits that the many natural leaders in the group, men like Ives, Moseley, Woodhouse and Garnett, drew on their past wartime experiences to lead and encourage others through the difficulties. There were also talented entertainers like young Jack Griffin, who could step to the fore on special occasions and raise spirits by organising musical and other entertainments using whatever resources they could make or muster.

As the relicts of a defeated colonial power the Australians would have also suffered ridicule and humiliation, including bowing to guards and the Rising Sun flag, and arbitrary face-slappings and beatings when they failed to show proper respect. The camp routine would have included drawn-out musters and roll calls, particularly during the occasional inspections of the camp by senior naval officers, all designed to lower the prestige of the discomfited Australians.[12]

As the fortunes of war elsewhere in the region turned ever more against Japan after mid-1942, and as Japan's lines of supply became increasingly interdicted by Allied naval and air activity, the lot of isolated island units like the 14th Naval Base Force in Kavieng became ever more severe. For the ordinary Japanese sailors and soldiers, living conditions became harsher than ever before, in an atmosphere of growing fear, anger and uncertainty. Neglected at the very bottom of the supply chain, the Kavieng internees would have become greatly overworked and malnourished, and more vulnerable to ever-present tropical disease and the diseases of protein deficiency.

The most common sicknesses were caused by the poor quality and insufficient food, combined with the stress of internment: weight loss, diarrhoea and dysentery. Added to the miseries suffered from these were those inflicted by exposure to the abundant bacteria, viruses and parasites of a tropical environment without the benefit of medication and proper treatment.[13] The most common, and recurring, tropical disease was malaria, but the men were also troubled by constant skin ailments, including tropical ulcers which could open up flesh to the bone. In these circumstances it is remarkable there was only one definitely recorded death at the Australian camp during the eighteen months of confinement, and it is probably true that the medical skills of Bill Garnett, Henry Topal and Leigh Lightbody played a significant part in this success. Tragically, Lightbody's was the single recorded fatality.[14]

Despite all of their privations after June 1942, the lives of the Australian internees in Kavieng were apparently never threatened by their captors. In the midst of a growing number of atrocities committed against prisoners of war and civilian internees throughout the occupied territories, and despite the worsening war situation, it appears the Japanese believed the Kavieng inmates were sufficiently energetic, useful and harmless to permit their continuing existence.[15] In other parts of the occupied territories, when internees and prisoners of war were deemed to be useless to the Japanese and had become their competitors for available food, shelter and medicine, they were quickly allowed to die of disease or starvation, or deliberately disposed of.

On 18 March 1943 the Japanese naval destroyer *Akikaze* arrived in Kavieng carrying almost seventy adult European missionaries, their families, and a considerable number of Chinese children in their care who had been collected from Kairiru Island and Manus Island further to the north-west in the Bismarck Sea. None of the civilian internees was disembarked in Kavieng, because secret orders had been received by radio from Japanese fleet headquarters in Rabaul to immediately execute the entire party. After the *Akikaze* left Kavieng later that day for Rabaul, and commencing at a point about 100 kilometres out to sea off the west coast of New Ireland, the men, women and children were moved in ones and twos to the rear of the ship, hung by their wrists from a frame, and machine-gunned. Their bodies were cut down and pushed overboard into the ship's wake, while a 5-year-old Chinese child was tossed overboard, still alive. A ruthless decision had been taken that such a large group of useless civilians was most likely to become an unwelcome drain on available space, food, and medical supplies at the Japanese internment camps in Kavieng and Rabaul.[16]

Because they were useful, productive, well organised and well led, the Australian men and young David Topal were permitted to live imprisoned in their dreadful circumstances at Kulangit, as were the missionaries at Panapai. Then, in February and March 1944, their little forgotten corner of the war abruptly changed forever.

chapter 8

The American offensive

The mid-1942 successes of the US navy in checking further Japanese advances in the Pacific encouraged America's war strategists to begin a large-scale offensive to reclaim all occupied Pacific territories. These included the Australian Mandated Territory of New Guinea. For the purpose of ejecting the Japanese from New Guinea the Americans would lead the campaign, in an alliance with the much smaller Australian military forces. From the perspective of the United States, Australia would play the role of a minor, albeit important partner in this great venture, with the bulk of Australian forces limited to land operations on the island of Papua. At the same time as our little group of Australians and Germans was beginning to be rounded up for internment in Kavieng, the US Joint Chiefs of Staff met in Washington in July 1942 to order a general offensive to be prepared, with the immediate objective being the reoccupation by Allied land forces of Papua (by Americans and Australians), and New Britain, New Ireland and the Bismarck Sea area (by the Americans).

With this plan a US invasion of the Australian territory of New Ireland was early made a central part of the strategy, and although there were numerous intermediate challenges to be met, including recapture of the Solomon Islands, the New Ireland objective was to remain one of the firm cornerstones of that strategy.[1] If the Australians still trapped on New Ireland were going to be rescued, it was probably going to be by US marines, not Australians—although the internees had no way of even guessing that might be the case.

Under a sometimes awkward arrangement, separate military tasks in the South-west Pacific were allotted evenly to the US-led armies,

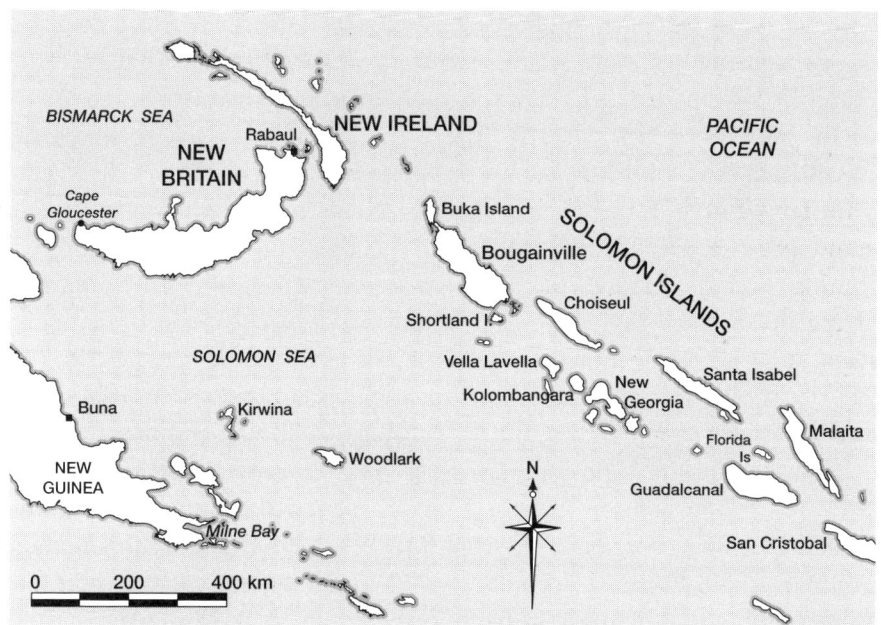

The Solomon Islands and Bismarck Archipelago areas, showing many of the islands and locations targeted by US forces during offensives from 1942.

including its army air forces (USAAF), all under the command of General Douglas MacArthur; and to the US-led naval forces, including the US Marine Corps and navy air wing, all under the command of Admiral Ernest King. The first step in this US army-navy campaign was to recapture the large mountainous island of Guadalcanal, about 800 kilometres south of New Ireland in the Solomon Islands group. In mid-1942 an Australian coastwatcher on Guadalcanal had reported that the Japanese occupiers had commenced construction of a strategically important airfield[2], so on 7 August 1942 the US 1st Marine Division landed on the island to seize control of this valuable asset. Their arrival provoked the first, longest and one of the bloodiest land, sea and air battles of the Pacific campaign. The fight for Guadalcanal would last just over six months, with the eventual American victory coming at great cost in lives, equipment and ships, especially to the defenders.[3] However, the loss of Guadalcanal and its prized airfield began a long, slow northwards retreat by Japanese forces which would continue for the next two and a half years. Each battle fought during this retreat would follow the Guadalcanal pattern. There would be an isolated Japanese garrison of soldiers weakened by disease and starvation which could only be reinforced, re-supplied or evacuated with great difficulty, the troops fighting stubbornly and enduring extraordinary casualties, and prohibited from surrender even though their cause was futile.

In January 1943, shortly after Guadalcanal was resolved, the Casablanca Conference in Morocco between President Roosevelt, Prime Minister Churchill and their respective chiefs of military staffs set the grand priorities for Allied strategy in Europe and the Pacific for the coming period. Among the many decisions made was reaffirmation of the importance of reclaiming the Bismarck Archipelago at an early stage, now not as an objective in itself but as a stepping-stone towards securing more northerly positions from which land-based aircraft could directly attack Japan. As a result, in February 1943 General MacArthur's headquarters in Brisbane completed new plans for the attainment of this objective, proposing among other things an encirclement of Rabaul and New Britain with an advance by US forces through the Solomon Islands to Kavieng and Rabaul in the east, and a complementary advance in the west by US and Australian forces along the north coast of Papua.

Later in 1943, following considerable debate at the Quebec Conference in Canada between Roosevelt and Churchill, approval was given to the latest plans for the American-led offensive in the South-west Pacific. These included MacArthur's gaining control of the Bismarck Archipelago, neutralising but now not yet recapturing Rabaul, and capturing Kavieng and the Admiralty Islands. By October 1943 MacArthur's staff had produced a more detailed plan and timetable for this venture, now incorporating as a specific target the recapture of Kavieng by 1 March 1944.

The Americans were now interested in little Kavieng for the same reasons as the Japanese before their invasion in early 1942—its strategic position, the deep-water all-weather harbour, and the airfields there and at Panapai from which the USAAF could threaten Japanese possessions further north in the Pacific and attack the huge garrison to the south at Rabaul. Under MacArthur's plan, after its seizure Kavieng was supposed to become a minor fleet base, a patrol-boat base and a major air base expanded to six airfields.[4]

In January 1944 detailed plans were developed by MacArthur's staff to complete the encirclement of Rabaul. This was to be achieved by firstly invading the western portion of New Britain; then seizing the Green Islands to the east of New Ireland; then the Admiralty Islands; and finally Kavieng itself and then the whole of New Ireland. Because of logistics issues the date for the Kavieng operation was adjusted from 1 March to 1 April, and orders were written for a concentrated, protracted preliminary air and naval bombardment of Japanese military positions throughout February and March. A principal objective of the American strategy was to achieve air superiority as quickly as possible, which included the destruction of all enemy aircrew, aircraft and the ground facilities which supported them. Kavieng had a Japanese seaplane base and two airfields. These would immediately come under intense scrutiny by US reconnaissance aircraft, and then be destroyed by bombing.

At this stage of the Pacific campaign the US war economy was moving into high gear. Affluent America was expending about half of its vast annual economic production on the war, and American industry was manufacturing ships, aircraft, vehicles, munitions and all manner of other military supplies at an extraordinary rate. There were almost 750 000 US servicemen in the South-west Pacific area, supported by over 400 000 Australians and New Zealanders. The military resources, energy supplies and technology that could be employed by these allies to dislodge the Japanese forces had reached an unprecedented volume and level of sophistication. The main technique being used was the application of relentless, concentrated, large-scale air and naval bombardment of Japanese positions and shipping, served by a seemingly inexhaustible high-volume logistics chain from US factories to the front line right across the Pacific Ocean. The Allies were beginning to enjoy almost total superiority in the air, and their navies were asserting increasing dominance over the seas.

As the fortunes of the Allies soared, the fortunes of Japan plunged. Increasingly deprived of energy supplies, war resources, and food and medicines in the face of this relentless and growing application of force, and facing an unbearable loss of face, Japan's leaders deliberately seized upon the only course of action open to them. To slow down the Allied advance they would begin progressively expending the 'one hundred million lives' of their own servicemen and citizen population[5], and the lives of the millions now under their control within the Co-Prosperity Sphere. The military leadership in Tokyo was, once again, misjudging the situation, believing that the vigour of the US allies would eventually dissipate in the face of such large-scale and blatant sacrifice of life, and that they would be drawn to an 'honourable' negotiated settlement. This policy was just another of the tragic outcomes of Japan's ultimately self-defeating militarist culture. The logic was that no matter how hopeless their circumstances the Japanese people and armed forces were to be coerced to achieve 'victory', irrespective of the cost, even if that eventually meant the destruction of Japan.[6]

As a consequence of this policy, the treatment of prisoners by increasingly frustrated and angry Japanese authorities and troops worsened. From 1943 the Japanese High Command began issuing directives for contingency preparations to be made for the 'disposal' of POWs and civilian internees should the military situation deteriorate to the point where 'prisoners could be deemed expendable'.[7]

For the officers and sailors of the 14th Naval Base Unit at Kavieng there would be further dispiriting news. In order to preserve ships, planes and crews, commencing in late 1943 Japan began moving many of its key naval and air force assets and personnel out of the now highly vulnerable New Guinea and Bismarck Sea areas to a new defensive line much further to the north, running through the Palau, Marianas and Caroline island groups. This withdrawal could not include the large numbers of soldiers and sailors on New Britain and New Ireland, who were thus abandoned to their fate.[8] In February 1944 the last remnants of the Japanese air forces—both men and machines—were withdrawn from Rabaul and Kavieng, including most of the float-planes at Kavieng. It would not take long before individual servicemen at these bases began to realise what was happening to them.[9]

By early 1944, vast numbers of Japanese servicemen trapped on islands and bases around the Bismarck Sea were being killed and maimed in their vulnerable garrisons while a frustrated Japanese High Command could do nothing to withdraw them to safety. From the point of view of the navy and army garrisons now under sustained attack on New Ireland, the almost daily rain of high-explosive bombs and shells simply added to the growing perception that they were doomed, unable to escape yet unable to ward off the threat. Progressively, following the fall of Guadalcanal, the nearby Japanese-held islands and bases of Bougainville, Buna, Lae, Salamaua, Finschafen, Nadzab, the western Solomon Islands and the western end of New Britain had all fallen with massive loss of life for the defenders, who gave up their lives by the tens of thousands. The Imperial Japanese Navy defenders of Kavieng and the Imperial Japanese Army forces on New Ireland clearly understood that an invasion by the all-conquering Americans, Australians and their allies would probably mean there would be no hope of survival.

chapter 9

War returns to Kavieng, February 1944

In February 1944, as American actions to recapture Kavieng played out, the war returned to the town with a fury. It was now just over two years since the Japanese occupation took place, and the violence was returning as the Allied line of advance pushed relentlessly northwards. The Americans had prepared three large-scale operations in the New Ireland area: occupation of the Green Islands, 400 kilometres to the south-east, by 15 February; occupation of the Admiralties, 300 kilometres to the north-west, by 29 February; and the frontal seizure of Kavieng itself by 1 April. Long before, the US Navy had allocated Kavieng the locality codename 'Forearm', and its planned invasion was now given the title Operation Forearm.[1]

To prepare the way for these operations the US Navy and USAAF began conducting wide-ranging attacks from sea and air on Japanese airfields, garrisons and shipping around the Bismarck Sea, staged from newly constructed forward bases in the Solomon Islands and Papua. To carry out these operations the Americans were equipped with a generous supply of aircraft, crews and armaments, and were becoming highly adept at using low-level bombing techniques to sink Japanese ships. They were also easily tracking enemy shipping movements using secret radio intelligence, and hunting the ships by day and night in any weather using the newly-perfected technology of air-borne radar.[2]

Many successful attacks were staged in the waters near Kavieng by US aircraft in early 1944. On 3 February the cargo vessel *Nichiai Maru* was sunk near New Hanover Island; on 16 February a Japanese convoy escorted by the submarine-chasers *Cha 39* and *Cha 16* was attacked by

The Kavieng Massacre

Kavieng, New Ireland, March 1944. A Japanese ship under attack by B-25 Mitchell bombers from the 5th Air Force, USAAF. Bombs from the aircraft have struck the ship but have not exploded. AUSTRALIAN WAR MEMORIAL NEGATIVE NUMBER AWM 127666

B-25 Mitchell aircraft near Kavieng, with the cargo ship *Sanko Maru* being sunk and the *Kashi Maru* forced to beach; on the same day the cargo vessel *Taisyo Maru* was sunk by B-25s near New Hanover. On 19 February the submarine chasers *Cha 34*, *Cha 22* and *Cha 40* and the cargo ships *No. 1 Shinto Maru* and *Shinkiku Maru* were also sunk by B-25s near Kavieng.

On 21 February, immediately to the north-west of Kavieng, American B-25s attacked a small convoy which had set out from Rabaul the previous day evacuating Japanese air force personnel to Palau, further to the north in the Central Pacific. This convoy included the submarine-chaser *Cha 38*, the converted submarine-chaser *Cha 48*, another submarine-chaser named *Naguara*, and two passenger/cargo ships, the *Kokai Maru* and *Kowa Maru*, carrying the service personnel. The *Kokai Maru* and *Kowa Maru* both received direct hits which killed or injured hundreds of passengers and started large fires. During the night as the ships slowly sank, the survivors watched from their lifeboats until they were picked up by the *Naguara*, which was itself sunk the following morning by surface ships of US Destroyer Squadron TG39.4. The sinking of the

War returns to Kavieng, February 1944

New Hanover, Bismarck Archipelago, 16 February 1944. An attack by B-25 bombers on a Japanese patrol craft. AUSTRALIAN WAR MEMORIAL NEGATIVE NUMBER AWM 043126

Kokai Maru, *Kowa Maru* and *Nagaura*, although completely unrelated at the time to the fate of the Kavieng internees, would much later turn out to be of enormous significance to their story.[3]

Apart from attacking shipping, for the first time in the war the Americans began massive air raids on land targets on New Ireland. In support of the Green and Admiralty islands landings, and in preparation for the re-taking of New Ireland, from mid-February 1944 the 5th and 13th USAAF air forces conducted many large raids, dropping hundreds of tons of bombs on targets around the town of Kavieng, particularly on the two airfields. On the night of 11 February, fifty B-24 Liberators heavily bombed and strafed the Kavieng airfields; on 13 February thirty-five B-24s again attacked the airfields; on 14 February forty B-24s bombed the Kavieng area; on 15 February over seventy B-24, A-20 Havoc and B-25 aircraft bombed and strafed the town area, harbour and shipping; on 16 February thirty B-24s attacked the airfields again; and yet again on 17 February, with forty B-24s conducting the raid.[4]

Air raids on this massive scale on little Kavieng were extraordinary and frightening experiences for everyone on the ground, particularly for the hapless Japanese forces, who became increasingly frustrated and angered. Day after day and night after night, the din of aerial warfare erupted over and around the town: the roar of US aircraft engines and

Kavieng, New Ireland, March 1944. A Japanese ship under attack by B-25 Mitchell bombers from the 5th Air Force, USAAF, with bombs exploding in forecastle and hold. AUSTRALIAN WAR MEMORIAL NEGATIVE NUMBER AWM 127667

guns, the bark of Japanese anti-aircraft artillery, and the crash of bombs. Apart from bombs other things fell from the sky, including debris from the Japanese barrage, crashing aircraft and aircraft parts, and parachuting aircrew, who became special targets for Japanese reprisals. The two airfields at Panapai became the graveyards of scores of Japanese aircraft, and the runways, taxiways and revetments blown up. Some American aircraft also crashed into the surrounding waters, and occasionally the survivors were picked up by daring rescue missions using Catalina flying boats.[5]

On 18 February 1944 the first US navy attacks on Kavieng commenced with a shore bombardment by 23 USN Destroyer Squadron. On 22 February USN Destroyer Squadron TG 39.4 bombarded the airstrips, pier area and anchorages, and while in the vicinity sank the minelayer *Natsushima*, a large tug, the submarine-chaser *No. 8 Tama Maru*, and two cargo vessels, the *Choryu Maru* and *No. 9 Tokuyama Maru*. On 25 February 12 USN Destroyer Squadron also bombarded the Kavieng area, sinking the cargo ship *Tatsugiko Maru* while en route to the target.

The officers of 14 Naval Base Force and 83 Naval Garrison Unit in Kavieng were alarmed by the ferocity and impunity of these US attacks,

War returns to Kavieng, February 1944

Kavieng, New Ireland, March 1944. Aerial photograph of a strafing run on Japanese floatplanes by B-25 Mitchell bomber aircraft from the 5th Air Force, USAAF. AUSTRALIAN WAR MEMORIAL NEGATIVE NUMBER AWM 127669

Kavieng, New Ireland, March 1944. Aerial photograph of bombs bursting at the main Japanese base. A floatplane is blazing in the water beyond the town. AUSTRALIAN WAR MEMORIAL NEGATIVE NUMBER AWM 127664

which they correctly interpreted as precursors to an invasion. Hundreds of Japanese sailors had been killed or injured. Many of the buildings in the town had been badly damaged or destroyed, the harbour installations were a tangled mass of broken piers and sunken ships, and the landing strips and aircraft storage areas at the two airfields were pockmarked by hundreds of bomb craters. The headquarters of 83 Naval Garrison Unit had been forced to relocate into the bush east of the town between Kavieng and Panapai, away from the bombs and shells, and the Japanese sailors had begun living in underground bunkers, caves and concrete pillboxes for protection.

After twenty months of relative peace, the Australian internees and German priests, now held together in the Kulangit camp[6], suddenly found themselves once again located in the middle of a very active war. The abrupt arrival of so many American planes overhead and ships off the coast was the biggest boost to their spirits since their captivity began. Surely this would mean the war would soon end and they would be delivered to safety. The sole concern of the internees became staying calm and alive during the ferocious bombardments. With thirteen ex-diggers in the group, men who had survived massive artillery shellings during World War I, the internees knew what to do. Like the Japanese, they quickly dug deep trenches and dugouts in the grounds at Kulangit, as far from the prominent bungalow buildings as possible, and huddled in the darkness below ground level each night while the earth rocked and shook with the bomb blasts and shrapnel whizzed through the trees.

But the internees could not know that these American naval and air attacks had initiated a sequence of secret actions by the Japanese naval officers in Kavieng which would determine their immediate fate. They could not know that the senior officer ultimately responsible for deciding what to do with the internees was being openly pressured by his immediate subordinates to make a quick decision about their 'disposal'.

chapter 10

Captain Tamura's instruction

In February 1944, as they continued preparations for what they thought would be their final defence, serious questions arose among senior officers at the Kavieng headquarters of the Imperial Japanese Navy regarding the Australians and Germans at the two internment camps. Lieutenant Kyoji Mori, Executive Officer of 83 Naval Garrison Unit and simultaneously Commander of the Sea Defence Department, was the officer immediately responsible for the camps, although he rarely visited them, and the person now becoming the most agitated about the foreigners' presence. Ever since the general order regarding disposal of prisoners and internees had permeated down the Imperial Japanese Navy chain of command the previous year, Lieutenant Mori had informally discussed the matter with his fellow officers. Now that the Allied offensive had apparently reached Kavieng, Mori once again approached his immediate superior, Commander Shozo Yoshino at 14 Naval Base Force headquarters, to remind him yet again of the existence of the internees and to seek more formal advice regarding what to do with them.[1]

Yoshino had been Senior Staff Officer of 14 Naval Base Force since December 1943, and because of Mori's frequent reminders knew the problem the internees' presence posed if an Allied invasion should eventuate. He had already signalled by radio two or three times to South-East Area Fleet headquarters in Rabaul requesting that the Europeans be sent there, thus passing responsibility for them to a completely different command. Understandably, no reply had ever been received, headquarters being completely preoccupied with their own, similar defensive predicament. Following repeated heavy air raids in February

Kavieng, March 1944. Low-level aerial shot from a US bomber of a large camouflaged house used as Japanese officers' quarters. It was destroyed by following planes of the 5th Air Force, USAAF. The house was probably a pre-war plantation bungalow.
AUSTRALIAN WAR MEMORIAL NEGATIVE NUMBER AWM 127665

and March 1944, American intelligence would estimate in April that only 200 of the original 1400 buildings in Rabaul were still standing, while Simpson Harbour was littered with the hulks of dozens of burnt and broken Japanese ships.

Yoshino's immediate superior in Kavieng, Captain Ryukichi Tamura, held simultaneous overall command of 14 Naval Base Force and 83 Naval Garrison Unit. Captain Tamura was an experienced 53-year-old career officer and supreme commander of all naval and civil affairs units in the Kavieng area, including the naval base and garrison of 4000 sailors; land, sea and air defence units; supply, construction, repair and transport units; and a number of naval vessels, including a small fleet of landing barges. He had been in the Japanese navy since his enlistment as a youth, had joined his first ship in 1913, and risen steadily through the ranks until appointment in 1922 to his first command, the submarine

SS-21. By 1944 he had commanded numerous naval vessels and shore installations and had seen service throughout the Pacific. He had become commander of 14 Naval Base Unit in October 1943 after postings immediately before at Rabaul and on Bougainville Island, and was soon to be promoted to rear admiral in May 1944. Within the vast ranks of the Imperial Japanese Navy, Captain Tamura was a very senior officer and regarded as an experienced, capable and respected leader.[2]

On 4 March 1944, following the waves of American air and naval attacks, and in response to Mori's reminders, Commander Yoshino approached Captain Tamura for instructions regarding the internees.[3] Tamura was well aware of the two internment camps, having inspected them early in his appointment, and was also of the opinion that the internees should have been sent out of his command to Rabaul. However, he was also painfully aware of the many losses of Japanese ships, and that the sea lanes between Kavieng and Rabaul had become very dangerous because of Allied dominance of air and sea. He knew that the few valuable ships still available to him could not be risked transporting a small group of valueless internees to safety. Getting the internees out of his area of responsibility and off his hands was now completely out of the question.

However, Captain Tamura was not yet prepared to make a decision. As senior officer in a military headquarters besieged with all the myriad problems of an imminent defensive battle, a final decision about the fate of the little group of internees was not a high priority. So, in response to Lieutenant Mori's request, Yoshino was unable to obtain any instructions from the Captain, and again the matter lapsed.

In mid-March 1944, as the Americans pondered what to do about their final plan of attack for Kavieng, a lull occurred in their air and naval raids on the town. This gave the Japanese a respite to consider their situation and pay attention to the details of their defense. On the morning of 15 March, and again prompted by the increasingly anxious Lieutenant Mori, Commander Yoshino once again went to Captain Tamura to point out the difficulty posed by the presence of internees.

This time Tamura was able to give some attention to the problem. Two days later, and impelled by what he would later describe as a 'military necessity', on Friday 17 March Tamura issued a verbal order to Yoshino that 'in the event of an Allied landing the foreign internees were to be executed secretly'.[4] The military necessity to which Tamura was referring was the doctrine of destroying absolutely anything that

Rear Admiral Ryukichi Tamura, photographed in Kavieng in October 1945. AUSTRALIAN WAR MEMORIAL NEGATIVE NUMBER AWM 098442

could be of use to enemy invaders, including people, which was one of the pillars of Japanese military thinking. When faced with an imminent defensive battle against a more powerful enemy, Japanese admirals and generals were required to 'prepare the battlefield' in a way which would concede nothing to their opponents in the event of a defeat. Apart from fixed installations and weapons, ammunition, vehicles, food and general supplies which could not be evacuated, Japanese forces were also required to destroy any person who might be of assistance to the enemy, if necessary including their own sick and injured, and their prisoners.

This was wartime Japanese logic being seriously applied in early 1944 by a senior, well-educated naval officer, who having been so indoctrinated in the military ideal of self-sacrifice thought that it was quite acceptable that everyone under his command should die, including harmless civilian prisoners in his 'safekeeping'. A rational response in the face of a terrifying military defeat would have been to fly the white flag and surrender. A humane response would have been to release the internees and allow them to escape from the battle area into the hills. But these were options that Tamura could not even contemplate.

During 1944 and 1945 the desperate logic of self-sacrifice would increasingly be expressed in suicidal *banzai* charges by the infantry; the *nikudan* 'human bullet' acts of suicide bombers who strapped explosives to themselves to blow up the enemy; the *tai-atari* pilots who rammed their planes into American B-29s, and the *jibaku* pilots who blew up themselves and enemy planes in mid-air; and the infamous *kamikaze* pilots who deliberately crashed onto the decks of American aircraft carriers.[5] By 1945 the Japanese government would be making serious plans for the self-sacrifice of their entire population, the 'one hundred million', which would of course automatically mean the deaths of scores of thousands of POWs and civilian internees.

Tamura's secret order was never subsequently provided in writing, the intent being that it would remain entirely off the record and known only to his immediate subordinates. But it was an order made by a very senior and responsible officer, and because of this was not open to discussion and could not be ignored. It had been made to be obeyed unquestioningly.

Commander Yoshino transmitted the Captain's verbal order to Lieutenant Mori shortly after it was given. Again, nothing was put down in writing about the matter for Mori's benefit. It was made clear by Yoshino that the initiative for carrying out the order would be left entirely with his subordinate, based on Mori's own appreciation of the likelihood of an invasion at the time. Thus was the immediate fate of the internees quickly passed from captain to commander to be placed in the hands of a young officer who firmly believed that his life and the lives of his men would shortly and violently come to an end.

By mid-March 1944 unsubstantiated rumours began sweeping through the Japanese forces all over New Ireland that Allied landings had already commenced. The apprehensive Mori and his agitated fellow junior officers and men were now certain that invasion of the Kavieng area was inevitable, and that they should begin to prepare for the ultimate test of their young and now probably short lives.

Then, suddenly, against this tense atmosphere of excitement and foreboding, a remarkable event occurred which would impel Mori to act against the internees. On the morning of Monday 20 March 1944 the US Navy delivered an unprecedented and fantastic display of firepower aimed directly at eliminating the Japanese forces in Kavieng, an attack so huge and impressive and vicious it could only be interpreted by Mori as the immediate prelude to an Allied landing.

chapter 11

A change of plan: the great bombardment of Kavieng, 20 March 1944

At almost exactly the same time in early March 1944 when Captain Tamura, Commander Yoshino and Lieutenant Mori were contemplating the disposal of the Kavieng internees, a long-running debate which had been raging between senior officers of the US Army and US Navy was about to reach its climax. This debate, which involved New Ireland, revolved around what was known as 'island bypass' strategy, or more popularly as 'island-hopping' or 'island leapfrog'. Its sudden resolution in mid-March would have a direct bearing on the tragedy now inevitably overtaking the Kavieng internees.[1]

The Americans and their allies had learnt from bitter experience during the protracted campaigns to retake the southern Solomon Islands and Japanese-held areas on Papua that their opponents were prepared to accept extraordinary battle losses before they could be subdued. Because of the impossibility of escape in large numbers from besieged islands and bases, and the elimination of surrender as an honourable option when faced with imminent defeat, the only acceptable choice for thousands of Japanese servicemen was deliberate self-sacrifice in battle. Defeating an enemy who was prepared to do this was proving to be a protracted and costly exercise: the suicide tactics of the Japanese were forcing the Americans to take suicidal risks to defeat them. From mid-1943 US planners had begun considering alternative measures for maintaining the northward momentum of their advance without incurring these pointless losses.

It had been General MacArthur who had first seized upon the idea of 'island bypass' during the campaign to retake the Solomon Islands. After finally reclaiming Guadalcanal in the far south in early 1943, and New Georgia and Vella Lavella later that year, he faced the prospect of an equally bloody fight over every Japanese-occupied island in the

General Douglas MacArthur, photographed in Australia in 1944. AUSTRALIAN WAR MEMORIAL NEGATIVE NUMBER AWM P00444.112

chain, including Santa Isabel, Choiseul and Bougainville, until he reached New Ireland and New Britain, the biggest obstacles of all. To accelerate progress he decided to skirt many of these southern islands, particularly Choiseul with its strong enemy garrison, and go straight for Bougainville. This decision took Japanese Imperial Headquarters in Tokyo completely by surprise.

The theoretical elements of a successful bypass operation were the existence of a large, well-defended island garrison which could no longer depend on friendly air cover or re-supply by Japanese ships; dominance of the surrounding air space and sea lanes by the Allies; and an alternative location nearby which offered strategic advantage and which could be occupied and developed as a forward base with minimal cost. If completed successfully, a bypass operation could quickly convert strongly-held islands into isolated compounds of vulnerable Japanese exiles located far behind the line of advance, condemned to starvation and demoralising inactivity. In effect, bypassed islands could become large POW camps which would require only an occasional air raid or naval bombardment to remind their inmates of their complete helplessness.

A great US army-navy debate during 1943 over the proposed taking of the daunting Japanese fortress at Rabaul was precipitated by these considerations. Although Rabaul had been a clear military objective since 1942, and although MacArthur had calculated that he could shorten the war through its immediate seizure, the navy had thrown up so many objections that by mid-1943 the Americans were no longer talking about Rabaul's seizure but instead were proposing its neutralisation or isolation—in other words, its bypassing.

As well, since October 1943 Admiral William 'Bull' Halsey, commander of the US South Pacific Force, had also been questioning the advisability of proceeding with General MacArthur's plan for the seizure of Kavieng and invasion of New Ireland. As commander of the naval and marine forces tasked with carrying out Operation Forearm, Halsey had begun drawing up the detailed plans necessary, including estimates of the force to be required, the logistics, and the requirements for construction of new naval and air bases there. As they worked their way through the problems and contingencies, Halsey and his senior staff began wondering if it might be far less costly to seize the unoccupied but equally suitable Emirau Island, about 100 kilometres to the north, for the same purpose. With a large garrison of well-entrenched and by now increasingly desperate Japanese sailors and soldiers concentrated mainly around Kavieng and Namatanai, in Halsey's considered opinion New Ireland was highly suitable to be bypassed.

General MacArthur's plans for the attack on Kavieng and occupation of the island were well advanced when Halsey, technically his subordinate, put forward his Emirau Island proposal. Whether or not to bypass New Ireland became yet another argument between US Army and US Navy, between the stubborn MacArthur and his generals and the feisty Halsey and his fellow admirals. During a conference at Pearl Harbor in late January 1944 when the matter was discussed, MacArthur's representative and Chief of Staff, General Richard Sutherland, had made it clear that MacArthur was insistent that capture of Kavieng was a key and well-established element in his campaign plans and should not be changed. In the face of MacArthur's obdurate refusal to seriously consider Halsey's Emirau proposal, the plan was put to one side.[2]

Thus preparations for the Kavieng invasion continued unabated, with the allocation of a large naval fleet including aircraft carriers to cover the landings, a force of marines to mount the invasion, and base construction units to rebuild the new port and airfields. It was also arranged at this time that the USAAF would commence the preliminary heavy attacks on Kavieng during February.

However, the persistent Halsey was not to be deterred by MacArthur's stubbornness, and he was prepared to take the debate to the highest levels in the US military. Before long he was lobbying hard in Washington for acceptance of his own proposal, and he soon had the ear of his naval colleague Admiral King, and especially that of Admiral Chester Nimitz, the American Commander in Chief of all Allied Forces in the Pacific Ocean Area, and technically MacArthur's immediate superior. Having heard Halsey's arguments, which seemed to make excellent sense, Nimitz also began questioning the advisability of attempting Operation Forearm. New assessments of Japanese strength had made it apparent to him that considerable advantage could be achieved through completely bypassing not just Kavieng but Rabaul as well. The rapidly evolving military situation was about to permit a major change to the strategy which had been firmly set since mid-1942.

When they met in Washington on 12 March 1944 to decide on the issue, the US Joint Chiefs of Staff had been sufficiently influenced by Halsey, King and Nimitz. To MacArthur's annoyance they ordered that his Kavieng plan be immediately cancelled, that Emirau Island be taken

A change of plan: the great bombardment of Kavieng

Vice-Admiral William Halsey, photographed in 1942. AUSTRALIAN WAR MEMORIAL NEGATIVE NUMBER AWM 013638

Rear Admiral Robert Griffin (left), who led US Navy Task Force 37 during the bombardment of Kavieng on 20 March 1944. At the time this photograph was taken, in January 1945, Admiral Griffin was based in the US west coast port of Seattle and is seen welcoming Admiral Royal E. Ingersoll for a base inspection.

instead, and that Kavieng and Rabaul be isolated with 'minimum force'. At Emirau a light air and naval base was ordered to be established from which the Bismarck Archipelago could be blockaded, and from which operations to neutralise Kavieng and Rabaul would continue.

Thus, with this decision, a tragic future had unwittingly been set in motion for the Kavieng internees. Just five days before Captain Tamura would issue his fateful order of 17 March to execute the Kavieng internees 'in the event of an Allied landing', and unbeknown to Tamura and his officers, the Americans called off Operation Forearm. There would be no Allied landing, and no rescue of the internees by US marines. Something completely unexpected, a deliberately induced Japanese misunderstanding of American intentions, would now take place to seal the final fate of the Australian and German internees.

Preparations for the invasion of Kavieng had been brought to a very advanced stage of readiness when the Joint Chiefs cancelled the

A change of plan: the great bombardment of Kavieng

operation, and two days later issued new orders for the occupation of Emirau. The US 4th Marine Division was ready at Guadalcanal for Operation Forearm, under the command of General Alfred Noble; and the navy was assembling a powerful task force of vessels to escort the marine landing force and deliver a pre-invasion bombardment. Forearm was meant to have been a major amphibious landing supported by many arms of the US military, designed to subdue a large, well-fortified target.

From late February 1944 the naval task force for the Kavieng attack had begun assembling at the big new US naval base at Majuro Atoll in the Marshall Islands, captured from the Japanese earlier that month. The task force, codenamed TF37, was under the command of the American Rear Admiral Robert M. Griffin.[3]

TF37 consisted of thirty warships and a large number of troop carriers transport the 4th Marine Division. The warships were four large battleships, two aircraft carriers and 24 destroyers, a formidable force. The four battleships were all over twenty years old, having been constructed in the dying stages of World War I or shortly after the 1918 armistice.[4] They were the almost identical BB40 USS *New Mexico*, BB41 USS *Mississippi*, BB42 USS *Idaho* and BB43 USS *Tennessee*. These great 32 000-ton vessels were huge floating artillery platforms, each over 600 feet long and manned by over 1000 sailors, and each capable of inflicting immense destruction. Mounted aboard each ship were twelve 14-inch guns in four huge turrets, among the largest naval guns of the time, each shell fired capable of demolishing a building. Each battleship also mounted fourteen 5-inch guns, formidable enough in themselves, and a variety of other armaments including torpedoes and anti-aircraft artillery. By 1944 these old ships were regarded as too slow and cumbersome to participate in the high-speed naval manoeuvres of the time, but with their immense firepower were ideally suited to pre-invasion shore bombardments.[5]

To provide air protection for the battleships, and to add to the bombardment, two 8000-ton escort aircraft carriers were assigned. These were CVE61 USS *Manila Bay* and CVE62 USS *Natoma Bay*. For Operation Forearm each carried about thirty FM-2 Wildcat aircraft to be used for fleet air cover, artillery spotting, and bombing and strafing of the target. The carriers were armed for self-defence with a 5-inch gun, sixteen 40-mm automatic cannon and twenty 20-mm cannon, many of which could also be used against onshore targets if necessary.

Three of the US battleships which bombarded Kavieng on 20 March 1944, at Pearl Harbor in December 1943. From left to right: *Idaho* (BB-42), *New Mexico* (BB-40) and *Mississippi* (BB-41).

Finally, to screen the battleships, aircraft carriers and troop transports against any hostile surface ships or submarines, 24 fast destroyers were added to the fleet, each carrying many of the standard 5-inch naval guns which could also add to the pre-invasion bombardment, as well as torpedoes and automatic cannon.

When the Joint Chiefs of Staff signalled Admiral Halsey in Noumea to cancel Operation Forearm and proceed with the much smaller Emirau operation, he immediately reallocated a section of the marine force in Guadalcanal to take responsibility for the new landing arrangements, and detached some of the originally allocated troop transports to Guadalcanal, escorted by nine of Admiral Griffin's destroyers detached from the main fleet. This landing force set sail from Guadalcanal on 18 March, scheduled to conduct the occupation of undefended Emirau Island on Monday 20 March.

In 1944 Admiral Halsey was deservedly famous for his aggressive leadership in most of the great naval campaigns of the Pacific war, starting

A change of plan: the great bombardment of Kavieng

USS *New Mexico*, with 14-inch ammunition laid out on the deck. Each shell is as big as a man.

with his command of the task force which delivered the Doolittle raid to Japan in April 1942. Part of his fame rested on his extreme opinions about the enemy. Always ferociously and publicly anti-Japanese, at one point he told American newsmen that 'the only good Jap is a dead Jap', and when the Pacific war ended abruptly in August 1945 he expressed

USS *New Mexico* firing her after turret 14-inch guns.

disappointment because 'there are still too many Japs alive'. Halsey was always looking for a chance to strike at the Japanese, and in the cancellation of Forearm he spotted an opportunity for a king-hit. He decided to save one part of the original invasion plan, the preliminary naval bombardment of Kavieng, his intention now being to create a major diversion by forming an unmistakable impression in the minds of the Japanese occupiers that a landing on New Ireland was imminent, while quietly occupying and fortifying Emirau with minimal losses. The bombardment would also wreck the isolated Japanese garrison at Kavieng, and hopefully permanently remove it from the war. So Halsey immediately issued instructions to Admiral Griffin to proceed directly from Majuro to Kavieng with his battleships, carriers, and his remaining fifteen destroyers, and conduct a massive bombardment on the morning of 20 March to coincide with the Emirau landings.

In the meantime, attacks on targets on New Ireland by the 13th Air Force of the USAAF had been continuing unabated. Since mid-February there had been many air raids on the Kavieng airfields by swarms of B-

A change of plan: the great bombardment of Kavieng

USS *Idaho* (Battleship BB-42).

24s, P-38s, P-39s, P-40s and US navy fighters, although there had been a lull in activity in mid-March following the cancellation of Forearm. Further to the south, heavy air raids were staged on the Rabaul area almost every day and night. Finally, on the night of 19 March 1944 there was a particularly heavy raid on the airfields by twenty-four B-24

USS *Tennessee* (Battleship BB-43) in 1943.

Liberator heavy bombers, causing considerable damage to the runways. Following the cancellation of Operation Forearm this would be the last and most destructive American air raid of the 'pre-invasion' series'; from this time on USAAF interest in Kavieng targets practically ceased, and for a very good reason—the Japanese defences were about to be hit so hard by the US Navy they would never recover.

A change of plan: the great bombardment of Kavieng

Admiral Griffin's bombardment fleet put to sea from Majuro and headed for Kavieng, arriving off that coast early in the morning of Monday 20 March 1944. The four great grey battleships, the two carriers with aircraft on deck armed and readied to fly, and the fifteen fast destroyers zigzagged out from the rain squalls and mist shrouding the area and cautiously approached the target. For the agitated Japanese force observing this ominous spectacle from the shore, it was the moment they had expected and feared—after all the waiting, after all the punishment they had received from the air raids, this was to be the day they would finally join battle with Allied land forces and throw the despised Americans back into the sea. Finally the chance had come to prove in glorious battle that they were indeed the Emperor Hirohito's warriors.

At 8 am artillery spotting planes were launched from the American ships and were soon out of sight in the rain and mist. Half an hour later the battleships opened fire with 14-inch salvoes, and as the range between ships and shore slowly decreased the 5-inch guns gradually joined in. A few Japanese shore batteries began counter-firing, but just as they began to get the correct range the guns of the *Tennessee* began accurate fire on them. This artillery duel, which lasted only ten minutes, was the only opposition encountered; nothing more was heard from the Japanese guns.[6]

For four long hours the American ships steamed slowly back and forth off Kavieng, shelling the fortifications, airstrips, port and town, guided by the spotting aircraft circling over the targets. Visibility continued to be a problem all morning, for adding to the rain and haze were the huge clouds of smoke and dust thrown up by the bombardment. The artillery spotters on the ships and in the air often had difficulty seeing through the murk, and on a number of occasions artillery barrages needed to be 'walked' from a visible point of reference onto the target area.

Finally, when the barrage was lifted, flights of fighter-bombers from the escort carriers further out to sea swooped low over Kavieng, bombing and strafing at will.

At 12.30 pm Admiral Griffin called a halt to the onslaught. In four hours his task force had fired over thirteen thousand high-explosive shells into Kavieng, over a thousand 14-inch shells and over twelve thousand 5-inch shells[7], plus hundreds of bombs from the aircraft and automatic cannon fire. This extraordinary display of firepower had been directed at a comparatively small and, as it turned out, comparatively defenceless target. The aerial attack mounted by the Japanese immediately before their invasion just over two years before had been extremely modest by comparison with what the Americans had just unleashed.[8]

Quite understandably, the unprecedented US shelling of Kavieng would be remembered and discussed for years to come by both the Japanese occupiers and the Melanesian inhabitants, and in many ways was a defining moment for them. Time was now to be measured as being 'before' or 'after' the great American naval bombardment. They did not know, as they watched Admiral Griffin's great fleet sail away over the horizon at around lunchtime on that fateful day, that it carried away with it the last American military interest in New Ireland for the remainder of the Pacific war.

chapter 12

'Kill the Europeans!'

The damage to Kavieng was immense. On average, for every minute of the four hours of the American bombardment over fifty shells had exploded somewhere in the vicinity of the town and airfields. Many of the buildings were now collapsed, the roads torn up, power and telephone lines destroyed, the two airstrips shattered (they would never be used again), fortifications exploded and thousands of coconut palms shredded and splintered. Dead and injured Japanese sailors and soldiers were everywhere. The beautiful little harbourside town of pre-war years had been turned into a churned-up mess of shell craters and rubble, with a pall of smoke, ash and dust hanging over all.

The remaining Melanesian townsfolk had fled in terror down the coastal road or into the jungle as soon as the shells began to land. As Admiral Griffin's bombardment fleet slowly disappeared over the horizon, thousands of stunned Japanese sailors and soldiers began emerging from their bunkers and tunnels and caves to face the enemy invasion they presumed was imminent; and somehow, still alive at the Kulangit internment camp in their muddy trenches and dugouts, were all the Australian internees and the seven German priests.

Although no great invasion fleet had yet appeared over the horizon, for Lieutenant Kyoji Mori and his men, now thoroughly aroused and stirred with fighting spirit, the great bombardment was quite obviously the prelude to an invasion which would arrive at any moment, probably on the flat coastlands south-east of the town near Panapai, adjacent to and aimed at seizing the airfields. While there was still time left Mori felt the moment had finally come to urgently carry out Captain Tamura's order given a few days earlier—'Kill the Europeans!'

Over the preceding days since he had received the Captain's verbal order from Commander Yoshino, Mori had many opportunities to quietly discuss a plan of execution with his own immediate subordinate, Lieutenant Soichi Ichinose of the Land Defence Party, 83rd Naval Garrison Unit, a marine-like naval unit staffed with sailor-soldiers trained for action on land. He had thoroughly briefed Ichinose about the secret order, instructing him to think about ways of carrying it out which would not attract attention or arouse suspicion, particularly that of the victims. In his turn, Ichinose had already mentally allotted the executions to the young men of his Security Detachment, commanded by Sub-Lieutenant Mochizuki Hichitaro.[1]

Shortly after the bombardment ceased Mori discovered that, miraculously, all the internees had survived the bombardment and were still at Kulangit camp. He summoned Ichinose to immediately carry out the secret order. By this time a method for its accomplishment had already evolved. Because the executions were to be conducted out of public sight and hearing, it had previously been decided by Mori and Ichinose that the internees would be taken by barge to the well-used execution ground on Nago Island and shot, and their bodies buried in the shell holes and bomb craters there. In the heat of the current situation, this plan now underwent a number of urgent revisions.[2]

Ichinose suggested that because of the need for secrecy it might be better to dispose of the dead internees at sea by weighting them and dumping them overboard in deep water. Mori quickly agreed with this idea and directly instructed Petty Officer Jutaro Takata, second in command of the Sea Defence Party, 83rd Naval Garrison Unit, to prepare for immediate sailing two of four still-undamaged small motorised Daihatsu 'Type A' naval barges, on which were to be loaded about thirty pieces of 5 mm steel cable each about 5 metres in length and the same number of large concrete sinkers, to stand by at Kavieng South Wharf later that day.[3]

Later in the afternoon, with rumours of an American invasion beginning to circulate, Lieutenant Mochizuki called a conference for 2.30 pm at Security Detachment Headquarters to convey orders to his three platoon commanders.[4] Ensign Suzuki Shozo, commander of the artillery platoon, was appointed overall supervisor of the executions, to be assisted by Petty Officer Horiguchi. Warrant Officer Muraoka, commander of the machine-gun platoon, volunteered to be responsible

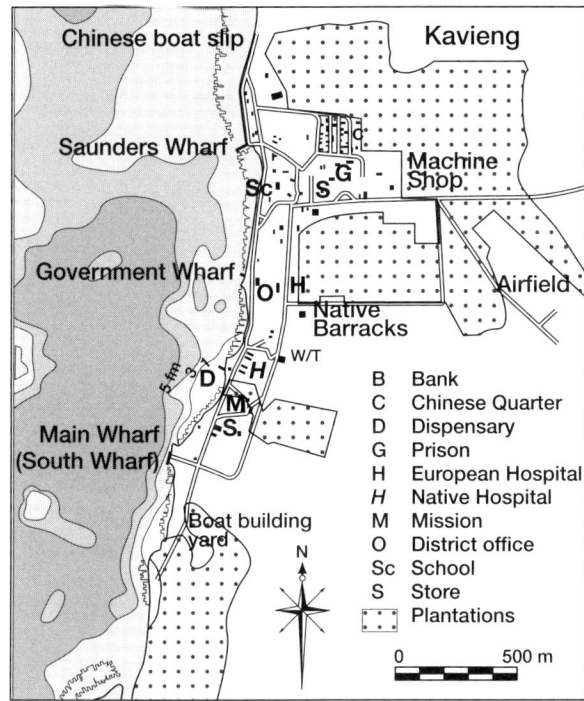

1943 British Admiralty chart showing the location of the four wharves at Kavieng, including the Main Wharf, called by the Japanese the 'South Wharf'.

for the actual executions. Warrant Officer Takada, commander of the two infantry platoons, was placed in charge of the guard.

When the chosen method of execution had been described to the platoon commanders Warrant Officer Muraoka proposed an even better plan. Instead of shooting them on Nago Island before dumping them in the sea, the internees should be taken to the partly damaged South Wharf soon after dark and quietly killed by 'silent jujitsu methods' by a number of sailors in the platoons of the Security Detachment who were experts at jujitsu and could easily kill with their bare hands. At a later stage Muraoka would further refine this plan, deciding that a more reliable method would be to have the internees strangled to death using thin cord, and he set about searching for suitable materials to make the nooses.

Ensign Suzuki then proposed that to lure the internees down to the wharf without raising their suspicions they should be lied to. He would tell them that for their own safety they were to be taken that night to Kavieng South Wharf and transferred by barge to a passing Japanese cargo ship which would convey them to Rabaul. To ensure that this

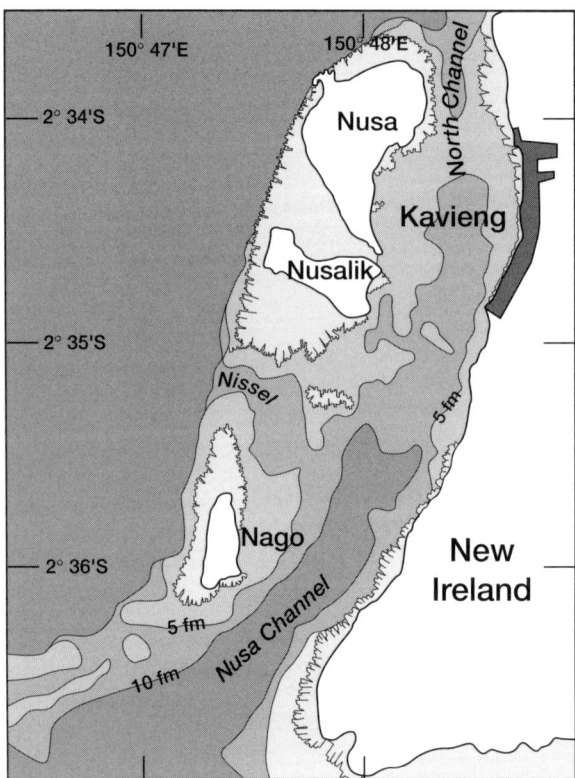

1943 British Admiralty chart showing the small islands offshore from Kavieng, including Nago Island. The bodies of the Kavieng massacre victims were secretly disposed of in waters just south of the Nusa Channel (bottom).

lie continued to deceive the internees until the last moments of their lives, all members of the execution party would need to be rehearsed in it and continue acting as if it were true right through the operation. Lieutenant Mochizuki readily agreed to these suggestions and instructed Ensign Suzuki to proceed with the arrangement.[5]

At 5 pm the three platoon commanders and 24 of their sailors assembled at the Security Detachment area to be addressed by Lieutenant Mochizuki who, without providing detail, instructed them that they would form an execution party that night, that Ensign Suzuki was in command, and that they were to promptly carry out whatever assignment Suzuki was to give them. Rumours had continued to circulate since the bombardment that an enemy invasion had already begun somewhere on the island, and the sailors knew there would be much killing ahead for them, beginning with the European prisoners.

The execution party drove in two trucks to a small coconut grove where Suzuki informed them of their urgent task, of the silent method to be used, and of the lie he would tell to the internees to lure them to their deaths. The men became very emotional. After all the waiting and wondering during their years at Kavieng, they would finally get a chance to prove themselves as warriors before giving their own lives for the Emperor. The enemy would meet their deaths that night.

Just after 5 pm they drove to the internment camp where Suzuki addressed the hastily assembled Australians and Germans. Communicating using halting English—'All men go to Rabauru [Rabaul]'—and sign language[6], he explained how the situation in Kavieng was now dangerous. Pointing at his watch, he indicated that the internees should pack up their possessions without delay and be ready to move in thirty minutes.[7] As a final theatrical touch, Suzuki told them that because of the urgency only one small suitcase could be carried by each prisoner.

Since the start of the American air raids the month before, the internees' lives had been more than usually awful. They had frequently gone without sleep, their nerves and general health suffering from the stress and uncertainty. The massive American shelling that morning, which could quite easily have killed them as they lay in their trenches and dugouts, had been the last straw. They were elated to hear Suzuki's 'news' and, believing they were shortly to be delivered from danger, chose from among their meagre possessions the most important, most personally valuable items to take with them to safety.

After their long incarceration and the privations they had suffered, the Australians and Germans were painfully thin, many of them ill from the ravages of malnutrition and tropical disease. They were still wearing the now ragged and frequently-repaired clothing they had brought with them when rounded up for internment in September 1942. The American raids and the shelling had frightened them, although they knew that the terror could also mean that the war might soon be over. They had all done remarkably well to survive this far, and were excited by the welcome turn of events this evening.

As the sun slowly set over the Steffen Strait they climbed aboard the two trucks with their suitcases and were driven with their guards along the darkening coast road through the wreckage of the town to the vicinity of the South Wharf, dismounting with their luggage a short distance from the pier.

chapter 13

The vision of Hell

That afternoon the crews of the Daihatsu naval barges No. 1 and No. 2 which had been hurriedly ordered to Kavieng Central Wharf had loaded the lengths of 5 mm steel cable normally used as components in mine-sweeping gear, and the heavy concrete sinkers, usually used by the navy to anchor channel marker buoys. Approximately fifteen sets of cables and sinkers had been carried aboard each barge under the supervision of Chief Petty Officer Jutaro Takata, Second in Command of the Sea Defence Department.[1]

The snub-nosed timber Daihatsu barges, named after the manufacturer Toku Daihatsu, were about 20 metres long and displaced about 15 tonnes. They were powered by two 6-cylinder diesel engines, and each had the capacity to carry cargo, motor vehicles or nearly 200 troops. They were normally crewed by eight or nine sailors under the command of a chief petty officer, and were the standard small cargo vessel used by the Japanese navy throughout the Pacific.

No. 1 Barge was captained by Chief Petty Officer Haruo Miyamoto, and crewed by Chief Petty Officer (Engineering) Yashichi Mori, Engine Hand Azuma, and other sailors. Warrant Officer Takada was in charge of the guards on the barge.[2]

No. 2 Barge was normally captained by Petty Officer Class II Kubo, but that day Petty Officer Riohei Kambe was in charge, and his crew included Chief Engineer Unoharu Yamao and three leading ratings, among them Seaman Kinjoro Jitsukawa, the youthful second engine hand.

Kavieng South Wharf had a low gallery specially designed for loading small ships with a low freeboard, like the Daihatsu. No. 2 Barge had been made fast adjacent to the wharf with No. 1 Barge tied up alongside.

The vision of Hell

Postwar shot of the wrecked Kavieng main wharf, taken in October 1945. AUSTRALIAN WAR MEMORIAL NEGATIVE NUMBER AWM 098451

Here the crews waited in the tropical evening until darkness descended. Because of the threat of enemy action no lights were permitted anywhere, but the rain and haze of that morning had blown away and the moonless night was clear with good visibility in the starlight.

Shortly after dusk the two trucks arrived from the internment camps and halted on the roadway about 50 metres from the wharf. Ensign Suzuki and Warrant Officer Horiguchi jumped down and began shouting instructions to the barge crews. The sailors who would shortly do the killing noisily moved to the wharf with Warrant Officer Muraoka. The internees dismounted from the trucks with their baggage and stood waiting, guarded by armed sailors under the supervision of Warrant Officer Takada, the wharf shielded from sight by a large naval buoy which stood on the ground.

Suzuki hurried about, arranging the placement of his men and the materials to be used. Aware that the imagined US invasion could happen at any moment, he was anxious to complete the assignment quickly and smoothly and return his men to their shelters. When he was satisfied that all arrangements were complete, he returned to the internees. At

6 pm the first internee, carrying a suitcase in one hand, was led forward in the darkness to a point about halfway between the wharf and the road. There, for 'security purposes' a blindfold was tied around his eyes by Horiguchi, who then took him by the free hand and led him to the low gallery below which No. 2 Barge was moored.

There the blindfolded man was handed over to Muraoka, the chief executioner, who told him that the deck of the barge was below the level of the wharf, and that he should sit on the edge of the wharf before stepping down to the barge deck, about a metre below. His suitcase of personal possessions was placed to one side. Some of the barge crew, not involved in the actual killings, watched expectantly.

Warrant Officer Muraoka had prepared a noose of a thin cord taken from Japanese kitbags; this was placed carefully over the head of the unsuspecting and blindfolded prisoner so as not to alarm him.

Muraoka then gave the signal. Two or three Japanese sailors at each end of the rope pulled suddenly with all their weight. Their victim was completely unprepared for this assault. As the rope tightened around the startled man's throat his hands tore at the noose and clutched at the sailors murdering him, his legs thrashed, his body contorted in shock. For a few minutes he struggled and convulsed before finally going limp and collapsing onto the decking. Muraoka bent to feel his heart and confirm death. The body was then dropped unceremoniously onto the barge.

For three long hours the sequence was repeated again and again—the walk from the road with suitcase in hand, the blindfolding, the blind walk to the wharf led by Horiguchi, the handover to Muraoka, the suitcase placed to one side, the strangulation and struggle. However, the plan to kill silently and secretly was proving to be very time consuming and untidy, and soon there were indications that the internees still waiting their turn to go 'on board' were becoming restless and more suspicious with every passing minute.

At some later point, when the slowness of proceedings began to frustrate the now impatient Suzuki, faster methods of killing the internees were resorted to, including clubbing them with lengths of timber and iron bars, and bayonet stabs to the heart; the screams of the victims could be clearly heard by the barge crews, who had now become witnesses to a terrible scene.

When the bodies of about half the internees had been thrown onto the mounting pile on No. 2 Barge it cast off and its place was taken

The vision of Hell

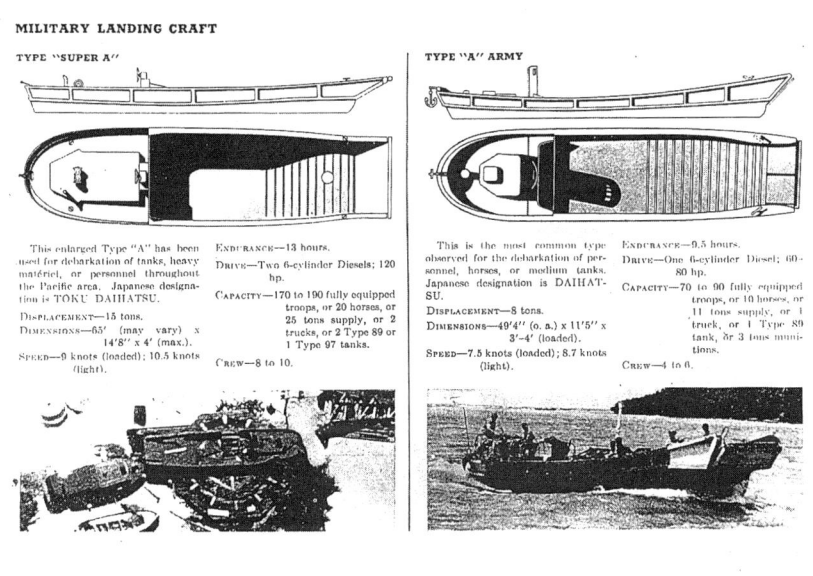

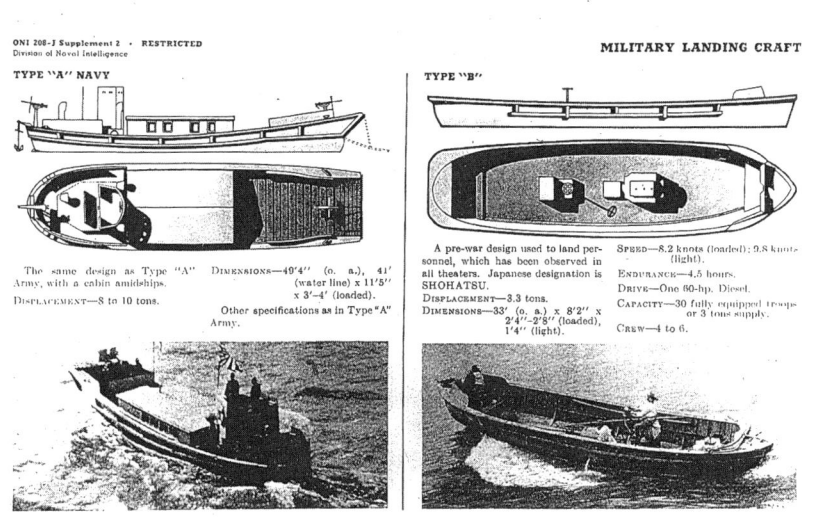

US Navy intelligence leaflet describing types of Japanese naval barges. The Daihatsu 'Type A' barge, used during the Kavieng massacre, is shown lower left.

at the wharf by its sister vessel. No. 2 Barge moved out to sea to the south, in the direction of Edmago Island. While en route to the disposal area, members of the execution party attached the cables and sinkers to the bodies in readiness. Less than an hour later, about 5 kilometres from the wharf, they stopped. For ten to fifteen minutes, with motors idling, the barge drifted while the bodies, sinkers and wire were dropped overboard in the deep black waters of the Eickstedt Passage in the middle of a triangle formed by Nago, Edmago and Usien islands. No. 2 Barge then proceeded back to the South Wharf.

Some time later, when the killing of the second group was over and loading of the bodies completed, No. 1 Barge cast off and moved southward towards the same area, passing the now returning No. 2 Barge in the darkness out to sea. Sailors attached the cables and sinkers to the second load of bodies, and at the disposal point they too were dropped overboard. In the darkness it was discovered by Warrant Officer Takada that somehow there were not enough cables and sinkers for the number of bodies to be dumped, and panicky attempts were made to push underwater the last corpses tossed overboard.[3] When this was finally and clumsily accomplished, No. 2 Barge headed back to the South Wharf. The execution parties disembarked, and the two barges returned together to the Central Wharf, making fast close to midnight. Before retiring for the night the barge crews washed the decks with seawater to remove the large amounts of congealed body fluids that had spilt from the piles of victims.[4]

Before finally departing the South Wharf, the execution party collected the pile of suitcases filled with the internees' most valued possessions—the family snapshots, the diaries, books and bibles and tattered clothes and Jack Griffin's drawings—and tossed them in a heap into one of the trucks. Then they drove back to their shelters and turned in for the night.

The bodies of Albert Moseley, Bill Attwood and Bill Garnett, Bob Furlong, Boyd Whitehead, Charlie and Max Ostrom, Claude Chadderton, Frank Consterdine, Henry and David Topal, Jack Griffin, Jim Naughton, John Bell, Len Woolcott, Leon Williams, Leonard Pinnock, Les Gordon, Lon Davies, Phil Levy, Ray Heming, Vivian Ives and Walter Heydon now drifted in the night darkness near the deep sandy bottom of the Eickstedt Passage, about 2 kilometres off Cape Sivisat, close by the bodies of Father Franz, Father Heinrich, Brother Heinrich, the two Fathers Josef, Father Karl and Father Paul.

Planters, ex-diggers and priests—all had died utterly alone in horrible circumstances, with just a few wild and awful moments to comprehend what was happening to them.

The story of their survival in the internment camps, their sudden and violent deaths, and the location of their watery gravesite would remain unknown to their families and wives and children for a very long time to come.

PART II
The concealment

chapter 14

The fabulous lie

The following morning, Tuesday 21 March 1944, the Kulangit internment camp was completely deserted and unguarded. A resident of Kavieng, Anton de Silva, happened to make one of his periodic visits that morning and managed to enter the camp grounds. Much later he reported: 'I found clothing, suitcases, papers and shoes, and other personal belongings torn up and strewn about the three houses', the aftermath of the rush to leave the previous evening.[1] He also found a large bloodstain in one of the dugouts in the gardens.[2] The same morning, at the nearby 83 NGU Security Detachment Headquarters, Ensign Suzuki supervised a party of sailors to burn the internees' suitcases collected at the wharf the previous evening. There was no Melanesian or other local witness to this act of concealment, this final obliteration.

The same morning Lieutenant Mori verbally advised Captain Tamura that the executions had been completed, but no formal report was made to South-East Area Naval Headquarters at Rabaul, for the incident was now to remain a secret held only by the men of the Kavieng garrison.

Commander Shozo Yoshino had not been in Kavieng on the day of the murders. Two days before, on Saturday 18 March, he had been ordered by Captain Tamura to drive far to the south to Namatanai, and confer there with the Army Brigade Group, commanded by Major-General Takeo Ito, regarding the defence of New Ireland. At Namatanai he had stayed for two nights with his colleague Commander Koshin Takeda at the headquarters of 89 Naval Garrison Unit, setting out for the long return journey on Tuesday 21 March. On the way to Kavieng his car was stopped by anxious soldiers who told him that American marines had landed further to the north near Kavieng and that it was dangerous to proceed. Yoshino decided to drop by the local army headquarters near Lemakot Plantation to obtain further information, but was reassured by the area commanding officer, Colonel Sakanoto, that there was no truth to the invasion rumours. He then drove on to Kavieng, witnessed the extensive damage as he entered the town, and that night returned to Captain Tamura's 14th Naval Base Force headquarters. Here he discovered that his fellow officers were also under the impression that the enemy had landed on the coast further to the south, from whence he had just come.[3]

He now learnt that the US naval bombardment had badly damaged the electrical, telephone and wireless communication facilities. It was this that had caused all the rumours to go unchecked by anyone in authority, and he was thus the first to inform his fellow officers that no invasion had yet occurred anywhere on New Ireland's east coast.

The following day he was told by a colleague, Staff Officer Hiratsuka, that during his absence at Namatanai, Lieutenant Mori had carried out Captain Tamura's order and the internees had been killed.

Of course, the American invasion of New Ireland would never transpire, although on many occasions right until the end of the Pacific war in August 1945 more excited rumours would suddenly spread among the occupying sailors and soldiers that US marines were on the way, and would just as quickly fade away. The sad irony was that while the last-minute change of plan to cancel the invasion of Kavieng had saved the lives of Captain Tamura and most of his officers and men, Admiral Halsey's decision to proceed with the diversionary bombardment had been a death sentence for the internees. Seventeen months later, in August 1945, following Emperor Hirohito's unexpected and unprecedented radio broadcast announcing a sudden and unconditional Japanese capitulation[4], the bypassed garrisons on New Ireland were still largely intact, although reduced in numbers to about 11 000 men, including over 4000 sailors. Cut off from all sources of re-supply since early 1944, they had survived by engaging in a massive food-production effort, feeding themselves from vast vegetable gardens tended by the troops. After all the years of fear, hunger, sickness and inaction, the sailors and soldiers eagerly awaited repatriation home to Japan.

However, there were going to be delays in accomplishing this. Nothing could happen until the formal surrender of Japan had been taken by

General MacArthur in Tokyo Bay on 2 September 1945 and, most importantly, witnessed by the Japanese people. That historic ceremony opened the way for the formal surrender of thousands of Japanese military units throughout the Asia-Pacific area, involving millions of men. With such vast numbers surrendering through the months of September and October 1945, it would be quite some time before their repatriation could begin. The highest priority for Allied shipping was moving hundreds of thousands of American, British, Australian and Dutch prisoners of war, civilian internees and servicemen back to their home countries. With the almost complete destruction of the Imperial Japanese Navy and merchant navy there were no ships left to take Japanese personnel home, and they would have to wait their turn.

The long delays between the official Japanese surrender in Tokyo on 2 September, the arrival of Allied forces to take control of the defeated troops scattered across vast geographical areas, and their eventual repatriation to Japan and discharge many months later, gave much time and plenty of opportunities for those who had engaged in wrongdoing to cover their tracks. All throughout the Asia-Pacific area where atrocities had been committed against American, British, Australian and Dutch soldiers and citizens, a vast secret effort was begun to conceal anything which might arouse the interest of Allied investigators. Much thought, ingenuity and effort was to go into making these defiant acts of concealment.

For the naval and army units on New Ireland there was a respite of more than a month before the Australian military could organise a high-level delegation to travel there and take a formal surrender. These arrangements needed first to be made by Australian military representatives in Port Moresby with General Imamura, Commander in Chief of all Japanese military units in the New Guinea area, and then communicated to the outlying commanders, including Tamura in Kavieng, who by now had been promoted to the rank of Rear Admiral. Finally, early on 19 September, the Australian naval sloop HMAS *Swan* embarked from Rabaul carrying Major-General Kenneth Eather, General Officer Commanding the 11th Australian Division, to take the Japanese surrenders on New Ireland, accompanied by his staff officers, interpreters and some native troops. Later that day at Namatanai, Lieutenant General Ito was brought out to HMAS *Swan* for the surrender of his army. The ship then moved on to Fangelawa Bay close to Kavieng where, on the beach, Rear Admiral Tamura formally surrendered the Japanese naval forces in the Kavieng area to General Eather's Chief of Staff, Lieutenant Colonel Nyman.[5]

Arrangements were made at the same time to begin concentrating the surrendered forces from all over New Guinea into what grew to be thirteen vast holding camps at Rabaul, in preparation for their repatriation to Japan when sufficient transport could be made available. This movement commenced shortly afterwards and by the end of 1945 most of the surrendered forces had been relocated to Rabaul, including the men of 14 Naval Base Force and 83 Naval Garrison Unit from Kavieng, still under the command of Rear Admiral Tamura.

In the month of interregnum preceding the surrender ceremony at Fangelawa Bay, Rear Admiral Tamura and his officers and men were not idle. Shortly after the mid-August capitulation announcement in Tokyo, Tamura received a signal from Imperial Japanese Navy fleet headquarters in Rabaul requesting that a representative be urgently sent from Kavieng to attend a conference to plan local area surrender arrangements and other matters including the disposal of military equipment, munitions, records and anything else that should not fall into the hands of the Australians.[6] Commander Yoshino was chosen for this duty and was immediately flown to Rabaul where during his stay he conferred with Captain Sadaru Sanagi, Senior Staff Officer at South-East Area Fleet headquarters. In the course of their discussion Sanagi asked Yoshino whether 'any acts in violation of international law' had taken place within the jurisdiction of 14 Naval Base Force. Yoshino revealed that about thirty civilian internees had been secretly killed at Kavieng the previous year by sailors of 83 Naval Garrison Unit because an American invasion had been expected. This was startling news; Sanagi immediately grasped the implications and instructed Yoshino that 'steps should be taken to prevent revelation of the facts' in compliance with the secret orders he knew had been received earlier from higher up the chain of command.[7]

Yoshino and a small group of officers at Fleet Headquarters immediately began research to determine the best way of concealing the now highly embarrassing Kavieng massacre. Firmly fixed in their minds were the 'friendly-fire' incidents involving American and Allied units which had accidentally killed their own soldiers and citizens. There had been scores of accidental bombing, torpedoing, strafing, shelling and mining incidents involving attacks by US planes, ships and submarines since the Pacific war had begun, and thousands of Allied

The fabulous lie

Namatanai, New Ireland, 19 September 1945. The surrender of General Ito (fifth from left), Commander in Chief of Japanese army forces on New Ireland, to Major General K.W. Eather (left), General Officer Commanding 11th Australian Division, on board the sloop HMAS *Swan*. AUSTRALIAN WAR MEMORIAL NEGATIVE NUMBER AWM 305708

soldiers, sailors, airmen and citizens had been killed and injured by their own side. The Japanese naval officers at Rabaul clearly remembered the extraordinary *Montevideo Maru* sinking in 1942, where torpedoes fired by the US submarine *Sturgeon* had killed over 1000 Australian soldier and civilian prisoners of war being moved from Simpson Harbour to Hainan on the unmarked ship. In August 1945 the Japanese were still the only people who knew the details of this disaster.

They remembered the numerous examples throughout the Asia-Pacific area when Allied aircraft had mistakenly bombed POW camps containing their own soldiers and citizens—some of these incidents had occurred in the Rabaul area.[8] The Japanese had also heard of the US submarine attacks on unmarked Japanese convoys moving Allied prisoners of war from South-East Asia to Japan after completion of the Burma railway, and the carnage this had caused. In June 1944, close to the port of Nagasaki, the *Tamahoko Maru* was in the final stages of its long journey from Formosa, carrying over 700 Australian POWs originally captured on Java, when it was attacked by the US submarine *Tang*.[9] Over 500 of the Australians had been killed. In September 1944 two Japanese ships, the *Rokyu Maru* and the *Kachidoki Maru*, were transporting over 2000 Australian and British POWs from Singapore for slave labour in Japan in an escorted convoy. Three US submarines, *Growler*, *Pampanito* and *Sealion*, attacked the convoy in the Formosa Strait, and another 500 POWs had died.[10] Many Allied prisoners had also been killed in Japan during the B-29 air raids in 1944 and 1945. In fact, if the truth could be stretched to the limit, the murders at Kavieng after the US navy bombardment might themselves be characterised a consequence of American 'friendly fire', if an ingenious explanation could be invented to prove it.[11]

The challenge facing Commander Yoshino and his colleagues at Fleet Headquarters was to come up with a plausible friendly-fire incident to explain the sudden overnight disappearance of the Kavieng internees. Could they claim that the internment camp had been bombed during the air raids of February and March 1944, with total loss of life of the inmates? Could they say that all internees had been killed during the US naval bombardment on 20 March that year? Unfortunately there were no bodies or graves to offer as proof of burial, and what were the chances anyway of every single prisoner in the Kulangit camp being accidentally killed by the rain of naval shells that day?

Prompted by Captain Sanagi, a naval Lieutenant Commander, Hideshi Matsumoto, attached to 8 Naval Base Unit in Rabaul, offered a suggestion. He recalled from a naval report that in February 1944, about a month before the US naval bombardment of Kavieng and disposal of the internees, the Japanese cargo and passenger ships *Kokai Maru* and *Kowa Maru* had been sunk together on the same day by American aircraft quite close to Kavieng. More research followed and before too long Commander Yoshino had the fabricated story he was looking for. The official navy report had concluded that the *Kokai Maru* and *Kowa Maru* had gone down immediately following the bombing with the loss of all hands, although at Rabaul headquarters there was some doubt if this had actually been the case with *Kokai Maru*. No witnesses... It was now just a matter of placing the internees on the *Kowa Maru* about the time of the sinking. You ask about the internees? Sadly, they were killed by American bombs just as we were sending them to safety.

Before leaving Rabaul, Yoshino called again on Captain Sanagi and received his blessing for the cover-up. He promised to provide further details of the story after he had conferred with Rear Admiral Tamura and his staff back in Kavieng. A few days later Yoshino met with Tamura to explain what had happened. To strengthen the plausibility of the story they were about to concoct they agreed to combine many actual incidents with a few invented by themselves. It was true there had been heavy air raids on Kavieng in mid-February 1944. It was true there had been a strong desire to pass responsibility for the internees to higher authority in Rabaul by sending them there. It was also true the *Kowa Maru* had passed Kavieng in mid-February on the way south from Japan to Rabaul, and true that it had been sunk by the Americans with all hands on 21 February 1944 near Kavieng, after leaving Rabaul to return to Japan. Finally, although admittedly a month later, the internees had been told they were being evacuated to a waiting ship and had definitely been taken to the South Wharf with their belongings and placed on barges which had embarked to sea at night.

Shortly after, Rear Admiral Tamura called a conference in Kavieng with Commander Yoshino and three of the younger officers directly involved in the killings: Kyoji Mori, by now promoted to lieutenant commander; Lieutenant Soichi Ichinose and Mochizuki Hichitaro, now promoted to full lieutenant. They agreed that the *Kowa Maru* story was an excellent and plausible subterfuge; the internees' disappearance would be explained by telling any enquirers that, after a particularly bad American air raid in mid-February 1944, for their own safety they had been taken to the wharf and placed on motorised barges which had conveyed them under cover of darkness to the *Kowa Maru*, waiting offshore in the shelter of a small island, and the ship had then safely delivered them to Rabaul. To increase the plausibility of this story, the officers decided it would not be necessary for anyone to explain that the ship had later been sunk after leaving Rabaul with the loss of all on board. It would be left up to Allied investigators to work that out for themselves. If questioned on this point, it would be best if the Japanese coyly denied any knowledge about the sinking.

The challenge now was to immediately identify within 83 Naval Garrison Unit all remaining witnesses to the massacre, have them learn the lie until they could repeat it verbatim, and swear never to tell the truth to anyone. To achieve this result, and sustain the conspiracy over the coming months and years, would require great discipline and outstanding acting skills. About seventy officers, non-commissioned officers and sailors were quickly identified as having knowledge of the event—the planners and organisers, the execution party, the sailors who had helped gather the cables and sinkers, the barge crews, drivers and guards, and those who had been party to gossip during the days immediately afterwards.

By the time Rear Admiral Tamura's formal surrender was accepted by the Australian army at Fangalawa Bay, almost a month later, all seventy witnesses from the Admiral down to the lowest, youngest and dullest had been thoroughly ordered-threatened, briefed and re-briefed, and rehearsed to tell the false story. For many, a false memory of the event had been induced by their officers, and the coaching and coercion would continue until the men were moved to Rabaul later in the year, and during the long wait there for repatriation back to Japan during 1946.

An outrageous, fabulous lie had been invented and then memorised by each conspirator. It was so good and strong and the men so clever at repeating it that they began to believe it as the truth. Some time later in Rabaul, Captain Sanagi at Fleet Headquarters would be so taken by the opportunities presented by the loss of the *Kokai Maru* and the *Kowa Maru* that he would decide to place more 'disappeared' civilian internees on the ships. He had been particularly troubled trying to conceal other acts of wrongdoing, especially executions of prisoners of war and the massacre of civilians at sea onboard the *Akikaze*, and decided that he would pretend that at least some of them had also been embarked from Rabaul on *Kowa Maru*.[12] Without providing too many details, Sanagi confided to his immediate superior, Vice-Admiral Junichi Kasuka, Supreme Naval Commander in Rabaul, that the *Kowa Maru* and *Kokai Maru* sinkings were being used to conceal the unaccountable disappearance of some civilian internees in New Guinea and that Kasuka should remember this if he was ever questioned.

The story of what happened to the Kavieng internees is essentially a story about truth and lies. The lies which had been used to carry out and conceal the crime were not isolated acts of creative genius on the parts of Yoshino, Tamura and Sanagi. They were products of an entire military culture which actively fostered dishonesty. They replicated similar deceit used elsewhere, and were only two of an unimaginable number of lies invented by Japanese military officers between 1941 and 1945.

During the Pacific war the Japanese military became very adept at using falsehoods whenever it suited their purposes. The two lies which had been concocted by the officers at Kavieng during the commission of their crime, the simple lie told to the internees on the evening of the murders to obtain their cooperation to leave the camp and be taken to the South Wharf, and the more complicated lie to later conceal what had really happened there, were quite typical. The lie told to the internees echoed scores of similar lies told to prisoners to obtain their cooperation throughout the occupied territories. Allied POWs in Singapore were repeatedly told that if they volunteered for construction work on the Thailand-Burma railway project their living conditions and diet would significantly improve and the work would be 'light'. When inmates of the many awful POW camps along that railway needed to be moved to a different site, they were promised that the new camp would be much better and have 'extra food and facilities'. Scores of thousands of Asian girls and young women kidnapped for forced sexual servitude as 'comfort women' were routinely told they were being recruited for well-paying jobs in restaurants and factories.[13]

Following the military setbacks suffered by Japan from mid-1942 and the start of high-order face-saving, official lying intensified until it was difficult for even many in high authority to tell the difference between truth and falsehood. By 1945 such a massive tangle of self-deception had been created that it was only a matter of time before it would collapse under its own weight.

It is, of course, common in wartime to use deception as a legitimate military strategy. During World War II many clever disinformation campaigns were used by both sides to deceive the enemy regarding their true intentions. The diversionary naval bombardment of Kavieng on 20 March 1944, designed to disguise actual US marine landings on Emirau Island, was a perfect example of a successful deception. The Japanese fully expected an invasion of New Ireland because so many signs pointed to it; the bombardment confirmed that expectation; and the deception was so convincing it caused Lieutenant Mori and his men to act as they did against the internees.

But in the end, the lying, deception and disinformation practised by Japan's government went far beyond military tactics. These behaviours were largely aimed at its own citizens and soldiers, not the Allies, and were all about saving face for Emperor Hirohito and his generals and admirals. To avoid the humiliation and disgrace of admitting their miscalculations in launching and then losing the war, the Japanese government at all levels routinely lied to the Japanese nation about the war's progress, thus prolonging the suffering. Face-saving logic meant that disastrous military defeats were boasted about as victories, and Allied losses wildly exaggerated, even with the enemy on the threshold of Tokyo. According to Japanese propagandists, Allied navies, armies and air forces were still being totally annihilated, crushed, blasted, hammered and slashed in mid-1945, when exactly the opposite was occurring. Great efforts were made to prevent Japan's citizens from ever knowing the truth, and the closed, conforming nature of Japanese society at the time made this coercion and deception possible. In the mad world of wartime Japan it was considered a disloyalty to think otherwise, and there were punishments for anyone questioning the official version of events.[14]

As conditions worsened on the battlefield, Japanese army and navy officers routinely lied to their men. By 1944 much of Japan's far-flung army and navy had effectively been abandoned by the generals and admirals in Tokyo. Like Admiral Tamura's isolated 14 Naval Base Force in Kavieng, hundreds of thousands of stranded servicemen faced disease, starvation and death all across the Pacific area. But Japanese face-saving logic dictated that they could not be told this, or even be permitted to suspect it might be true. So the sick and dying men were fed a stream of encouraging lies by their officers. Non-existent reinforcements and supplies of food and medicine were always 'immediately on their way to the front'. Fictitious new weapons had been developed 'to turn the tide of battle'. Thousands of imaginary Japanese aircraft and ships were being held in secret locations in readiness for a great offensive. When they failed to materialise it was because 'they had been diverted to achieve a great victory elsewhere in the theatre of operations'. Credulous servicemen died in droves as a result.[15]

The variety and extent of Japan's self-deception and the suffering it caused were well known to the Allies. The gulf between internal portrayals of what was occurring and external reality became a psychological weakness to exploit. Early in the Pacific war, the combined Allied Intelligence Bureau had established under Australian control a secret organisation nondescriptly called the Far Eastern Liaison Office (FELO), a so-called 'psychological warfare' unit. FELO's major function was to help shorten the Pacific war by finding nonviolent ways to exploit the widespread self-deception practised within the Japanese forces, and in particular to weaken the morale of Japanese servicemen in the field by exposing them to the truth. Later in 1944 the Americans created a counterpart organisation, the Psychological Warfare Branch (PWB), with a parallel function. As the war became progressively more catastrophic for Japan and the self-deception intensified, FELO and PWB expanded and refined their activities.[16]

They did this by repeatedly telling the Japanese servicemen in the field the truth in ways which could be understood and which were credible. Information about the actual battlefield circumstances and living conditions, military setbacks, the private thoughts and miseries of individual Japanese soldiers, was obtained, analysed and then used to induce in them feelings of insecurity and hopelessness and, hopefully, evaporation of the will to fight. Information about the intimate thoughts of the soldiers was obtained from letters and diaries recovered from the dead, captured military documents, from radio eavesdropping and interrogations of prisoners, and from secret surveillance. This enabled the creation of timely, cleverly written and culturally appropriate Japanese-language leaflets for precisely targeted air-drops, Japanese-language radio broadcasts and public address announcements which were relentlessly delivered to the troops in their jungle positions. Quite early in this FELO campaign it was decided as formal policy that because of the depth and extent of Japanese self-deception, only the unvarnished truth would be presented to them. If truth-telling was done repeatedly and credibly, over time individual soldiers would begin to draw their own conclusions about who was presenting the real facts.

The dishonesty of the Japanese generals and admirals enabled the truth to be used against them. When all their lies were repeatedly pointed out to be patently false, ordinary soldiers and sailors began to lose both confidence in their officers and the will to fight. The Japanese-speaking men and women of FELO and PWB became experts in understanding the dishonest acts of enemy leadership, and were able to turn this knowledge against them in increasingly devastating ways. Instead of truth, famously, becoming a 'casualty of war'[17], truth-telling became a formidable weapon for shortening the conflict and alleviating further suffering on both sides.

The important truth-telling work of the Far Eastern Liaison Office would, in time, have a direct influence on the Australian investigation soon to be launched into the disappearance of the Kavieng internees. A key wartime member of FELO, a Japanese-speaker with a passion for uncovering the truth, would end up eventually leading that investigation.

PART III
The crime revealed

chapter 15

A very difficult investigation

The difficulties facing Australian war crimes investigators pursuing Japanese war criminals from 1945 onwards were substantial. There were many contributing factors for this situation, and given the number of obstacles it is miraculous that so many successful prosecutions were eventually concluded.

As the Pacific war began to slowly turn in favour of the American-led allies, evidence emerged of Japanese maltreatment of military prisoners of war including acts of assault, torture and murder; and maltreatment and murder of Australian, European and Overseas Chinese civilian internees and other inhabitants of the occupied territories. Beginning in 1943, the Australian government began quietly investigating these allegations, with an expectation that the perpetrators would be prosecuted as soon as the Allies secured victory. As deliberate policy, efforts were made to prevent the atrocities from becoming public knowledge in Australia, partly to limit undesirable reactions from thousands of families of prisoners of war and internees, and partly to maintain the fighting morale of the sailors, soldiers and airmen who were at risk of capture.[1] This policy was maintained until the end of the Pacific war, and accidental revelations were carefully managed by government and military to limit damage to morale. Helpfully, the Japanese surrounded all matters to do with Allied POWs with a wall of secrecy and silence, only occasionally releasing carefully and cynically stage-managed messages from some prisoners to their families, messages which invariably painted a picture of the men's happiness and health—and which sometimes came from prisoners who had already died of disease and maltreatment.

In June 1943, Sir William Webb, Chief Justice of Queensland, was appointed as a commissioner under the National Security (Inquiries) Regulations to report on whether there had been breaches of the established international rules of warfare by Japan. This enquiry was to be the first of three conducted by Justice Webb, in 1943–44, 1944, and 1945–46. After the war Justice Webb went on to become President of the International Military Tribunal Far East (IMTFE), the major war crimes court in Tokyo to prosecute the most senior leaders of wartime Japan.

As a result of his enquiries Justice Webb became Australia's pre-eminent authority on war crimes, especially those committed by Japanese against Australians. Immediately following the war, and to provide a legal framework to enable war crimes investigations and prosecutions, in October 1945 the Australian Parliament enacted the *Australian War Crimes Act*. Drafting of this legislation was a response to the Webb enquiries, and its purpose was to provide legal authority for the Australian army, under supervision of the Adjutant-General of the army, to conduct military courts to try Japanese accused of war crimes against Australian citizens, wartime allies[2] and British subjects. The Act authorised the military courts to award the penalty of death or a lesser penalty. Anticipating problems likely to be caused by the wartime deaths of so many victims and witnesses, and problems of arranging attendance in overseas courts by potential witnesses, the rules of evidence were relaxed to permit evidence to be provided indirectly by witnesses without their being physically present in court and available for cross-examination.[3]

Among other things, the *War Crimes Act* also enabled the establishment, under the Australian Army Directorate of Prisoners of War and Internees in Melbourne, of a new military unit capable of investigating crimes involving the Japanese military. This was to be called the Australian War Crimes Section, later to have two overseas branches, 1 Australian War Crimes Section, initially based in Singapore and later in Hong Kong; and 2 Australian War Crimes Section, based in Tokyo and associated with the Allied Occupation Forces in Japan. The war crimes sections were to be staffed by Australian military officers with appropriate legal, investigatory and language expertise, and their work was to partly depend on close cooperation with counterpart organisations in the US and British military.

From the time of the first Australian-managed war crimes trial, which commenced at Wewak, New Guinea in late November 1945, until the last trial on Manus Island in 1951, over 900 Japanese ex-servicemen were tried during almost 300 trials, most of which lasted no more than a few days. Between 1945 and 1951 trials were conducted at eight locations including Rabaul, Manus Island and Wewak in New Guinea, and Hong Kong, with the Rabaul military court by far the most active, the scene of almost 190 trials. The Rabaul court was kept busy partly because of the numerous crimes which had occurred in the New Guinea area; but mainly because of the vast numbers of surrendered Japanese forces which had been concentrated in the thirteen internment camps in the Rabaul area, including the almost intact garrisons from New Britain and New Ireland. At the Rabaul court between December 1945 and August 1947 almost 400 Japanese stood trial, and most were convicted, 87 being executed, usually by hanging in Rabaul.

Of the Japanese ex-servicemen tried at all Australian court venues, over 600 were declared guilty and nearly 300 acquitted. Of the guilty, almost 150 were executed. The rest, almost 500 men, received prison sentences ranging from under ten years to life. The vast majority of these convictions related to crimes conducted against Australian and Allied servicemen, usually when prisoners of war.

Comparatively few trials were conducted and convictions obtained for crimes against civilians in the occupied areas, particularly against Europeans. Most of the fifty trials involving civilian victims related to crimes against indigenous people and Overseas Chinese in New Guinea. Only six of the fifty trials were for crimes committed specifically against Australian civilians.

Had the Australian government and military been able to fully placate the outrage of the Australian people and news media, there would have been far more investigations, trials and convictions, until as many Japanese as possible involved in atrocities against Australians had been brought to justice, no matter how long this took to accomplish. Immediately following the war and the lifting of official censorship the Australian people had begun learning about the terrible fates of thousands of their countrymen while in Japanese hands, and there was a public outcry for the perpetrators to be caught and severely punished. Vast numbers of unforgiving returning servicemen and prisoners of war added their voices to the calls for punishment, and a politically powerful organisation, the Returned Sailors', Soldiers' and Airmen's Imperial

League, became a vigorous and influential lobbyist on their behalf. However, public demands to leave no stone unturned in the hunt for war criminals could not be so easily satisfied.

In circumstances where thousands of war crimes were alleged or were suspected to have occurred, major obstacles to successful investigations were the absence of either perpetrators to prosecute; direct witnesses to atrocities believed to have been committed; or material evidence. Although substantial evidence existed that many war crimes had definitely occurred, on investigation it was discovered that the perpetrators had subsequently died, or that witnesses had also died or could no longer be found. One of the most notorious crimes in the view of the Australian public, the machine-gunning of Australian army nurses at Bangka Island in the Dutch East Indies after the fall of Singapore, could not be brought to justice because the Japanese officers and soldiers involved had been killed during subsequent military actions in Burma. In such cases, a great deal of investigatory effort eventually led nowhere.[4]

In other cases, absence of material evidence confounded investigations and led to their abandonment, or to later acquittal of the accused. A great deal of effort was devoted to the search for graves, bodies and Japanese documentary records, mostly without success. The absence of material evidence was partly caused by Japanese inefficiency and carelessness with record-keeping during the war; and partly by the widespread practice of concealing wrongdoing, either at the time of the incident or immediately after the war. This included the deliberate falsification and destruction of whatever records had been maintained, as well as destruction of human remains and the personal property of victims. Also impeding investigations were the shielding and delaying tactics used by surviving Japanese soldiers, sailors and airmen, officers and lower ranks alike. It was unusual for suspects to be cooperative and remember details clearly, and numerous lies, half-truths and selective admissions were told to deliberately mislead investigators.

Information about alleged crimes was, on investigation, quite often found to be based on hearsay or misunderstanding, much of it generated by indigenous men and women and a small number of surviving European witnesses who either genuinely misunderstood what had actually happened; could not exactly remember names, dates and places; or for a variety of personal reasons deliberately made complaints which could not be legally substantiated. A great deal of time was lost by investigators attempting to verify the unverifiable.[5]

To achieve a successful prosecution in a trial and satisfy the army's Adjutant-General that due process had been followed, the War Crimes Section required a still-living Japanese perpetrator, preferably a still-living reliable witness and, if possible, a range of material evidence. Although huge numbers of Japanese servicemen had been killed during the last years of the war, in late 1945 there were still large numbers of survivors being concentrated into holding camps throughout the Asia-Pacific region. Before their repatriation to Japan during 1946 much effort went into correctly identifying each surviving serviceman and obtaining details of his military service and unit attachments. This information could then be made available to investigators in the War Crimes Section.

However, the single major factor which eventually severely impeded Australian prosecution of Japanese war criminals was growing international pressure on the Australian government to conclude its entire war crimes investigation program. Very early in the occupation of Japan by the US-led allies the supreme commander, General MacArthur, and his pragmatic civilian advisers had decided that to more speedily achieve the twin aims of Japan's demilitarisation and democratisation it would be necessary to preserve some of the peak institutions of Imperial Japan. In particular, the position of emperor would need to be retained, and Emperor Hirohito used as a living symbol of Japan's continuing 'polity' and unity. The rationale behind this decision had its genesis in a standing wartime policy not to physically attack the person of the emperor. For example, the Doolittle air raid in 1942 and all subsequent air attacks on Tokyo had specifically avoided bombing the Imperial palace. The psychological warfare programs waged by the Psychological Warfare Branch and Far Eastern Liaison Office during the last few years of the war, which had been intended to weaken the resolve of Japan to continue, also carefully avoided mentioning the emperor. Because PWB and FELO believed that the Japanese worshipped and revered Hirohito as a living god, and were prepared to die in droves defending his name, it was decided to avoid making provocative personal attacks on him in Allied propaganda.[6] Allied propaganda thus targeted the militaristic clique, the generals and admirals, even though the Allies knew that Hirohito was just as culpable as they for waging the war, having, among other things, issued an Imperial Rescript on 8 December 1941 giving his personal instructions and authority to initiate hostilities. Hirohito's only known creditable action during the war was his last-minute manoeuvring of the war cabinet into accepting Japan's unconditional surrender in

August 1945 against strong resistance from the military, an action which should have been taken years earlier.

To ensure that the postwar occupation proceeded smoothly and to obtain the full cooperation of the Japanese people, particularly the influential conservative elites, the symbolic figurehead of Hirohito would need to be saved, humanised and rapidly converted into an enthusiastic promoter of pacifism, democracy and civil society, and friend of the United States. By late 1945 all the elements were in place for this public conversion by US occupation authorities of Hirohito from wartime god-warrior to postwar pacifist, with the enthusiastic collusion of Hirohito himself and his imperial retinue.[7] To assist with this rewriting of history, Hirohito was to be portrayed as a person who had been duped and threatened by his military leaders before and during the war, a blameless figure who was as much a victim of the miscalculations of the generals and admirals as the ordinary people and servicemen of Japan. The logic used by the United States to save the Emperor from prosecution as a war criminal, and his subsequent refusal to ever accept any personal responsibility, would eventually introduce a huge moral weakness into efforts to prosecute thousands of 'war criminals' who had committed their crimes in his name, and under his ultimate authority.

A consequence of arranging Japan's rapid demilitarisation and democratisation using Horohito as a living symbol would be the inherent contradiction in being simultaneously friendly towards and forgiving of 'good' Japanese, while at the same time wanting to punish so many of the 'bad' militarists and their subordinates. By late 1946, just over a year since the war concluded, strong opinions were being expressed within the US government that continued prosecution of Japanese war crimes was becoming counterproductive within the framework of America's overall diplomatic and strategic goals in East Asia. By this time it had also become clear that a key wartime ally, the Soviet Union, was going to be a major adversary for some time into the future; and there was a strong possibility that another wartime ally, China, was collapsing into civil war and could easily turn Communist. An active Communist movement had emerged in postwar Japan as well, a consequence of the political openness and freedom which came with democracy. The exigencies of this new 'cold war' between the US-led 'free world' and the Communists meant that Japan was needed as a staunch ally and bulwark of democracy in East Asia. As well, the numerous American military bases now located in Japan had turned the country into a valuable strategic asset should push come to shove with China and the Soviet Union. In these circumstances the full cooperation of the Japanese people, polity and business community was required, and continued prosecution of war criminals was seen to be less important than achieving the much more important and noble goals of forgiveness and reconciliation.[8]

From 1947, the United States, now joined by Great Britain, began giving notice they intended to begin winding down war crimes investigations, even though thousands of war criminals would probably go unprosecuted. The Australian government, still driven by strong public opinion, wanted to continue but was very much dependent on the larger US and British occupation forces in the practical work of tracking down suspects, arresting them for interrogation, and conducting trials. Eventually, following execution of key 'Class A' war criminals in December 1948, US and British support and cooperation would be rapidly withdrawn from ongoing Australian investigations. In the face of these developments, Australia needed to obtain as many arrests and convictions as possible before the two allies brought a complete halt to proceedings.

The small group of Australian army officers who in 1945 began investigating the disappearance of the civilian internees at Kavieng would need to overcome all these impediments to their enquiry and, unbeknown to them, would also need to break through the biggest obstacle of all, the fabulous lie crafted by the Japanese in Kavieng to conceal their crime. Kavieng would turn out to be a very difficult investigation.

chapter 16

I am a naval officer and will speak the truth!

In September 1945 the *Pacific Islands Monthly*, the immensely popular magazine produced in Sydney covering the affairs of New Guinea and the south-western Pacific[1], published a list of over 700 Australian civilians known to have disappeared during the Japanese occupation of eastern New Guinea and the Solomon Islands, and the names and addresses of their immediate next of kin. Jack Griffin's name was included, listed as 'J.K.V. Griffin—Miss Griffin, c/o Manufacturers Mutual Insurance Co. Ltd., 14 O'Connell St., Sydney'.[2] The name of every other Australian held at the Kavieng camp was also on the list, but no one at this early stage knew they had been interned there from September 1942 until March 1944.

The list had been compiled during the war years from numerous reports and enquiries received by the Australian Department of External Territories, and its final contents had been coordinated by a Sydney-based volunteer organisation called the Prisoners Welfare Section. The purpose of the PWS was to identify missing persons and eventually arrange for their safe recovery from Japanese hands at war's end. It was the centre of a cooperative effort involving the Australian government, the Pacific Territories Association, the Australian Red Cross and the New Guinea Women's Club. The activities of the PWS were of enormous interest to the families of those who had disappeared, including the many wives and children evacuated from Port Moresby, New Britain and New Ireland in 1941. It was optimistically expected that immediately following the Japanese surrender in August 1945 most of the missing civilians would be recovered alive from internment camps.

132

The families of all the Australians stranded on New Ireland had received almost no information about their men since 1941. The last reliable news received was the partial information and personal correspondence carried to Australia in April 1942 by Harry Murray and Jerry MacDonald after their successful escape. Since then, and despite considerable efforts, every enquiry had drawn a blank. Australian army and naval intelligence had from time to time since 1942 received fragments of information about the whereabouts and condition of some of the men, but this had not been passed on to their families.

In its September 1945 report the *Pacific Islands Monthly* speculated that a possible explanation for such a large number of missing persons was the reported evacuation of many internees in an unknown ship from Rabaul in about June 1942, and the apparent loss of this ship while en route to Japan. Also in September came the news from Tokyo that an Australian army investigator, Major Harold Williams, had turned up important information.

In Tokyo, as the very first competent Australian investigator on the job, one of Major Williams' most urgent tasks was to obtain information about the missing New Guinea civilians, a job for which he was eminently suited. He was one of the small number of unusual and especially talented people employed by Australia in the war against Japan, having spent much of his life living in that country. Raised in Melbourne, he had studied medicine, but had also developed a private, abiding interest in Japan and taken Japanese language lessons. In 1919 young Williams visited Japan on holiday to improve his language skills, but delayed his return home when he found employment with a foreign firm in Kobe. Twenty-two years later, and with hostilities imminent, he returned to Australia in August 1941 and immediately enlisted in the army, eventually serving in Australia, Africa, the Pacific and Burma. In August 1945 he found himself in Japan with the Allied occupation forces, eventually being attached to 2 Australian War Crimes Section. Having lived in pre-war Japan for so long, and being an avid student of Japanese language, culture and psychology, he was one of Australia's most knowledgeable experts on the country.[3]

In late September 1945 Williams had almost miraculously succeeded in rapidly tracking down and translating the Japanese-language nominal list of passengers on the *Montevideo Maru*'s last voyage[4], not in government files but with the vessel's owners, Osaka Shosen Kaisha. Over 800 Australian servicemen and over 200 civilians who drowned

The Japanese vessel *Montevideo Maru*, which left New Britain on 22 June 1942 carrying Australian prisoners of war and civilians. In Tokyo in September 1945 Major Harold Williams learnt that all were lost when the ship was torpedoed on 1 July 1942 off Luzon Island in the Philippines. AUSTRALIAN WAR MEMORIAL NEGATIVE NUMBER AWM 042334

in this miserable friendly-fire incident could now be identified.[5] He also discovered that a number of New Ireland men had died on the *Montevideo Maru*. Major Williams and the families could not know at this stage that these included many of the men who had tried to escape from Kavieng in January 1942 and had been subsequently apprehended by the Japanese and sent to Rabaul.

But there were many other missing New Ireland civilians who could not have perished on the *Montevideo Maru*, and Williams' early investigations in Tokyo into their fate yielded nothing. By January 1946 the *Pacific Islands Monthly* could still list the names of more than 100 New Guinea civilians whose whereabouts remained unknown, including about 25 Australian men believed to have been interned at Kavieng.[6] What had happened to them? On behalf of the Australian government, a series of investigations was begun by the Australian army in New Guinea to find answers to this question.

The first Australians to handle the Kavieng case on the ground in New Guinea were young regular army officers not particularly qualified or experienced for handling what would later turn out to be criminal investigations of Japanese suspects, and who were completely dependent on interpreters and translators in their dealings with these suspects. The young officers began arriving on the scene in the previously occupied territories from August 1945, months before the army had properly established its new war crimes investigations section. They were assisted in their work by civilian district officers of the Australia-New Guinea Administrative Unit, ANGAU, which had begun re-establishing a system of territorial administration that month. The Australians faced a difficult task from the outset. There were just too many missing persons cases and alleged crimes to investigate in a situation of general chaos, and numerous other pressing matters to attend to. In particular there was an urgency to obtain convictions and punish Japanese wrongdoers in response to the growing public pressure in Australia. The cases to be resolved first would be those where all elements of a successful prosecution could be quickly assembled. The difficult cases were going to have to wait until later, and as it turned out the Kavieng investigation would prove to be particularly troublesome.

The first officer assigned to re-establish Australian administration on New Ireland after the surrender was Captain Frank Warner-Shand, a former New Guinea resident, who arrived in Kavieng in October 1944. As leader of an ANGAU team, one of his principal duties was to organise the removal of the thousands of Japanese sailors still in New Ireland to Rabaul. Captain Warner-Shand met with Rear Admiral Tamura and his senior officers to discuss this relocation. Although there is no record of Warner-Shand pressing Tamura at this stage about the missing internees, presumably this did occur, and presumably Tamura's explanation would have been the *Kowa Maru* lie. Warner-Shand's discussions with Tamura involved laborious interpretation between English and Japanese, which would have given the Admiral an enormous advantage. Warner-Shand needed to obtain Tamura's cooperation over a host of administrative matters of much higher priority regarding the identification, disarming, feeding and relocation of the Japanese sailors.

Investigations among the few surviving European civilians and Melanesians on New Ireland began slowly with interviews of the handful of elderly nuns who had survived the war at Lakuramau Plantation. Although they were able to confirm that many of missing men had been interned in September 1942 and were subsequently sighted on a number of occasions in the Kavieng area until early 1944, the nuns were unable to cast any light on what had eventually happened to them.

Three civilian males who had not been interned in Kavieng were also interviewed. The German Richard Hermann, before the war manager of Numanne Island Plantation, had miraculously survived because of a pre-war friendship with a local Japanese resident. In mid-1942 he had had many dealings with the Kavieng internees and was able to provide the names of 23 of the men held there at that time. Not immediately interned himself, he was caught by the Japanese in August 1942 smuggling goods to the prisoners, and arrested. His life was spared after intervention by his Japanese friend, and he was sent to Rabaul where he survived the war growing vegetables for his Japanese gaolers. Hermann also was unable to say what had eventually happened to the Kavieng internees.[7]

Another civilian, Julius Lundin, also saw some of the internees in Kavieng in early 1942, shortly before he was sent by the Japanese to New Hanover Island; he did not return to Kavieng until April 1944. Although he heard news of some of the executions on Nago Island, he had learnt nothing about the disappearance of the civilian internees.

Kavieng, 20 October 1945. Rear Admiral Ryukichi Tamura in conference with Captain F.N. Warner-Shand, of the Australian New Guinea Administrative Unit. The unidentified man standing at the end of the table is a Japanese interpreter. AUSTRALIAN WAR MEMORIAL NEGATIVE NUMBER AWM 098442

I am a naval officer and will speak the truth!

Lossuk Bay, New Ireland, October 1945. Captain F. Warner-Shand ANGAU, Lieutenant P. Mollison RAN, and Lieutenant-Commander S.J. Benson RAN talking to unidentified Japanese naval officers on the beach following the arrival of postwar Australian occupation forces. AUSTRALIAN WAR MEMORIAL NEGATIVE NUMBER AWM 098431

Another survivor of the Japanese occupation of New Ireland was Rudolph Diercke. He was a German-Samoan member of one of the pioneering European families in the Rabaul-Kokopo area and had been employed by W.R. Carpenter & Co. as a plantation manager at Komalu on the west coast of New Ireland. He had survived the war still working at Komalu Plantation and repairing roads for the Japanese, until his eventual internment near Bo village in March 1944. Diercke provided a statement to investigators in October 1945 in which he said that he was 'the last European person in Kavieng in May 1942', but afterwards had heard about the internees only second-hand from others, including Melanesians. He said he had been told that the internees were still in the Kavieng camp until early 1944.[8]

The investigators soon became aware of rumours suggesting there was a mass grave somewhere in the Kavieng area, allegedly containing about thirty bodies. They began questioning the Melanesian and Chinese inhabitants, and although none had actually witnessed any incidents involving a mass murder, their evidence seemed to confirm the probable existence of an unmarked burial site. Searches on Nago Island led to the bodies of thirteen people being exhumed from a number of graves. Seven of the bodies were positively identified, including those of the coastwatchers Bill Kyle, Greg Benham, Con Page and Jack Talmage; the Catholic priests Father Karl Martin and Father Michael Murphy; and a local identity, 'Sailor' Herterich from Tabar Island. But there was no evidence that any of the other civilian internees were buried on Nago. Over the coming year numerous attempts would be made to uncover the 'mass grave', and convincing accounts would continue to be provided to investigators suggesting that such a grave existed.[9]

The investigators had also learned of the *Akikaze* incident in 1943, where a large number of civilian internees from Kairiru Island and Manus Island had been executed by machine-gun fire. When it was learnt that the *Akikaze* had called at Kavieng on the day of these killings, suspicions were immediately aroused, and a new path of enquiry opened. Had the internees been embarked on the *Akikaze*?

Finally, in late 1945 the Australian investigators began questioning the Japanese servicemen from Kavieng, now in one of the large military internment camps at Rabaul. Since September various captured naval officers in Rabaul had been informally questioned about the missing internees, and they had begun providing vague details of the air raids and bombardments during February 1944, and of the *Kokai Maru/Kowa Maru* story. By December the time had come to make a more thorough interrogation of Rear Admiral Tamura. On 10 December 1945 his lengthy signed statement of interview was obtained in Rabaul by Lieutenant Alfred Havilland of the Australia-New Guinea Administrative Unit. Through this first formal process, Tamura was able to begin selectively revealing more of the details of the fabulous lie. Communicating with

I am a naval officer and will speak the truth!

Kavieng, October 1945. A Japanese Daihatsu landing barge requisitioned by ANGAU is drawn up alongside HMAS *Kiama*. It is quite possible that this barge had been used during executions of the civilian internees the previous year. AUSTRALIAN WAR MEMORIAL NEGATIVE NUMBER AWM 098452

Havilland through a Japanese-American army interpreter, here is Tamura answering some of the questions put to him:

> HAVILLAND: What oath is binding to the Japanese?
>
> TAMURA: In Japan we have no such custom. I am a naval officer and will speak the truth.
>
> HAVILLAND: Were you in command at Kavieng at the time of the naval and air bombardment on February 11th 1944?
>
> TAMURA: Yes, the bombardment took place from 11th February and for five days after.
>
> HAVILLAND: How many Europeans, internees or prisoners were in the Kavieng prison on 11th February 1944?
>
> TAMURA: There were European internees in Kavieng. There were 23 prisoners. They were housed in two houses in the bush near Chinatown, Kavieng. One house was for Neutral civilians and the other for Allied civilians.

HAVILLAND: Are you sure that there were 23 civilians or could there have been more?

TAMURA: There were 23 Allied civilians and nine civilians from neutral countries. I am sure that there were 32.

HAVILLAND: Where are those 32 civilians now?

TAMURA: The bombing became so severe that on February 16th 1944, after consulting the Supreme Commander in Rabaul, I sent the 32 civilians to Rabaul. They were sent by barge to Doi Island about 60 miles from Kavieng where the Japanese ships in convoy on their way from Japan to Rabaul were sheltering from aerial bombardment. The 32 civilians were put safely on board. I cannot definitely name the ships in the convoy, there were two and their names were something like 'Kowa Maru' or 'Koa Maru'. My signalman was listening in on the radio and by accident heard from Rabaul that the ship named above arrived safely. This would be two or three days after the 32 prisoners had embarked.

HAVILLAND: Is it customary to receive a receipt for a prisoner handed over?

TAMURA: Yes, it is customary.

HAVILLAND: Did you receive a receipt for the 32 prisoners?

TAMURA: No, I did not receive a receipt for the 32 prisoners because communications were cut off between Rabaul and Kavieng by sea and air.

HAVILLAND: Can you give any reason for not receiving acknowledgement from Rabaul HQ by radio signal?

TAMURA: On account of the air bombardment I was too busy to communicate with Rabaul.

HAVILLAND: As you only know that the ships arrived safely, how do you know that the 32 people were on the ship that arrived safely?

TAMURA: We heard that the convoy arrived safely, so I assumed that the 32 people were safe in Rabaul.[10]

Another quite separate investigation into the fate of the Kavieng internees had also been underway. Apparently unbeknown to the Department of External Territories, the Army or any of the families involved, throughout the war the Royal Australian Navy had been accumulating secret intelligence information about the invasion and occupation of Kavieng. The RAN was particularly interested in understanding the system of Japanese harbour defences, including minefields and anti-

At Malaguna, New Britain, 20 September 1945. Rudolph Diercke being interviewed by a war correspondent after his release from New Ireland following the Japanese surrender. Diercke had been on New Ireland for the duration of the Japanese occupation, managing plantations and mending roads until interned in March 1944. AUSTRALIAN WAR MEMORIAL NEGATIVE NUMBER AWM 096855

submarine boom nets, and the state of Japanese navy shipping and shore installations. For this purpose RAN officers from time to time interviewed people who might have been in the Kavieng area. In October 1944, Lieutenant Commander Eric Feldt, the head of the RAN coastwatching organisation, interviewed Harry Spanner at his home in Queensland. Spanner was an elderly Australian who had been a plantation worker on New Ireland. When the Japanese arrived he pretended he was German, and because of his age and apparent nationality had been given considerable freedom. Eventually he was assigned by the Japanese to work at the leprosarium on New Hanover Island, from where he made a successful escape to Australia.

Harry Spanner provided Feldt with information about the Kavieng internees which he had received from local natives, including a report that 'European prisoners were shot in retaliation for casualties in air raids' and that it was also rumoured that 'several prisoners were taken away in a Japanese warship and that the ship had been sunk, the prisoners being lost'.[11]

In October 1945, after cessation of hostilities, the RAN sent a naval intelligence officer from Rabaul to Kavieng to survey the entire situation, including any atrocities which may have been committed. As well as conducting a survey of the harbour and port facilities, Lieutenant J. Mollison interviewed scores of people and prepared a detailed report of his discoveries.[12] He learnt from native eyewitnesses about the executions of Australians as 'spies' on Nago Island, and also learnt that 'the other group of Europeans stated to have been put to death were said to have been taken after a heavy Allied bombing or shelling to a nearby bomb crater, bayoneted, and buried in the crater'.

Thus by the end of 1945 all the key elements which would mislead the investigation were in place. It was believed by the Australian investigators that the internees had probably disappeared from Kavieng around February 1944, although it could have happened much earlier; and three possible explanations seemed to exist. The internees could have been killed and buried in a mass grave somewhere in the Kavieng area; they could have been loaded onto the *Akikaze* and executed; or they had been sent to Rabaul in the manner described by Rear Admiral Tamura and disappeared some time afterwards. For the next year the investigation would be completely bogged down chasing these three promising but eventually unproductive leads.

In the meantime, the families of the disappeared Kavieng internees began besieging the Department of External Territories in Canberra for news of the whereabouts of their men. In turn, the Secretary of that Department, James Halligan, began writing what would turn out to be a long sequence of letters to the Secretary of the Department of the Army in Melbourne, pressing for more information. But very little of the information gathered in all these investigations would ever be provided to the families.

chapter 17

A neat, diminutive, wiry young man of unusual intelligence and curiosity

The one person who would eventually, and almost single-handedly, exert most influence over the investigation was, by the most fortuitous and unusual of circumstances, the perfect person for the job. Albert Klestadt was born in Essen, Germany on 30 October 1913, and raised and educated in the Baltic seaport of Hamburg, where his father was a manufacturer. The family was of part-Jewish descent, and shortly after the accession of Adolf Hitler to power in 1933 came under the scrutiny of the Nazi authorities. By 1935 the Klestadts had been ruined by official anti-Jewish discrimination, and Albert's parents advised him to leave the country. So, along with thousands of other German Jews, he became a refugee.[1]

Klestadt was a neat, diminutive, wiry young man of unusual intelligence and curiosity, with a practical way of dealing with life's problems.[2] Among the strong attributes with which his character was endowed, two in particular would shape the direction of his life over the next decades. The Klestadt family's weekend hobby in Hamburg had been sailing, and Albert had learnt to be confident from an early age handling small craft. The sea was not something that frightened him, although he learnt to greatly respect its changing moods, and he understood and was fascinated by navigation and seamanship and the preparation, responsibility and independence of action that was their heart and soul. Along with his love of sailing, Klestadt had also developed strong political beliefs, especially respect for individual freedom, rights and responsibilities. His ejection from Germany by a totalitarian regime which practiced a vicious form of racial discrimination against himself and his family had inspired in him a passion for human rights. He would become particularly sensitive to human rights abuses and injustices wherever he found them.

In 1935, the same year that Jack Griffin left Australia to start his own adventure in New Guinea, and at the age of 21 (Jack was 25), Klestadt departed Germany, disowned by the Nazis, a stateless person without passport or other identification papers. Not knowing exactly where he would end up, he travelled by ship from Hamburg to England. A German friend who was living on the other side of the world in Japan had earlier suggested that work might be available for him there. In England he quickly discovered that it was relatively easy for a person in his circumstances to gain admittance to Japan, and anyway he had always had a fascination with Asia, and knew as well that conditions in Japan were ideal for small boat sailing. So he scraped together enough money to purchase a third-class fare, and after just a week in London embarked on the passenger steamer *Haruna Maru* for the Japanese port city of Kobe. It did not take long for him to land a job with a German import and export firm in Kobe, and thus began six years of life in Japan.

Alone in Kobe while he attempted to arrange for first his mother, and then his brother Eric to join him from Germany, Klestadt lived the enjoyable expatriate life of a young, single European male. He began learning the Japanese language, and took up sailing on the Inland Sea with the purchase of a 21-foot sloop built of teak, which he named *Spray* after the yacht Captain Joshua Slocum had used to single-handedly circumnavigate the world for the first time thirty years before. He read widely, and collected books about sailing and famous seafarers, becoming especially an admirer of Lieutenant William Bligh. In 1789, following a mutiny on his ship HMS *Bounty* in the south Pacific, Bligh sailed a 23-foot, under-provisioned open boat crowded with a crew of eighteen loyal sailors, from near Tonga nearly 4000 nautical miles westward to safety in Kupang on the island of Timor in the then Dutch East Indies. That miraculous accomplishment is one of the greatest open-water navigation and ocean-survival feats of all time, and Bligh pulled it off by dint of his extraordinarily strong leadership, and daily attention to the health and hygiene of his crew, of whom only one died, not from ill-health as it happened but as a result of conflict with hostile islanders.

In mid-1938, after her marriage had failed and just as she was on the verge of departing from Germany to migrate to Japan, Klestadt's mother suddenly died of stomach cancer.³ The following year he was finally able to organise his brother's travel to Japan after Eric's release from a Nazi concentration camp, and there was a joyful reunion between the two in Kobe.

However, life for Europeans in Japan was about to take a turn for the worse. During the 1930s the Japanese government had itself become progressively militarised, totalitarian, racist and rabidly nationalistic. By 1937 Japan had started an ambitious war in China propelled by self-proclaimed racial and cultural superiority, complete with all the murderous violence, abuses and indifference to human suffering which it would soon visit on many other nations. At roughly the same time in 1941 that the Australians in faraway Kavieng were becoming suspicious of Japanese intentions there, in Japan Klestadt was able to observe at close hand the signs of a country preparing itself for a wider war, as economic activity gradually became subverted to the needs of the military, and the rights and freedoms of citizens became increasingly restricted. In particular, the signs of an official campaign of racial vilification directed at white people began to appear in government propaganda, directed particularly towards the citizens of Japan's perceived rivals in the Asia-Pacific area, the United States, Great Britain, the Netherlands and Australia.

In September 1939 Adolf Hitler had started the European war with his surprise attack on Poland, and in 1940, as Hitler was overrunning the rest of Europe, Germany and Japan had signed a mutual non-aggression treaty. Klestadt increasingly sensed that he had, in a slow-motion way, managed to escape from the racism and super-nationalism of Nazi Germany only to end up facing the racism and super-nationalism of pre-war Japan.

By mid-1941, Albert and Eric Klestadt's weekend yacht cruises on the Inland Sea were affording them unusual insight into Japanese war preparations. Maritime activity had become extraordinarily busy with the recall home of most of Japan's fleet of passenger and cargo steamers. In Kobe harbour these ships were now being repainted in drab military greys and blacks, and their names and other markings obliterated. The Klestadts decided that once again the time had come to move on, which they prepared to do by sailing *Spray* out of the Inland Sea into the open ocean and then across the Pacific to Canada. But this plan was blocked by the Japanese navy, which now strictly prohibited passage by non-military vessels through the only exit route, the Kii Suido Narrows, so the escape using *Spray* was abandoned.

As a young man with strong feelings about the evils of totalitarianism and racism, based on direct experience, Klestadt badly wanted to join in the fight against Germany, and Japan too if it came to that, and began actively seeking ways of getting to a country where he could be useful to a government opposing them. He had begun numerous unsuccessful attempts to be recruited into the British military in 1939, but his German background and statelessness had made it difficult for him to be accepted.

Eventually, in September 1941, with help from the British Consul in Kobe in the form of a half-promise of later work in Singapore, and directions to proceed with covert liaison for the British using his special language skills and knowledge of Japanese shipping movements, Albert Klestadt left Kobe for Singapore via Shanghai and Manila on one of the last regular passenger steamers to leave Japan. By December 1941 he was living in the YMCA in Manila, on Luzon Island in the Philippines archipelago, gathering information for the British government and awaiting his final journey on to Singapore. His brother Eric was to remain in Japan, stateless and unable to obtain an exit visa.

In the same way that Jack Griffin's final sea voyage from Rabaul to Kavieng in December 1941 had unerringly delivered him straight to a primary Japanese military target, in Manila Klestadt found himself squarely in the path of oncoming Japanese forces. The first air raids on Manila and the nearby US military bases began immediately following the December 1941 Pearl Harbor attacks, with the same intention of destroying American power in the western Pacific with an initial heavy strike. These raids were soon followed by Japanese landings on Luzon and Mindanao islands, and then an all-out state of war.

Klestadt's survival instincts were thoroughly roused by this dangerous new situation, and when informed by his British contacts that forward travel to Singapore was now out of the question, he began preparing to make a dash for escape from Manila and the Philippines, preferably to the nearest free British country, and join in the fight from that side. As he prepared his escape, he came to the realisation that he was probably going to have to achieve it unaccompanied. Although there was a large European expatriate community in Manila, among which he had good friends and acquaintances, Klestadt was unable to convince anyone to join him in his escape bid. Here among the expatriates in the Philippines in December 1941, in the midst of fast-moving events, he encountered exactly the same cautious attitudes that Harry Murray and Jerry MacDonald were to encounter among the remaining planters a short while later on New Ireland. How are we going to suddenly and safely leave? We need to look after our property. The war may not last long and the Japanese might quickly be defeated. If there is serious danger we believe our government will rescue us.

In January 1942, following the occupation of Manila, and using his German background and Japanese language skills, Klestadt acquired official identity papers passing himself off as a good German with a small business in a rural town south of Manila. Then, as Jack would do in his initial escape from Kavieng at exactly the same time, Klestadt acquired a car, maps and supplies, and set out alone to drive south from Manila as far away from the Japanese as he could manage. This road journey delivered him to a small coastal town from which he was able to leave the island of Luzon in a rented outrigger canoe, heading for the large island of Mindoro. Eventually, after much travel and many island-hopping adventures, which he would later relate in his 1959 book *The Sea Was Kind*, in late May 1942 Klestadt arrived undetected by the Japanese at islands off the Zamboanga Peninsula near Mindanao Island in the far southern Philippines, the land of the Moslem Moro people.

Here he acquired a small, open 24-foot native sailing sloop, the *Maring*, normally used for coastal trading in rice, sugar and corn, and commenced preparations and provisioning for a long single-handed sea voyage to Australia, nearly 3000 kilometres to the south-east. In mid-June 1942, just months before the planters on New Ireland were being rounded up for internment, Klestadt set sail alone for Australia, having estimated it would take him a few months to do the trip.

There was soon a major setback. It transpired that this time of the year, in the middle of the dry season with strong prevailing winds blowing from the south and south-west, was not a good time to attempt this long southwards voyage completely by sail. The combination of winds and currents made headway very difficult, the *Maring* was becoming unseaworthy from the battering it was taking, and Klestadt was becoming fatigued and dispirited. Eventually, not much further south but a month later, he was advised by expert Moro sailors from the Tawi-Tawi Islands that it would be far easier to make the voyage to Australia after October, when the prevailing monsoon winds would be

Albert Klestadt (centre), with Frank Young (left) and Sahibad, a Moro crewman, on the day *Kakugan* reached Arnhem Land.

more likely to blow a sailing boat to the south. So he reluctantly decided to hide for three months in these remote islands where the Japanese had not established a strong presence. Befriended and protected by the local people, he leased the *Maring* to a local Chinese trader to provide an income to live on, and settled in for the wait.

In October 1942, as Klestadt was once again preparing the *Maring* for sea, an extraordinary coincidence occurred when he learned that a stranded officer from the US Army of the Philippines, who wanted to sail to Australia to link up with US forces there, was looking for him. Second Lieutenant Frank Young turned out to be the 22-year-old Eurasian son of an American father and a Moro mother. Young had heard, through Moro networks, of Klestadt's small boat and of his navigation skills, of which Young possessed none. Very soon a partnership was formed in which Young would arrange for the supply of a Moro *cumpit* (traditional open sailing craft) and Moro crew, and Klestadt would provide his navigation skills, charts and compass to get them all safely to Australia. Reluctantly, Klestadt parted company with the *Maring*, selling her to raise funds for provisioning the journey on the 35-foot cumpit *Kakugan*, and with Young and his initial crew of three began revised preparations for the long voyage.

The *Kakugan* sailed on 24 October 1942 from the Sulu Islands, with Klestadt planning to head for Arnhem Land on the north coast of Australia via the Celebes Sea, the Molucca Passage through the eastern islands of modern-day Indonesia, and then due south through the Ceram and Arafura seas. Before losing sight of the last of the Philippine Islands, the *Kakugan* acquired three more Moro sailors as additional crew, and in early November sailed south-east into the Celebes Sea. For most of the journey south conditions were ideal for sailing, and despite some scares caused by Japanese aircraft and a patrol boat, and some tense disagreements between Klestadt and his crew[4], in early December 1942 *Kakugan* entered the Arafura Sea immediately north of Australia. On 8 December the little vessel crossed Lieutenant Bligh's 1789 east-west sailing track, and the following day made landfall on Goulburn Island just off Arnhem Land, about 300 kilometres to the east of Darwin. The men were directed by Australian Aborigines to a mission station managed by the Reverend L.N. Kentish for the Overseas Methodist Mission, from which they were soon picked up by a Catalina flying boat of the Australian air force and taken to Darwin.

Klestadt had successfully navigated the *Kakugan* nearly 2000 nautical miles in 47 days of sailing from the southern Philippines. In this long, hard journey, the sailor-man Klestadt had become one of only a handful of Europeans to escape from Japanese-occupied territory by small boat, and possibly the only one to have sailed all the way without motorised assistance, depending entirely on wind, currents and his meticulous navigation to deliver him and his crew to safety.

Despite this extraordinary accomplishment, and although still possessed with a burning desire to join the fight against the Japanese, new obstacles cropped up in the form of strong suspicions held by Australian military officers about Klestadt's antecedents and intentions. Here was a Japanese-speaking German without travel documents who had mysteriously arrived by small boat in the northern Australian military defensive zone at a time of a heightened alert. Klestadt was now going to be made to prove his bona fides. Young was immediately awarded the DSO for having made his successful escape to rejoin US forces and posted to a unit of the US Army in Australia; and later sent back to the Philippines by submarine to conduct secret duties with guerrilla forces. The Moro crewmen were initially housed near Brisbane at a special US Army intelligence base; they later disappeared and Klestadt never found out what became of them.

It took a very long time for Klestadt to persuade Australian authorities to accept him for what he was, and he was under surveillance for most of this period, and under threat of internment as an enemy alien. In the end, in Melbourne in May 1943, it was arranged for Klestadt to be recruited into the Australian Army Intelligence Corps with the rank of private, and he was immediately put to work as an analyst specialising in Japan. At this time, over two years after Pearl Harbor, Australian intelligence units still possessed very few people with a deep understanding of the Japanese language, culture and psychology. Klestadt was to prove over the next few years what an extraordinarily valuable asset his unique mixture of skills would be in the fight with Japan in the south-west Pacific.[5]

With his unusual background and talents it was probably inevitable he would be posted to the Far Eastern Liaison Office. In this capacity he worked with FELO for a long time in Australia, then in the field in the Solomon Islands, and finally in New Guinea. His observations of the appalling conditions suffered by Japanese troops in the field provided him with a deep understanding of the extent and depth of Japan's official dishonesty, and the many and varied methods used by Japanese officers to deceive their own men. In particular, he learnt that when handled skilfully the truth was a far more powerful weapon for inducing changes in enemy attitudes than was the farrago of lies told to them by their leaders.[6]

When the Japanese capitulation came in August 1945 Klestadt was a Warrant Officer Class 2 stationed with his FELO unit near Wewak on the north coast of New Guinea, directly to the west across the Bismarck Sea from Kavieng. In September he was involved in organising the surrenders of Japanese troops in the Wewak area to Major-General H.C.H. Robertson, General Officer Commanding the 6th Australian Division.

Given everything that had happened to Klestadt since his escape from Nazi Germany in 1935, his escape from Japan in 1941, and finally his escape from the Philippines to Australia during 1942, it

Members of FELO gathered at South Yarra, Melbourne. The diminutive Albert Klestadt is third from the left.

was an immensely satisfying moment for him to participate in this important surrender ceremony in the uniform of a Warrant Officer of the Australian Army. He had thrice been a refugee from racism, ultra-nationalism and militarism, and here he was in 1945 playing an important role in formally witnessing the defeat of these scourges of mankind.

In October 1945, still in New Guinea, he heard from an Australian army colleague in Tokyo that his brother Eric was alive and well and had lived out the war in Japan.[7] Klestadt immediately began to manoeuvre for a posting with the Allied Occupation Forces. He soon received a commission as lieutenant, and in early 1946 was posted as a language and intelligence officer to the 65th Australian Infantry Battalion stationed in Fukuyama in the south of Japan, and was reunited with his brother.

Also in October 1945 the Australian Parliament had passed the *Australian War Crimes Act*, authorising the army to establish the War

Crimes Section to investigate and prepare cases for trial, and 2 Australian War Crimes Section was firmly established in Tokyo by 1946. The War Crimes Section was going to need Australian officers who were fluent in Japanese and understood Japanese psychology, and were familiar with interrogation and investigation techniques. Later in 1946 the 65th Infantry Battalion was posted from Fukuyama to Tokyo to complete a routine month of guard duty at the Imperial Palace, just near the offices of 2 Australian War Crimes Section. Klestadt had met Major Harold Williams socially in Kobe before the war, and later in Melbourne after his arrival in Australia in late 1942.[8] In Tokyo they renewed their acquaintanceship, and Williams and other officers of 2 War Crimes

Cape Wom, New Guinea, 13 September 1945. Warrant Officer 2 Albert Klestadt and two Japanese staff officers arriving for a surrender ceremony at Cape Wom airstrip. Klestadt was the interpreter during this ceremony. AUSTRALIAN WAR MEMORIAL NEGATIVE NUMBER AWM 096450

A neat, diminutive, wiry young man

Cape Wom, New Guinea, 13 September 1945. The surrender ceremony at Cape Wom airstrip, with Lieutenant General Adachi, Commander 18th Japanese Army in New Guinea, formally surrendering to Major General Robertson, General Officer Commanding 6th Australian Division. Warrant Officer 2 Albert Klestadt assisted with negotiating this surrender. AUSTRALIAN WAR MEMORIAL NEGATIVE NUMBER AWM 096233

Section thought that Klestadt was perfectly qualified to help them solve the large number of outstanding investigations they were expected to handle. Before too long a transfer from the 65th Australian Infantry Battalion had been arranged, and in late 1946 Klestadt commenced duty at the Meiji Building in Tokyo as an investigator for Australia of suspected Japanese war crimes against Australians.[9]

The stage was now slowly being set for Albert Klestadt, a man who had pulled off a remarkable and risky escape from the Japanese-held islands of the southern Philippines in 1942 by sailing a small boat to Australia, to investigate the suspected murder at Kavieng in New Guinea of a group of Australian civilian internees. All the victims had earlier the same year made what turned out to be momentous personal decisions not to escape by small boat from that Japanese-held territory.

chapter 18

I am indeed sorry to have to inform you…

By early 1946 the Kavieng investigation had been sidelined by the many other more easily resolved war crimes cases. At Rabaul the Australian War Crimes Section had been busy accumulating evidence against hundreds of Japanese ex-servicemen held in the internment camps there, and there was no shortage of complainants and witnesses to their alleged crimes. The intention was to release for repatriation to Japan only soldiers and sailors who could be cleared of complicity in war crimes. Being cleared for repatriation meant freedom from prosecution, or so each relieved ex-serviceman believed. The Australian investigators were particularly interested in identifying very senior, living Japanese army and navy officers who could be held ultimately responsible, including for crimes committed by subordinates.

Held within a separate section of the Rabaul internment camps was a small group of those senior officers, including Lieutenant General Takeo Ito and Rear Admiral Ryukichi Tamura, who between them had held command of Japanese forces on New Ireland at war's end. Also held there was a group of senior army and naval officers who had been based in Rabaul, including General Hitoshi Imamura, Vice-Admiral Junichi Kasuka and Captain Sanagi. More senior officers were collected from other Pacific islands and brought to join them.

The first war crimes trial in Rabaul was held in December 1945 and by July 1946 nearly 170 had been completed in the first round. Among those convicted of serious crimes during these early trials was the comparatively lucky General Imamura, sentenced to just ten years' imprisonment. In May 1946 Lieutenant General Ito, made to accept responsibility for the actions of his Kenpeitai subordinates, was found guilty of the murder of Chinese civilians on New Ireland and sentenced to death.[1] A number of other senior officers were convicted in Rabaul for serious crimes at other locations in the Pacific.

But Rear Admiral Tamura and his senior officers from Kavieng were not to be caught up in this 1946 dragnet. Although occasionally questioned by investigators about the fate of the Kavieng internees, they all stuck to their well-rehearsed *Kowa Maru/Kokai Maru* story, which was corroborated by Vice-Admiral Kasuka and Captain Sanagi whenever they were questioned. When in July 1946 the first round of trials were completed at Rabaul, Tamura, Yoshino and all the other Japanese based in Kavieng had escaped prosecution, and many of Tamura's subordinates had already been sent back to their families and occupations in Japan.

Back in Australia, by mid-1946 the families of those who had disappeared at Kavieng had repeatedly approached the Department of External Territories for news of their men. By now many had given up hope their man would ever be found alive. Although still wishing to

Rabaul, New Britain, 5 December 1945. Suspected Japanese war criminals were rounded up and detained in a number of compounds in the 11th Division AIF area, and guarded by troops of the New Guinea Infantry Battalion. AUSTRALIAN WAR MEMORIAL NEGATIVE NUMBER AWM 099240

know what had happened they were being provided with almost no information by a curiously secretive government. Not only that, but nearly all were beginning to face legal and financial issues which could not be resolved without official certification that their relative was no longer still living.[2]

Some of the relatives had already returned to New Ireland to personally conduct a search, including Moya Chadderton[3] and Gwen Ives, and Harry Murray was also back in Kavieng to help in this endeavour. Those who could return to the island were heartbroken by what they discovered. As well as learning nothing useful about what had happened to their men, they witnessed the immense destruction that had been caused to their island paradise during the Japanese occupation. The towns of Kavieng and Namatanai had been reduced to rubble; roads, bridges and wharves destroyed; and all the neat pre-war copra plantations extensively damaged and looted. Many friends, neighbours and Melanesian employees had disappeared. To re-establish the family businesses they would need to start from scratch, and it would be mainly the Australian women who would have to lead this reconstruction effort.

The main problem for the Minister for External Territories, Eddie Ward, and his Departmental Secretary, James Halligan, was that of establishing legal certainty regarding each of the now presumed deaths. For this they turned to the Australian National Security (War Deaths) Regulations, which had been created by Parliament expressly for the purpose of enabling certification of the death of Australian citizens actually or presumed killed during the war. The urgency to provide legal certainty in the form of a death certificate for each of the Kavieng internees would now overtake the need to establish the actual cause of death through a successful investigation.

At the highest levels of the Australian government, no one knew with any certainty what had happened to the Kavieng internees. Many unsuccessful attempts had been made to discover the 'mass grave' in Kavieng, and there had been no success in linking the disappearances to the *Akikaze* massacre. The only plausible explanation was that provided by Rear Admiral Tamura in his statement, made in Rabaul in December 1945, that in mid-February 1944 the internees had been successfully loaded onboard the *Kowa Maru* or possibly the *Kokai Maru* for transfer to Japan via Rabaul. Separate investigations by the Australian army had confirmed that both of these ships had been sunk shortly afterwards by American aircraft.

I am indeed sorry to have to inform you...

TELEPHONE No.: CANBERRA 631.
TELEGRAPHIC ADDRESS: "TERRITORIES" CANBERRA.

DEPARTMENT OF EXTERNAL TERRITORIES,

Canberra, 17th October, 1946

In reply quote No. 16/3/408

Dear Mrs. Griffin,

        I desire to refer to previous correspondence concerning the fate of your brother, Mr. J.K.V. Griffin, who was reported to have been captured at the time of the Japanese invasion of New Guinea in 1942.

        It is sincerely regretted that it has not as yet been possible to make an official pronouncement concerning the fate of many former residents of the Territory. The lack of accurate and comprehensive Japanese records, however, has necessitated very extensive enquiries, both in the Territory and in Japan, and although the investigations are still continuing, it is expected that sufficient confirmatory evidence will shortly be available to warrant the presumption of your brother's death.

        I am indeed sorry to have to inform you that the information which has been received so far indicates that Mr. Griffin, together with 31 other civilians, was imprisoned by the Japanese in the Kavieng Internment Camp. A Japanese report claims that 32 civilian internees were sent from this camp by barge on 16th February, 1944, to an island 60 miles from Kavieng, and embarked in two transports which were proceeding to Rabaul, and which were bombed and sunk by the Allies before any internees had disembarked. Although this report lacks confirmation, it is considered reasonably certain that these civilians met their death on or about this date, as no further reports concerning them have been received.

        I am enclosing a Form of Information of Death, and will be glad if you will fill in the personal items and return the form to me, so that a Certificate of Death may be issued, under Regulation 5A of the National Security (War Deaths) Regulations, as soon as all the enquiries have been completed. This Certificate will be forwarded to you when issued.

Yours sincerely,

J R Halligan

(J. R. Halligan)
Secretary

Miss, Griffin,
C.- Manufacturers Mutual
Insurance Co. Ltd.,
14 O'Connell St., <u>SYDNEY</u> N.S.W.

Department of External Territories' first letter to Alison Griffin about the disappearance of J.K.V. Griffin, October 1946.[4]

In the absence of any other explanation, and to satisfy a pressing bureaucratic requirement to issue certificates of death, Tamura's sworn testimony was about to be given official status as a historical fact, and the mid-February 1944 timing of the internees' disappearance accepted as the true date. In October 1946 Alison Griffin, still Jack Griffin's faithful representative and advocate in Sydney, received the first formal government advice about her brother's fate, in the form of a letter from Secretary Halligan.

Just a few days after Secretary Halligan's letter was sent from Canberra, Rear Admiral Tamura was again briefly interviewed, now by the Australian War Crimes Section at the Rabaul internment camp. On 24 October 1946, Lieutenant Joseph Backhouse obtained another record of interrogation signed by Tamura which included the following exchange:

BACKHOUSE: Can you remember having 32 Allied PW [Prisoners of War] interned at Kavieng?
TAMURA: Yes, but to be precise they were internees, not PWs.
BACKHOUSE: What became of them?
TAMURA: From 11 February 1944 Kavieng was heavily bombed daily by a great number of Allied planes and almost all houses in the area were destroyed, and it was considered unsafe for the 32 Allied internees (all males) kept in Kavieng to remain there. I sent a message to South Eastern Fleet HQ asking for instructions, stating I thought it advisable to send the internees to Japan. The HQ replied by wireless that *Kowa Maru*, destination Japan via Rabaul, would anchor off Doi Island near Kavieng for the night and that the internees were to be sent on that boat. The internees were sent from the compound in the evening of 17 or 18 February to Kavieng wharf, where they got on a barge and were sent to Doi Island. Next morning, the 83rd Naval Garrison Unit reported by telephone that the barge had safely delivered the internees to *Kowa Maru* and had returned. I heard later that *Kowa Maru* after a short stay in Rabaul left for Japan.
BACKHOUSE: Do you know if the *Kowa Maru* reached Japan with the internees aboard?
TAMURA: I do not know, though I heard it arrived safely at Rabaul.
BACKHOUSE: Were the internees disembarked at Rabaul?
TAMURA: I do not know. I heard that after a short stay at Rabaul the *Kowa Maru* sailed for Japan.

BACKHOUSE: Did you ever hear about the sinking of the *Kowa Maru*?
TAMURA: No.
BACKHOUSE: Do you swear this story to be true and correct?
TAMURA: Yes.
BACKHOUSE: Then can you explain about the finding of a grave at Kavieng containing approximately 30 human beings?
TAMURA: I cannot.
BACKHOUSE: Could the barge commander have disposed of the internees in a manner other than your instruction unbeknown to you?
TAMURA: Definitely not; though I did not witness the internees' embarkation I am certain the barge commander obeyed orders most faithfully.
BACKHOUSE: What is the name of the barge commander?
TAMURA: I do not remember.
BACKHOUSE: Are there any other members of your naval force still in Rabaul?
TAMURA: No. They have all been repatriated.[5]

In this exchange, again made through the medium of an interpreter, Lieutenant Backhouse's completely untrue remark about discovery of a 'mass grave' in Kavieng only served to confuse the issue for months to come while more futile attempts were made to locate it. With each of his carefully managed and courteous interviews with Australian investigators, Tamura was successfully buying more time for himself and his men, and here was an Australian investigator unwittingly helping the process.

Just a few weeks later, on 6 November 1946, a relieved Rear Admiral Tamura was embarked at Rabaul on the destroyer *Hanazuki*, finally on his way back to Japan and reunion with a family he had not seen for years, the last of the Kavieng naval garrison to be repatriated. With his cautious, selective release of information under questioning, he felt he had been singularly successful in concealing the true story of the Kavieng murders, protecting his men from further questioning, and avoiding having to face the vengeful military courts in Rabaul. And unbeknown to him, his story was being accepted in Canberra as the best possible explanation for the internees' disappearances.

But, also unbeknown to him, just as the Rear Admiral was preparing for his repatriation home to Japan, a series of events was unfolding in Tokyo which would guarantee that his homecoming and family reunion would be seriously spoilt. At their quarters in the Meiji Building in

Tokyo, Japanese-speaking officers of 2 Australian War Crimes Section were beginning the process of checking all the facts surrounding the sinking of the *Kowa Maru* and *Kokai Maru* in February 1944. To facilitate a more thorough investigation they had access to thousands of repatriated Japanese servicemen, civilian contractors and merchant sailors. Not then realised by the investigators, many of these people knew nothing about the Kavieng incident, or of the secret conspiracy to conceal it, but they had been in Rabaul at the time the ships had sailed, and in some cases had actually been on board.

chapter 19

Extremely unlikely that Europeans would have been on the ship

On 2 December 1946 Lieutenant Albert Klestadt commenced working in Tokyo as an investigating officer with 2 Australian War Crimes Section, a unit which reported directly to the Australian army's Directorate of Prisoners of War and Internees in Melbourne. The Section had established an office on the seventh floor of the impressive Meiji Building, a surviving office building quite close to the Imperial Palace[1], along with war crimes and legal departments of other Allied nations. The Section was commanded by Lieutenant Colonel Duncan Goslett, who had come to this posting from years of outstanding front-line military service during the war.[2] For the volume of work being undertaken, the Section was quite small, comprising just twelve or thirteen staff at any one time, of whom only a handful were investigating officers, some of them with a legal background in civilian life, others with special knowledge of the Japanese and their language.[3]

Working in close cooperation with the Allied occupation forces and Japanese police, the duties of investigation officers included obtaining and analysing all kinds of Japanese records, identifying and interrogating repatriated Japanese servicemen, and preparing sworn Affidavits of Evidence to help build legal cases which could result in war crimes convictions at Australian Military Courts.

Cases were not permanently assigned to particular investigators to handle, but constantly moved around from officer to officer. At the time Lieutenant Klestadt commenced work in the Meiji Building, his colleague Major Harold Williams was handling both the Kavieng and *Akikaze* cases, and Klestadt was assigned a number of other investigations,

Lieutenant Colonel Duncan Goslett, Officer Commanding Number 2 Australian War Crimes section in Tokyo during the Kavieng investigation. This portrait was taken in Perth in 1943 when he was a major on the staff of Headquarters, 3rd Australian Corps.
AUSTRALIAN WAR MEMORIAL NEGATIVE NUMBER AWM 052876

including the 1942 Bangka Island Massacre of Australian Army nurses. Also, by sad coincidence, he was assigned to investigate the murder of the Reverend L.N. Kentish of the Goulburn Island Methodist Mission,

Extremely unlikely...

the man who had greeted the crew of the *Kakugan* after their landfall in Arnhem Land in December 1942 following Klestadt's escape from the Philippines and had arranged for their safe transfer to Darwin.[4]

By November 1946, fifteen months after the Kavieng investigation had been launched in New Guinea, not much progress had been made. However, following repatriation from Rabaul during 1946 of most of the Kavieng garrison to Japan, the centre of the investigation was now in Tokyo and, with Major Williams' excellent knowledge of the Japanese military psyche, the case was finally being handled by someone well equipped for the job. Unlike the Australian army officers who had conducted the earlier investigations and interrogations of Admiral Tamura in Rabaul, Williams possessed a much better understanding of the many subtle and persuasive methods used by Japanese ex-servicemen to lie when under interrogation. He also possessed broad knowledge of the murderous proclivities of the Japanese forces, particularly the gratuitous and random acts of violence against civilians of all races in New Guinea, where murder had been so commonplace it was highly likely the reason for many unexplained wartime disappearances.[5]

From the accounts already provided in Rabaul by Rear Admiral Tamura, Williams was aware that the Australian internees from Kavieng were alleged to have been on board the *Kowa Maru* or *Kokai Maru* at the time of their sinking, and had commenced an enquiry to determine if this could be verified. With cooperation from American counterparts and the Japanese police he was actively searching in Japan for passengers or crew who could reliably assist. At last a serious investigation could be launched into the fates of the missing civilians on New Ireland.

What was generally known from Imperial Japanese Navy reports obtained in Rabaul and Tokyo was that after a long and dangerous voyage from Yokosuka in Japan, the *Kowa Maru* and *Kokai Maru* had departed together on 12 February 1944 from the big Japanese naval base at Truk in a troop convoy southbound for Rabaul, guarded by a number of small warships. On both the 15th and 16th of February the convoy was spotted by Allied aircraft and attacked, with some ships suffering damage. To avoid further attacks the ships may have sheltered near Doi Island, near Kavieng, and on 17 February proceeded to Rabaul, moving into Simpson Harbour early the next morning. For the next two days both ships disembarked replacement troops and cargo, then at midday on 20 February began embarking hundreds of members of the Japanese Army Air Force who were being withdrawn with their aircraft further

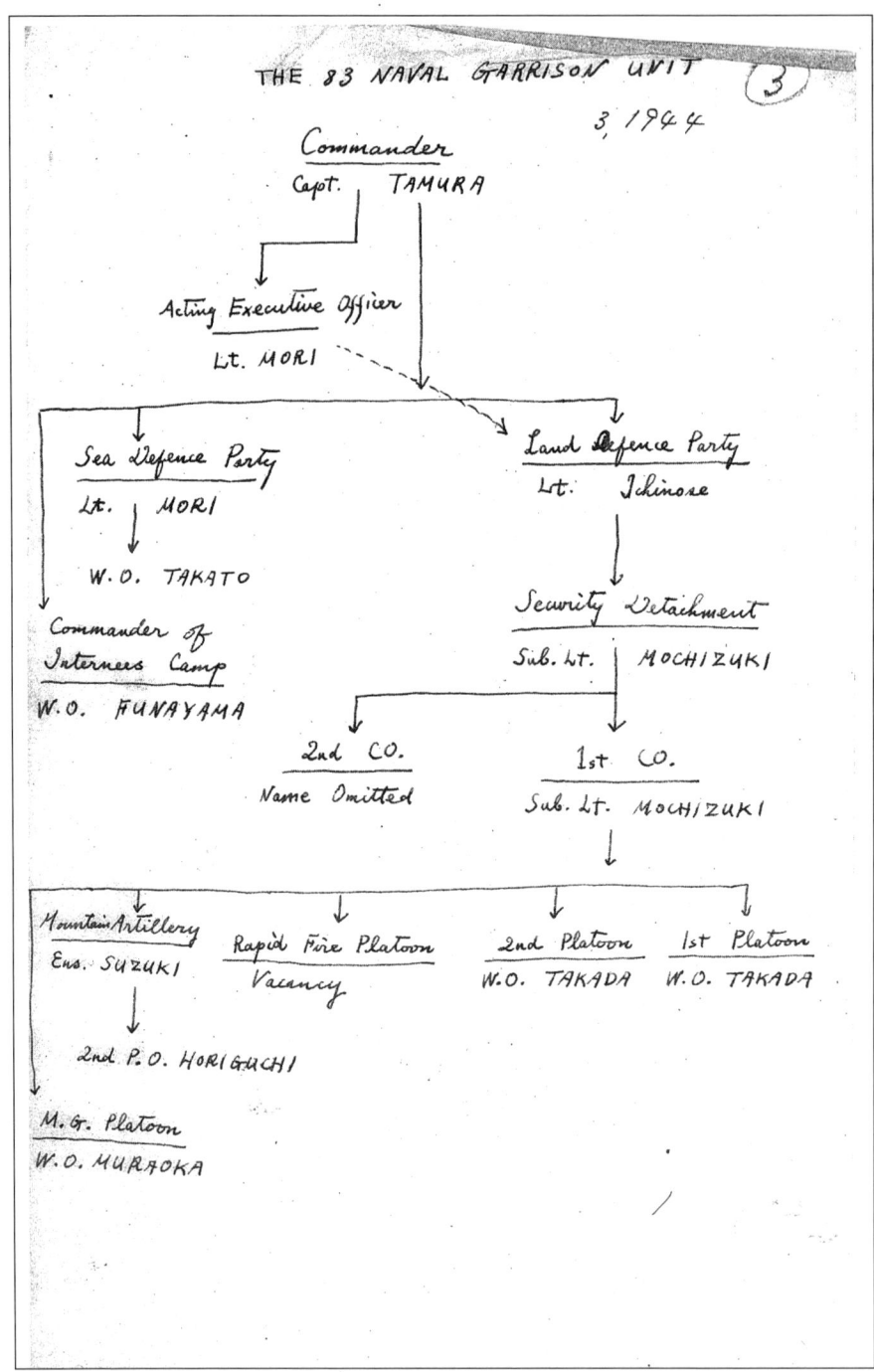

One of Albert Klestadt's handwritten diagrams showing the disposition of 83NGU in March 1944

Extremely unlikely...

to the north to Palau. Later that afternoon a new escorted convoy was formed outside Simpson Harbour, and the *Kowa Maru* and *Kokai Maru*, now fully loaded with air force personnel, took their places in it. During the night the convoy sailed northwards up the west coast of New Ireland and by midday on 21 February was between New Hanover Island and Mussau Island where it was attacked in two waves by a number of American B-25 Mitchell bombers, direct hits being taken by both the *Kowa Maru* and *Kokai Maru*, causing great loss of life, fires and serious damage. The Japanese naval records of this incident obtained by the investigators stated that the *Kowa Maru* had been immediately sunk with all hands, and that a few survivors from the *Kokai Maru* had been picked up by an escort ship, the submarine-chaser *Nagaura*, which itself was sunk the following morning, again, it was believed, with the loss of all on board.[6]

By cross-checking with the activity records of the USAAF, the investigators were able to confirm that the ships had definitely been attacked by B-25s in mid-February 1944 on their southbound voyage, and sunk by B-25s on 21 February as they made their return journey to the north. If the Japanese naval records were correct, the problem was going to be in establishing whether the Kavieng internees had been on board either of the ships—if there were in fact no survivors. Fortunately for the investigators, the carelessness of the naval record-keepers would now enable a breakthrough to occur which would raise the first real doubts about the veracity of Rear Admiral Tamura's explanation of events.

Despite the incompleteness of the records, it did not take long to begin identifying and locating in various parts of Japan some still-living survivors from the two ships in late 1946. By coincidence, Major Williams' interrogations of the first of these men to be brought to the Meiji Building occurred at exactly the same time Tamura was boarding the *Hanazuki* in Rabaul to be repatriated for reunion with his wife and adult children at their home near Tokyo. It had been a very long time since Tamura had seen his family, and by the time this finally occurred he was a very sick man. The deprivations and distress of so many years trapped on New Ireland, followed by the long imprisonment at Rabaul, had taken their toll on his health, and among other problems he was suffering from advanced tuberculosis. Once safely at home at Kamakura, in Kanagawa Prefecture quite near Tokyo, he began protracted medical treatment and convalescence in the care of his family.

Commencing on 5 November 1946, Williams began a series of formal interrogations of a small number of survivors from the *Kokai Maru* and *Kowa Maru* and the escort vessels of the ill-fated convoy. None of the first group of *Kokai Maru* survivors to be interviewed, including air force passengers, recalled any European civilians having been embarked on the ship in Rabaul or being on the ship at the time of their sinking. Similarly, three members of the Japanese air force who had been passengers on the *Kowa Maru* could not recall seeing any Europeans on board.

The first real breakthrough in Williams' investigation came on 12 November 1946 when Yoshio Otsu was brought in for questioning. Otsu was a former non-commissioned officer in the Japanese navy who had in 1943 been assigned to the *Kowa Maru* as a member of the ship's naval gun crew. Although a merchant vessel, *Kowa Maru* had been equipped with a deck gun for self-protection, and the naval gunners assigned to operate this weapon lived and worked near their gun station. If not killed in an enemy attack, they would certainly be among the first overboard if an order were given to abandon ship. It transpired that when the *Kowa Maru* was attacked and severely damaged by the American planes on 21 February 1944, Otsu saved himself by quickly jumping into the sea, and after seeing it and the *Kokai Maru* sink, was picked up later that night by the escorting Japanese submarine-chaser *Nagaura*, along with about a hundred other survivors. The following morning, as *Nagaura* steamed towards Palau, the ship was attacked by US warships and sunk. About fifty survivors were picked up by the American vessels and transported to Guadalcanal for eventual internment in the United States and Australia. Without Major Williams being able to grasp the significance of the occasion, in fact on this day he had before him the first member of the Japanese navy to be brought in for questioning who was not a party to the Kavieng conspiracy, and who was not associated with the navy units which had been in Kavieng or Rabaul.

When questioned whether European civilians had boarded the *Kowa Maru*, either near Kavieng during the ship's southbound journey to Rabaul, or later in Rabaul before the ship joined the northbound convoy, Otsu declared his strong belief that this had not occurred. He told Williams that the *Kowa Maru* was a relatively small ship, and that as a longstanding member of the crew with a position of responsibility he knew about practically everything that occurred on board, and that it would have been extremely unlikely that Europeans would have been

Extremely unlikely...

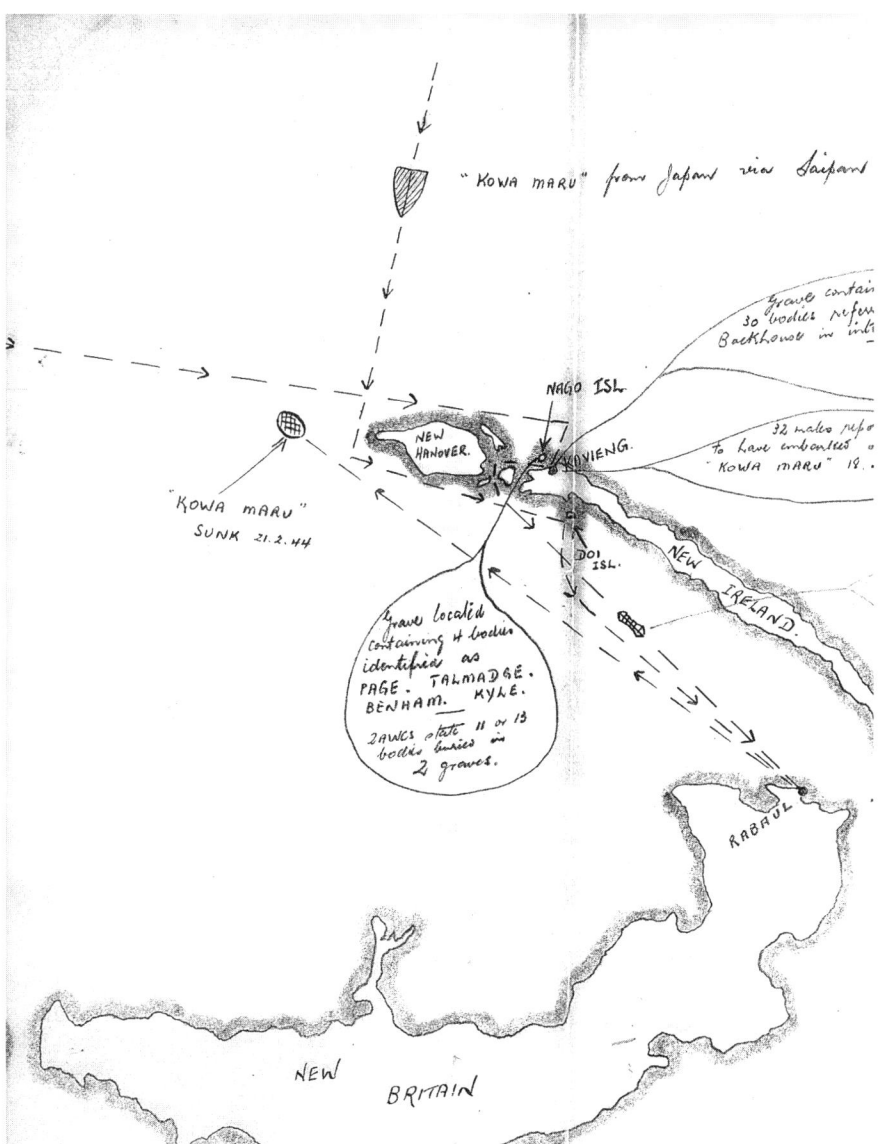

Sketch-map prepared by Albert Klestadt to demonstrate the track of the *Kowa Maru* west of New Ireland during its final voyage in February 1944.

on the ship without his hearing of it. Besides, even though he had been all over the ship he had personally seen no Europeans at any stage of its journey to and from Rabaul, nor in the water after the ship was attacked. Williams formed the strong impression that Otsu was a reliable witness, and emphasised his testimony in subsequent reports.[7]

In fact, a small miracle had occurred for the investigators. In February 1944, within the space of 24 hours in the Bismarck Sea, the honest sailor-man Yoshio Otsu had beaten the odds by surviving the successive sinkings of the *Kowa Maru* and the *Nagaura*, fortuitously been picked up by a US vessel, interned in the comparative luxury and safety of a US mainland camp, and later repatriated to Japan to eventually tell his story to Williams. This extraordinarily lucky man had now brought his good luck to the Kavieng investigation.

There was another breakthrough, on 18 November, when Major Williams interrogated Yajiro Kai, who as a naval lieutenant had on about 16 March 1943 embarked for naval headquarters at Rabaul as a passenger on the destroyer *Akikaze*. During that voyage Kai had witnessed the execution of a large number of blindfolded civilians by machine-gunning, their bodies falling into the sea. He had seen men and women, including married couples, and children being shot. He confirmed that although the *Akikaze* had called at Kavieng that day no European civilians had been taken aboard there, and that there were none on board when the destroyer arrived at Rabaul later that night. Williams believed that with this new information the *Akikaze* and Kavieng incidents could be assumed to be entirely separate events.

On 19 November 1946, Lieutenant Colonel Goslett wrote a report for his headquarters in Melbourne summarising the outcomes of Major Williams' investigations over the previous weeks. His report, entitled *Civilians in New Britain and New Ireland and Movements of Kowa Maru*, observed that no information had been provided which could substantiate Rear Admiral Tamura's claim that the Kavieng internees had been sent away on the *Kowa Maru*, or Vice-Admiral Kasuka's claim that civilians from the *Akikaze* had also boarded that ship. Finally, Lieutenant Colonel Goslett speculated that it was possible that Rear Admiral Tamura and Vice-Admiral Kasuka 'deliberately furnished false information in the belief that the *Kokai Maru* and *Kowa Maru* had been lost with all hands and in the hope thereby of covering up any responsibility of Rabaul HQ or other naval personnel for the massacre of 70 civilians on *Akikaze*'.

On 6 December 1946, Albert Klestadt was assigned to take over the Kavieng case from Major Williams. Klestadt would turn out to be a particularly good choice for handling this difficult investigation. Apart from his language skills, deep understanding of Japan, and experience as a sailor, he also possessed the special investigatory instinct and strong determination which would be needed to eventually break through the conspiracy. He began with interrogation of the Japanese merchant marine captain at the time of the *Kokai Maru*'s final voyage and two of his crew, who had been located and brought in for questioning. Toshio Ose had been the ship's master from mid-1943; Minoru Miyazaki had been the ship's longstanding cook from October 1941, and Yutaka Okumura an engine hand. Each was interrogated separately at the Meiji Building on 6 December 1946. As an experienced mariner, Klestadt was able to obtain a very detailed and, he felt, 'fairly reliable' written statement from Ose regarding his ship's movements from the time the *Kokai Maru* left Yokosuka bound for Truk and Rabaul, to the time of its sinking on 21 February 1944 near New Hanover, as well as details of how one group of survivors were brought to safety.

Under Klestadt's 'close and strict questioning and cross-questioning', Ose stated quite emphatically that:

> no non-Japanese persons, either prisoners of war or civilian internees were embarked in his ship, either at Rabaul or at any other stage of the voyage between Yokosuka or Rabaul, including the six hours during which the convoy sheltered near an island in the New Hanover Group.[8]

After the American attack on 21 February the *Kokai Maru* had taken over twelve hours to sink, an event observed during the night from Ose's lifeboat, which contained forty survivors, many of whom were badly burnt and injured. His group had not been picked up the following morning by the *Nagaura*, and the lifeboat had fortuitously drifted towards a group of nearby islands where they had made landfall. From here Ose was able to slowly guide his companions to safety and medical treatment in Kavieng three weeks later. They remained at Kavieng until the end of the war, growing vegetables, but as merchant marine outsiders who were unconnected to the regular navy men of 83 Naval Garrison Unit.

From Major Williams' interrogations of the four surviving passengers from the *Kowa Maru*, and his and Lieutenant Klestadt's interrogations of survivors from the *Kokai Maru*, two important things had been discovered. Firstly, it was clear that the Japanese navy had been wrong to report that the two ships had been lost with all hands. In fact, there had been many survivors rescued by the *Nagaura*, and another group led by Ose had managed to make their way to Kavieng. Secondly, it appeared to be confirmed there had been no European civilians on either the *Kowa Maru* or the *Kokai Maru* at the time of their loss. From now on, the statements obtained from Rear Admiral Tamura in Rabaul by Lieutenant Havilland and Lieutenant Backhouse were to be viewed with great suspicion.

On 10 December, 2 War Crimes Section sent an enciphered message to Army headquarters in Melbourne reporting these newly discovered facts, and, believing that Tamura and other officers of 14th Naval Base Force and 8th Fleet Headquarters were still in Rabaul, requesting their urgent re-interrogation at that location. Klestadt would soon discover that all these suspects were already in Japan, and well within his reach.

On 23 December Klestadt interrogated Hideshi Matsumoto, who had been a lieutenant commander attached to 8 Naval Base Unit in Rabaul from 1943 until 1945. Klestadt was not in a position to know that the former officer sitting opposite him in the interview room was actually the first senior member of the conspiracy to be brought in; or that he possessed vital knowledge about the affair and had been directly involved in helping concoct the *Kowa Maru/Kokai Maru* cover story with Captain Sanagi and Commander Yoshino at the time Yoshino made his rushed visit to Rabaul in August 1945. It was Matsumoto who had searched the records and discovered that the two ships had been sunk close to the location and time the Kavieng internees had been murdered, but Klestadt would not discover this until much later. As the first of the conspirators to face the more knowledgeable and persistent questioning of the Australian investigators in Tokyo, Matsumoto had to tread the tightrope of trying to maintain the fictitious story while at the same time not giving the appearance that he was involved in its creation, and would need to use a very skilful mix of truth and lies.

Matsumoto truthfully told Klestadt that he and his unit had not been connected in any way to the management of prisoners of war or internees, those matters being the responsibility of the ultimate naval authority in the area, Headquarters South-East Area Fleet. He truthfully related that he was never instructed to place prisoners or internees aboard the *Kowa Maru* or *Kokai Maru* in Rabaul in February 1944. But then came the lie: Matsumoto told Klestadt that he had 'heard rumours that prisoners had been aboard one or other of these ships' only after later learning that the convoy had been attacked and 'virtually wiped out', although the rumours were vague. He concluded by truthfully saying that he never saw or read anything definite about the incident.

Unable to be certain he had just been deceived, Klestadt could not draw any firm and useful conclusions from his interrogation of Matsumoto, signing off his interrogation report with the comment that 'the Senior Staff Officer, 8 NBU Rabaul has no definite knowledge of any Europeans having been placed aboard *Kowa Maru* or *Kokai Maru* in February 1944'.

On Boxing Day, 26 December 1946, Lieutenant Colonel Goslett filed his second report about the Kavieng case to Army Headquarters in Melbourne, enclosing copies of interrogation reports prepared in Tokyo by Major Williams and Lieutenant Klestadt, pointing out that the Kavieng and *Akikaze* cases were most likely unconnected, and reporting that the Japanese authorities had been requested to 'make available for interrogation repatriated officers of 14 Naval Base Force who were in Kavieng in 43/44'. He noted that 'investigations are progressing slowly due to delaying tactics by Japanese authorities in making available information and informants'. A few days later, and still without realising that all key suspects were now in Japan, Goslett sent another short enciphered message to Melbourne requesting that Rear Admiral Tamura and his senior officers be re-interrogated in Rabaul as a matter of urgency.[9]

The focus of investigation would shortly be concentrated entirely on the Rear Admiral, Commander Yoshino, Lieutenant Commander Mori, and scores of their subordinates who had been in Kavieng in February 1944. The 'fabulous lie' was about to be put to its biggest test.

In response to the requests from 2 War Crimes Section, throughout January 1947 the investigation continued with renewed urgency in New Guinea. Australian Army Headquarters in Melbourne sent a series of messages to the Eighth Military District in Rabaul instructing that if any of the named Japanese officers were still there they were to be re-interrogated, specifically mentioning that Tamura's story was suspected as probably false; and requesting any further information about the Kavieng case which might have been uncovered, particularly regarding the existence of the 'mass grave', and any eyewitness accounts of the purported embarkation of the internees. More enquiries were initiated on New Ireland, and more Melanesian and Chinese inhabitants were questioned, but to no avail. On 28 January 1947 Army Headquarters reported back to 2 War Crimes Section that none of the suspect

Japanese naval officers were still in Rabaul, and that the last officer held, Rear Admiral Tamura, had been repatriated to Japan over two months before. The message added that the story about the 'mass grave' in Kavieng was probably an unsubstantiated rumour, and ended with the inconclusive information that no person in Kavieng had apparently witnessed embarkation of the internees on the *Kowa Maru*.

Throughout January 1947, Klestadt's investigations in Tokyo intensified. With assistance from the Japanese police he had been able to track down and have summonsed to Tokyo from their homes throughout Japan some of Admiral Tamura's staff officers from Kavieng days, including Yoshino, Mori, Ichinose and Suzuki, and three of the non-commissioned officers. However, and without Klestadt understanding this, channels of communication between the conspirators had been open and highly active ever since their repatriation from New Guinea, and they had already been tipped off by Matsumoto that an investigation by the Australian War Crimes Section was underway at the Meiji Building, led by a troublesome officer who could speak Japanese. Matsumoto was able to describe the line of questioning used by Klestadt, and what he had said in reply. By the time Yoshino, Mori and the others faced Klestadt across the interview room table they knew exactly how to handle the situation, using the well-tried method of mixing truth with lies.

One by one they carefully repeated the story that Admiral Tamura had first provided to the Australian investigators in Rabaul—that after a series of heavy air raids on Kavieng in mid-February 1944 all European internees had been embarked from landing barges onto a ship, possibly named *Kowa Maru* or *Kokai Maru*, and evacuated to Rabaul. No, they couldn't be sure if the internees had definitely reached that destination but heard that they had; and no, they didn't know what had happened to the internees afterwards, but, yes, there were occasional rumours that the ship may have been later sunk by American planes. Each then signed a sworn record of interview, knowing it to be false.[10]

When these January 1947 interviews were over, and with a great sense of relief and satisfaction, the interviewees were released to return to their homes, from where they immediately began to secretly share their experiences through the network of old comrades from Kavieng. Before long, practically every conspirator, including Admiral Tamura, knew what was going on and how to handle the little Australian officer who spoke Japanese if they were ever ordered to Tokyo for interrogation by him.

Without knowing the size of the conspiracy he was up against, Klestadt felt these first interviews with the officers from Kavieng were highly unsatisfactory. Their responses to his questions were so similar that he was sure there was something distinctly odd going on. He shared his suspicions with Lieutenant Colonel Goslett and Major Williams, and together they became ever more convinced that the evacuation story was a fraud, and the internees had somehow been 'disposed of'. They realised that if the case were ever to be broken, a much more wide-ranging enquiry was called for, which would undoubtedly strain the resources of their busy office. After seeing such promising progress in the investigation since November, they had once again hit a dead end. They could not obtain lawful convictions in a Military Court on the basis of strong suspicion, being required by law to present evidence which conclusively proved that a crime had occurred. But the only witnesses to the disappearance of the internees appeared to be the perpetrators themselves, and it looked as though they were not going to talk. How were the Australians going to get a confession out of these obdurate men, and how long was it going to take to get it?[11]

So yet more signals were sent off to Melbourne requesting further assistance in New Guinea to track down anyone who might have witnessed what had happened to the internees in early 1944, and in particular, to confirm one way or another if the 'mass grave' in Kavieng ever existed. Interestingly, in January 1947 Klestadt also began researching secret naval signals intelligence to see if Allied codebreakers had ever eavesdropped on Japanese navy radio discussions about the Kavieng internees, but this path of enquiry also led nowhere.[12]

chapter 20

For official purposes his death has been presumed

For the families in Australia of the 23 missing men, over eighteen months had passed since the war in New Guinea had ended, and over five years since they had been separated in 1941. Despite all their representations to Secretary James Halligan at the Department of External Territories, nothing new had been turned up to bring closure to this long and awful wait. Like Alison Griffin, others had received the discouraging letter from Halligan in October 1946, and most were beginning to accept the inevitable, that they had indeed lost a son, husband, father or brother. There was a lot of bitterness as well, most of this directed against the Australian military and the Department of External Territories. Why had such large and apparently powerful organisations been so ineffective in obtaining and passing on information, and so reluctant to take responsibility for what had happened to the stranded men and their many surviving family members in Australia?

The seven German priests who had disappeared at Kavieng at the same time were not so well represented to the Department, either by their families or by the Catholic Church. Although their names appear on all the official lists of the missing, they received very little attention in the enquiries. Despite the fact they had been longstanding residents of New Ireland and important in the expatriate community, these remnants of the German colonial occupation of New Guinea were ignored because of their status as German nationals. As foreigners they were not covered by the provisions of the *Australian War Crimes Act*. Making them still more 'invisible', the priests had been single men without estates; any still-living relatives were located in a troubled and divided postwar Germany, unaware of and unable to participate in a secret enquiry being conducted on the other side of the world.[1]

For the Australian families there were many now-urgent practical problems brought about by the lack of official closure. Until they had in their possession official documents which confirmed the death of their men, it was impossible to move forward to resolve mounting legal, financial, insurance and pension matters. All through 1946 and into 1947 the Department of External Territories received a barrage of plaintive personal correspondence explaining these legal and financial predicaments, as well as letters from solicitors and trustee companies handling the estates of particular victims.

James Halligan was not an unkind, remote bureaucrat personally disinterested in the plight of the families. In 1946, for example, he had been influential in arranging war widows' pensions for the wives of men lost during the Japanese occupation. But he was sufficiently cautious, given the legal consequences of his actions, to want not to release certificates of presumed death for each of the men without first satisfying himself that every possible avenue of enquiry had been exhausted, and that none of the missing men was still alive. Halligan was, of course, completely unaware that the main obstacle to achieving progress in his inquiry was the now long-running silent conspiracy among the Japanese servicemen returned from Kavieng to prevent the truth being known. Because of their own abiding concerns about loss of face and disloyalty, the conspirators were preventing widows in faraway Australia and New Guinea from re-marrying, wills from being executed and estates settled, and affected families generally getting on with life.

Halligan had taken a keen interest in the progress of investigations by the Australian army and by district officers of his own department on the ground in New Guinea. Through frequent correspondence and conversations with his counterpart, the Secretary of the Department of the Army, he was thoroughly aware that only vague or inconclusive evidence had been gathered regarding the disappearance of the Australians at Kavieng. As well, his department knew that about 80 other cases of disappeared civilians from New Britain, other islands in the Bismarck Sea, Bougainville Island and the mainland remained unresolved. To prepare the way for a final decision regarding the issue of Certificates of Presumed Death, in early 1947 Halligan instructed his staff to make a last effort to gather as much information from all available sources and to try to make sense of what was so far known about all of these missing persons cases. So, from the Department of External Territories, a final push was commenced to bring the affair to a definite end.

For the Kavieng disappeared, this would involve methodically examining all the information so far unearthed by the Army in New Guinea, by 2 War Crimes Section in Tokyo, and by the Territories Department's own district and patrol officers on New Ireland, and then through a process of deduction eliminate the possibility that any could still be alive, and finally try to fix a place, date and cause of their presumed deaths.

This final review concentrated on establishing when each of the missing individuals was last seen alive and by whom, and whether any identifiable human remains or personal effects had ever been discovered. As the documentary evidence was assembled and analysed, further requests for clarification were cabled to the Department's representatives in New Guinea, especially for officials in Kavieng to determine for once and for all if the mysterious 'mass grave' really existed.

While all this was going on, 2 War Crimes Section in Tokyo had embarked on much the same path of enquiry. Klestadt wanted to know if the case could be more speedily resolved using evidence and testimony available from New Guinea before having to embark on what could be a frustrating and draining attempt to track down a Japanese person who was prepared to tell the truth. Klestadt knew that there had been 13 000 Japanese service personnel on New Ireland, and that trying to find even one honest individual might well be like trying to find 'a needle in a haystack'.

In April 1947, the two investigations came together when the Department of the Army and the Department of External Territories met to share what they knew about the Kavieng case, and hopefully set the stage for the issue of death certificates by Secretary Halligan.[2] The meeting reviewed in detail the summarised documentary products of the most recent enquiries by both departments, from which they understood that although inmates of the two internment camps had been regularly observed and generally identified by local people from mid-1942 until early 1944, no witnesses of any reliability could be found who could throw light on the abrupt disappearance of the internees after that time. The meeting also accepted that despite all of the digging and searching for the 'mass grave' that had occurred since 1945, there was still absolutely no sign that it existed. Finally, it was accepted that the internees had probably not been murdered on the Japanese destroyer *Akikaze*, and that this atrocity had occurred about a year earlier.

The meeting considered fragmentary information which had been gathered when the Department of Territories had been trying to learn the circumstances of the death of one of the internees, Ernest Russell 'Dusty' Miller, the planter and trader from New Hanover who was believed by some witnesses to have died of natural causes in early 1944. The October 1946 summary of that investigation reads as follows:

> Enquiries revealed that E.R. Miller was seen imprisoned in Chinatown, Kavieng (i.e. at Panapai) [sic], with other Europeans, Viz:- Ostrom, Gordon, and RC Priests, etc., at the eve of the shelling of Kavieng by Allied warships in February [sic] 1944.
>
> After the shelling, none of the Chinese or Malays [sic] saw any of the Europeans. Chinese Fong Chin Wah reported that a Japanese Native Police Boy, whose name he could not remember, told him afterwards that he saw a line of European prisoners were [sic] marched off to Saunders Wharf one morning after the bombardment and herded into a fishing boat by Japanese soldiers, presumably heading for Nago Island.
>
> It is generally believed that the Europeans were beheaded by the Japanese at Nago Island.
>
> The Chinese and Malays here do not know actually where Mr. Miller or the rest of the Europeans were killed or buried, but they are positive that prisoners were killed in the Kavieng area.[3]

With the perfect hindsight of sixty years into the future, within this summary of investigation are numerous errors of fact. The 'Europeans' are correctly located in 'Chinatown, Kavieng', but Chinatown is co-located with Panapai, actually 6 kilometres away and where the German missionaries were separately located. The US naval shelling of Kavieng is placed in February 1944, when in fact it was the more devastating shelling in March which led to the disappearance of the internees.

There was also a statement taken in October 1946 from A.J. Corlass, who said he was working in New Ireland in 1945 on a military intelligence assignment and made contact with the natives there. He had stated to investigators that 'according to native sources L. Gordon, H.J. Topal and Topal Junior were last seen in the POW camp in February

1944, but were missing from the camp in March, and that the natives informed him that they had been killed by the Japanese'.[4]

Then the meeting turned to the question of Rear Admiral Tamura's sworn testimony purporting that the Australians and Germans had been evacuated from Kavieng on either the *Kowa Maru* or *Kokai Maru*. Although it was known that these two ships had been sunk by American aircraft a few days later, it was still not known if the internees had definitely been on board, and strong doubts had recently been raised about this by 2 War Crimes Section in Tokyo. But Tamura's version of events was the only plausible explanation thus far, and apparently there was still no compelling evidence available to convincingly disprove it. The Department of External Territories officials at the meeting also knew that this explanation had already been provided to the families in letters sent the previous October.

In the end, the Department of External Territories summarised the outcomes of all enquiries in this way:

> Since the return of the Civil administration [to New Guinea] in October 1945, search has been made for the missing civilians without trace, and it is unlikely that we will ever know what happened to them.
> The National Security (War Deaths) Regulations were enacted for the purpose of authorising the issue of Certificates of Death in cases of this nature.[5]

Secretary Halligan was left to draw his own conclusions from this meeting. Although after all this investigatory effort there was still no conclusive explanation, the administrative realities were that much time had already passed and there was now an urgent necessity for everyone concerned to have legal closure. He decided to bring the matter to an immediate end, and issued instructions for a Certificate of Presumed Death to be prepared for each Australian believed to have disappeared from Kavieng, with the exact date of disappearance to be based on Admiral Tamura's estimate that 'evacuation' from Kavieng had occurred in mid-February 1944 at the time the *Kowa Maru* and *Kokai Maru* passed Kavieng en route to Rabaul.

Jack Griffin's family was still getting over the death of old George Griffin, passed away at the age of 86 just two months earlier, when in May 1947 Alison Griffin received Secretary Halligan's official and final notification about her brother's disappearance.

For official purposes his death has been presumed

TELEPHONE NO.: CANBERRA 631.
TELEGRAPHIC ADDRESS: "TERRITORIES" CANBERRA.

DEPARTMENT OF EXTERNAL TERRITORIES,

Canberra, 1 4 MAY 1947

In reply quote No. 16/3/408.

Dear Miss Griffin,

    I desire to refer to previous correspondence relative to your brother, the late John Kenneth Vicars Griffin, and regret to advise that exhaustive investigation has not brought to light any information further to that conveyed to you in my letter of the 17th October, 1946.

    After careful consideration of the available evidence, however, it has been determined that Mr. Griffin became missing on the 18th February, 1944, and for official purposes his death has been presumed.

    A Certificate of Death, issued under the provisions of Regulation 5A, of National Security (War Deaths) Regulations, has been forwarded to the Public Trustee, Box 7A, G.P.O., Sydney, who I am informed is acting on your behalf.

Yours faithfully,

(J.R. Halligan.)
Secretary.

Miss Alison Griffin,
16 Brunswick Avenue,
STRATHFIELD, N.S.W.

Department of External Territories' second and final letter explaining J.K.V. Griffin's disappearance, May 1947.[6]

So there it was. Over three years after his murder Jack Griffin was now officially deceased, and although nobody was to know or care at the time, the presumed date of his death in February 1944 was based on false information provided by the Japanese rear admiral who had in fact ordered his murder a month later. The wordy certificate, when it eventually found its way to the family from the NSW Public Trustee, gave away very little information:

```
                                                No. 386

                    COMMONWEALTH OF AUSTRALIA.

                 DEPARTMENT OF EXTERNAL TERRITORIES,
                              CANBERRA.
                              ──────────

                 NATIONAL SECURITY (WAR DEATHS) REGULATIONS.
                              ──────────
                 CERTIFICATE OF DEATH UNDER REGULATION 5A.

    WHEREAS I am satisfied from information available in the Department of
    External Territories that John Kenneth Vicars GRIFFIN, formerly of Rabaul,
    New Britain, Territory of New Guinea, was in a portion of the Territory
    of New Guinea at a time when that portion was occupied by the enemy and
    that the said John Kenneth Vicars GRIFFIN became missing on the Eighteenth
    day of February, 1944, and is for official purposes presumed to be dead.
    NOW THEREFORE, I, James Reginald HALLIGAN, Secretary of the Department
    of External Territories, being an authorised person within the meaning
    of regulation 5A of the National Security (War Deaths) Regulations, in
    pursuance of the powers conferred by that regulation, do hereby certify
    that John Kenneth Vicars GRIFFIN, formerly of Rabaul, New Britain,
    Territory of New Guinea, being aperson to whom that regulation applies,
    became missing on the Eighteenth day of February, 1944, and is for
    official purposes presumed to be dead.

                    DATED this Thirtieth day of April, 1947.

                                  J.R. Halligan,
                                     Secretary,
                             Department of External Territories.
```

Department of External Territories' Certificate of Presumed Death for Jack Griffin, issued in April 1947.[7]

But for anyone in Jack's family concerned enough to wonder about these things, there was still no detailed explanation about why, or how or where this gentleman had met his death, or where his remains and personal property might be. In May 1947 no one in the family knew anything about the ongoing investigation in New Guinea, or about the efforts of Albert Klestadt and Harold Williams in Tokyo. All information about the investigations was withheld from public knowledge by the Australian government. Neither did the family know anything about who was with Jack in the camp, about Rear Admiral Tamura and his men in Kavieng, about the American bombardment led by Admiral Griffin (who could have imagined such a coincidence?) or about the awful events at Kavieng South Wharf on 20 March 1944. They only knew that their irrepressible and adventurous Jack had gone off to New Guinea in 1935, had become a plantation auditor for Burns Philp, had never married, and had disappeared in the war.

chapter 21

We know you did it! How did you do it?

At about the same time Secretary Halligan was arranging for certificates of presumed death to be issued for each Kavieng internee, Albert Klestadt, now promoted to captain, was busy in Tokyo trying to find a way through the wall of silence built by the Japanese. Since his frustrating January 1947 interviews with Yoshino, Mori and the other ex-officers and men from 14 Naval Base Force and 83 Naval Garrison Unit, and despite his heavy case-load of other suspected war crimes, resolving the Kavieng case had become a personal challenge.

Klestadt was aware that the further investigations he had requested in New Guinea to find local eyewitnesses to the embarkation of the internees, or the 'mass grave', had not turned up anything useful. Since January he had interviewed many more of the ex-officers and men from Kavieng as they had been progressively located and brought in to the Meiji Building. Each had repeated the same story about evacuation of the internees by landing barge from Kavieng to either the *Kowa Maru* or *Kokai Maru* after heavy air raids in February 1944. Klestadt particularly wanted to re-interrogate Rear Admiral Tamura, who he had located quite near to Tokyo in his home at Kamakura, but Tamura was always too ill to face questioning.

The interrogations had, however, yielded considerable information about the individual backgrounds and general military roles and responsibilities of all the key officers and non-commissioned officers, because this was safe information they had felt they could truthfully provide. Klestadt had also obtained the nominal rolls of 14 Naval Base Force and 83 Naval Garrison Unit from Japanese navy records, and had drawn complicated diagrams which re-created the organisational

- 3 -

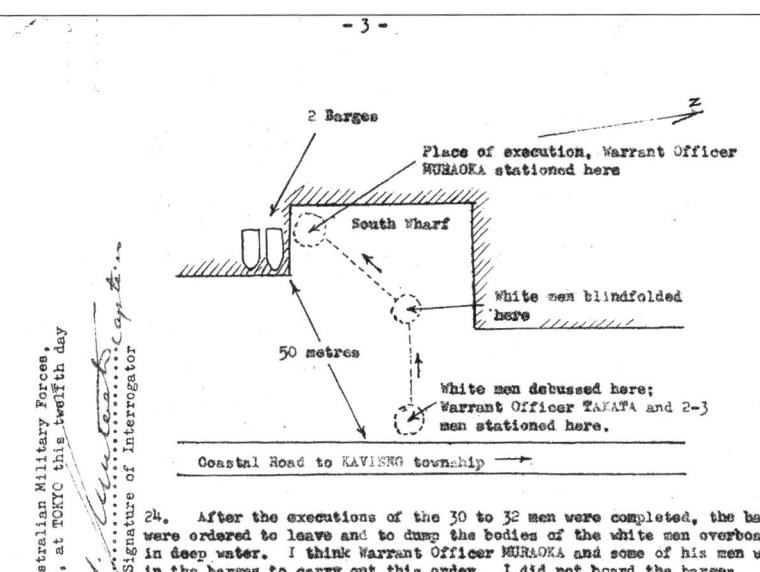

24. After the executions of the 30 to 32 men were completed, the barges were ordered to leave and to dump the bodies of the white men overboard in deep water. I think Warrant Officer MURAOKA and some of his men went in the barges to carry out this order. I did not board the barges.

25. After the barges had left I ordered a lorry back to the South Wharf. There I ordered the blankets and suitcases which the white men had brought with them to be loaded on the lorry. I then returned in the lorry to headquarters of the Security Detachment. On the way back we called at the internment camp and loaded the rest of the belongings of the internees.

26. On the day following the execution of the white men, we burnt their belongings near Security Detachment headquarters.

27. After the cessation of hostilities I received orders from Lieutenant MORI, Kyoji, then Executive Officer of 83 Naval Garrison Unit to the effect that if I was to be examined by Allied Officers, I was to say that the white internees at KAVIENG had been sent by barge to a place of rendevous with a ship named KOWA MARU which was to take the internees to RABAUL. It was this false story which I told an Australian officer when I was first interviewed at TOKYO on 2 May 1947, and again 26 June 1947.

28. Since being interned at SUGAMO prison I have thought much about my family and about religious matters. As a result of my deliberations I have now decided to make a full and correct statement of the facts which is contained in the above paragraphs.

In making this statement I acknowledge that it was made freely and voluntarily and that no threats were used nor promises made to influence my statement.

鈴 木 省 三
....
Signature of Deponent

I, VX 128203 Captain Albert KLESTADT, AUSTRALIAN MILITARY FORCES and now attached 2 AUST WAR CRIMES SECTION, hereby certify that I duly translated the whole of the above statement to the deponent in his own language prior to his signature which appears above and he then appeared to fully understand the same.

....
Signature of Interpreter

Page from the sworn statement obtained by Albert Klestadt in August 1947 from Shozo Suzuki, who directly supervised the massacre. It includes a diagram of the murder scene at Kavieng south wharf.

structure of these units, and the officers and men allocated to each of their sections in early 1944. The names and backgrounds of these servicemen had become very familiar to him.

In particular, Klestadt wanted to know the details of the 'evacuation by barge' in February 1944, in particular the names and whereabouts of the barge crew who had handled the evacuation. In 1945 Rear Admiral Tamura had first mentioned an evacuation, but had been unable to say who had been in charge of the barge. Since January 1947 the same thing had happened repeatedly. While all the interrogated men had perfect memories of the evacuation, none could recall who had crewed the evacuation barge. These missing names and faces were shaping as a crucial missing link in the story, so Klestadt set about reconstructing on paper the disposition of naval barges in Kavieng in early 1944. Delving through the records, and cross-checking information from interrogations, he learnt that there had been four of these small motorised vessels still intact in February 1944, Barge Numbers 1, 2, 3 and 4. He now needed to know which sailors had been allocated to which barge, to locate them in Japan if still alive, and have them brought in for questioning.

Among the leading conspirators, Klestadt's narrowing-down of the investigation to focus on the barge crews was greeted as an alarming development. They had not anticipated this turn of events when they had cooked up their alibi in August 1945. They also could not know that the Australian investigators had already discovered that the *Kowa Maru/Kokai Maru* story was probably false. The word was quickly spread among old comrades on the 83rd Naval Garrison Unit grapevine in Japan to warn the barge crewmen—former Chief Petty Officers Haruo Miyamoto and Yashichi Mori, former Engine Hand Azuma, former Warrant Officer Takada, former Petty Officer Riohei Kambe, former Chief Engineer Unoharu Yamao, and all junior sailors, including former Seaman Kinjoro Jitsukawa and any others who could be found. Now living on farms and in fishing villages all around the country, they needed to be quickly told that an exceptionally troublesome Australian investigator in Tokyo was hot on their trail.

The problem for the conspiracy leaders, who as ex-senior officers had the most to lose if the conspiracy unravelled, was that they might now be depending for their protection on the most junior and most poorly educated of their non-commissioned officers and men, the same men they had so ruthlessly bullied and bossed around for all those years on New Ireland. As well, although the weakest part of the cover story concerned the purported transfer of the internees by barge to the *Kowa Maru* or *Kokai Maru*, it was the part of the story that was least well rehearsed. What would these junior members of the conspiracy say when exposed to close questioning in Japanese by Klestadt? Would they each be able to plausibly and consistently lie in a way which did not expose further weaknesses in the story? To save their own skins when the questioning became difficult, would they abandon protecting their officers, take the least line of resistance, and start revealing the truth? Thus it was that when warnings eventually reached the ex-barge crew members that they would probably face interrogation, they were overlaid with menace and with hints about loyalty and discipline and duty.

By June 1947, more than 70 interrogations had been conducted in New Guinea by Australian army officers and in Tokyo by Albert Klestadt and his colleagues at 2 War Crimes Section. Dozens of signed Records of Interview and sworn and signed Affidavits of Evidence had been taken from the ex-Rear Admiral Tamura and his ex-officers and men from Kavieng, ex-officers from South-East Area Fleet Headquarters in Rabaul, and surviving crew and passengers from the *Kowa Maru* and *Kokai Maru*. This evidence contained glaring contradictions. On the one hand, the accounts of Tamura and his men upheld the story that the internees had been evacuated from Kavieng in mid-February 1944 and placed on board one of the two ships. On the other hand, the credible accounts of those who had been on the ships clearly suggested there had been no Europeans on board at any time, including when the ships sank. Klestadt's strongest instincts told him that the story parroted by dozens of Tamura's men was definitely false. He knew that the real explanation was more likely to be that the internees had somehow been 'disposed of' after leaving Kavieng. It all came down to the barge crews. They must have witnessed the event, although they might not have been directly involved.

So from early June 1947, 2 War Crimes Section once again enlisted the help of the Japanese police and now-exasperated American MPs to begin rounding up and bringing to Tokyo a small number of ex-sailors of the Imperial Japanese Navy who had been in Kavieng in February 1944, employed as crews of the barges which might have been used to transfer the civilian internees who had disappeared shortly afterwards.

Captain Albert Klestadt knew that the barge sailors being brought to him most probably represented his last chance to crack the case. Almost two years had gone by since the war ended, and over three

> J.3.10.J
>
> Inst of TAMURA Ryukichi and others
> Statt. [?] (3rd copy)
> Henry G. Quinn
>
> 6. 1 March, 1944, I received a [?] 1947
>   verbal report from Lieutenant (late
>   Lieutenant Commander) MORI, Keiji,
>   Executive Officer of 88 Naval Garrison
>   Unit to the effect that 2 or
>   three days earlier the internees
>   had been executed by strangulation.
>
> 7. MORI told me that he
>   had judged an enemy landing to
>   be imminent in view of the heavy
>   and repeated air raids and naval
>   shellings which were occurring about
>   this time and he had therefore caused
>   all the internees to be executed on
>   my orders.
>
> 8. After the cessation of hostilities
>   and expecting an investigation by the
>   Allied authorities into the disappearance
>   of the internees I became a party to
>   the fabricating of the story that the
>   internees had been taken from
>   KAVIENG by barge and placed aboard
>   the Japanese transport KOWA MARU en
>   route for RABAUL.
>
>   In making this statement I acknowledge
>   that it was made by me freely and
>   voluntarily and that no threat were
>   used and no promises made to influence
>   me in making this statement.
>
>   Tamura Kiukichi
>
> I, VX128203, Captain Albert KLESTADT,
> AUSTRALIAN MILITARY FORCES and now attached 2 AUST WAR
> CRIMES SECTION hereby certify that I have duly translated
> the whole of the above statement to the deponent in his
> own language prior to his signature which appears above and
> he then appeared fully to understand the same. A. Klestadt.

Page from Admiral Tamura's sworn statement handwritten in English by Albert Klestadt in August 1947 and signed by Tamura. In this statement Tamura admits to having issued the order for the Kavieng internees to be executed.

years had lapsed since the internees had disappeared. He was aware that in Australia the Department of External Territories had given up on the investigation and had already issued death certificates, effectively closing the case from the department's point of view. More pointedly, in the Meiji Building, relations between 2 Australian War Crimes Section and the American and British war crimes investigators still there were becoming increasingly testy. Under political pressure from Washington and London, the American and British investigators were beginning to wind down their enquiries. The main trials of Japan's wartime political leaders, with the notable exception of Emperor Hirohito, were still dragging on in Tokyo amid much controversy. Most of the trials of the admirals and generals, the leaders of the wartime military, had long ago been concluded, and many of the big names already convicted, some executed. America and Britain now wanted to put the war behind them, stop the endless persecution of Japanese ex-servicemen, and enlist the cooperation and friendship of a newly 'democratic' Japan. But in Australia, political pressure was still being applied for the army to keep going with investigations and prosecutions, and Australia's military leaders were happy to oblige. Although more than ready to do their duty, Lieutenant Colonel Goslett, Major Williams, Captain Klestadt and their colleagues in the Meiji Building also knew that time was fast running out before they completely lost the support and cooperation of their American and British allies and access to their extensive records, police contacts and administrative facilities.

Goslett, Williams and Klestadt also realised that the political and social landscape in Japan was rapidly changing, making it harder for them to catch war criminals. More and more ex-military figures were emerging as leaders of business and politics in the new Japan, including some they suspected of having shady wartime backgrounds. The evidence was everywhere that the tide was turning, that concern with righting past wrongs was being rapidly overtaken by a mood of reconciliation and reconstruction. They also sensed that the ex-servicemen they were attempting to track down and trap themselves realised that things were changing, and if these men could continue to avoid falling into the clutches of the Australian investigators they might soon stand an excellent chance of escaping prosecution altogether.

Thus as Klestadt began preparing to interrogate the barge crews, he knew that if he could not extract a confession very soon the Kavieng case would probably become yet another war crime investigation which was shelved for being 'too hard and too late'. He also knew that he would need to carefully plan and stage-manage these last-chance interrogations, and start with the crew member most likely to break under the pressure tactics he intended to employ. Who would be the ex-sailor most vulnerable when faced with his pointed questioning? Which of them was the most junior, frightened and blameless? Looking through the list, he quickly settled on the person he would concentrate on. It would be a young farmer, Kinjiro Jitsukawa, who Klestadt knew had been the assistant mechanic on No. 2 Barge in early 1944, and who in the hierarchy of 83 Naval Garrison Unit was the lowest of the low, a mere 'engine wiper'. Jitsukawa was in the process of being brought by the police from his family farm in Chiba Prefecture, very close to Tokyo.

But before Klestadt could start questioning Kinjoro Jitsukawa, he received some depressing although in its way most encouraging news. Information had just arrived at the Meiji Building that another sailor, ex-Warrant Officer Kazue Takada from No. 1 Barge, had committed suicide a few weeks earlier while travelling to a Tokyo meeting with Klestadt. He had been sent a telegram to report to the investigators, but had failed to show up. His father-in-law eventually informed the police that Kazue 'threw himself under a running train west of Fukroi station on the Tokaido line'.[1] Klestadt could not know that Takada had been the non-commissioned officer on No. 1 Barge who had supervised disposal of the bodies, including the clumsy attempts to sink them when the concrete sinkers and wire ran out. But the meaning of his suicide was unmistakable. Takada had seen something very bad happen that night in Kavieng and had taken his own life rather than be forced to talk about it.[2]

In contemplating the forthcoming interrogation of Jitsukawa, Klestadt would draw on his FELO experience, using clever psychological techniques to obtain the truth. He knew that for Japanese suspects used to wartime Kenpeitai interrogation methods, his normally polite and considerate manner would not appear particularly alarming. During the war the Kenpeitai had practiced their outrageous interrogations on anyone suspected of disloyal acts, including their own country's servicemen. The ferocious beating, sexual abuse, part-drowning, electrocution, burning and part-dismemberment of men, women and children had nothing to do with obtaining truthful accounts. These techniques were designed purely to inflict maximum physical suffering and obtain quick confessions irrespective of the truth. Thousands of Kenpeitai victims had, under torture, admitted to acts they had never committed, and had implicated other innocents in imaginary crimes, just to stop the assault on their bodies.

For young Kinjiro Jitsukawa's attendance at the interview room on 24 June 1947, Klestadt had stage-managed a psychologically intimidating welcome. Plucked straight from the peaceful rice fields of his hometown, on arrival Jitsukawa was quickly marched through the corridors by a brusque guard of Japanese police. It was bluntly explained to him, by the police, that he was a suspect in the murder of European civilians in Kavieng in 1944, and that it was best if he made a clean breast of it or he would be in very serious trouble indeed. Then, without being allowed to catch sight of any of the Australians waiting behind the scenes, he was seated at the table in the interview room, and left alone to think things over. Time passed, confused thoughts crowded his head, and the interview room became a strange and lonely and fearful place. He tried once again rehearsing in his mind the story he had been told to tell by his superiors long ago in Kavieng and Rabaul, those overbearing petty officers who still continued to make life difficult for him with their veiled threats. But he knew one thing for sure. He was not going to be blamed for what had happened, because he hadn't even seen it. That night in Kavieng in 1944 he had scurried down to the engine room of the barge as soon as the mayhem had started, and in this hot and crowded space had crouched sweating next to the diesel engine, all too aware of the thumps and bangs and muffled shouts up on the deck. He only found out later what they had done to the Europeans, but he, Kinjiro Jitsukawa, would swear that he had taken no part in it.[3]

Suddenly the door to the interview room flew open, and there, standing glaring before him, was the little Australian investigator who spoke fluent Japanese, the very one he had been warned about. Immaculately dressed in the uniform of a captain of the Australian Army, Klestadt drew himself up to his full height, glowering at the seated Jitsukawa, then suddenly shouted at him in Japanese: 'We know you did it! How did you do it?'

The startled Jitsukawa reacted precisely as Klestadt had hoped. Stammering and blushing as he spoke, out came the words that Klestadt had been waiting so long to hear. 'I knew nothing about it! I was not involved in it! You cannot blame me! I was below decks all the time when it happened and only learnt afterwards! Please do not blame me!'[4]

Now, handling the rest of the interview with great precision, and interspersing threats with praise, Klestadt carefully extracted the story from an increasingly relieved Jitsukawa. 'No,' he was able to reassure the frightened man, 'we do not seek to punish ordinary sailors like you, Jitsukawa. We want to know who were the ringleaders, the officers in charge that night!'

As it turned out, the story told by Jitsukawa was not entirely accurate, but he supplied so many names of the officers and men present at the scene of the crime that Klestadt finally had a host of solid leads to work on. Jitsukawa related how 'two or three days after the great air raid on Kavieng on 11 February 1944' he and the crews of No. 1 and No. 2 Barge had loaded the sinkers and wires and tied up at Kavieng South Wharf. Shortly after sunset, 'while it was still light enough to see faces', he saw 'white people board the barges', guarded by sailors of the Land Defence Department of 83 Naval Garrison Unit:

> While the passengers were boarding the barges I had to go into the engine compartment to look after the engine and did not see what happened aboard the barge. Before we left the South Wharf while I was already in the engine compartment I heard sounds as if people were being beaten with sticks and also human screams.

Jitsukawa related how, down in the engine compartment, he had received the order to engage the engine and go ahead. After a while, according to him 'ten minutes', he received the order to reverse the gearbox and slow the barge. Then an order was given to de-clutch the engine and the barge drifted for ten or twenty minutes, engine still running. He heard 'a lot of noise as if heavy weights were being dragged about, and also splashes as if large objects were being dropped into the sea'. Then he received the signal to go ahead, and the barge proceeded back to Kavieng and made fast at the Central Wharf. 'When we returned only Ensign Suzuki and the sailors got off the barge, the internees had disappeared.' He estimated that the entire trip took about an hour. Jitsukawa then told Klestadt that he had heard from fellow crew members that the 'internees were bound with belts, rope, and wire cable to the cement slabs and were pushed overboard'.

Finally, Jitsukawa revealed the details of the conspiracy to cover up what had happened. 'After the surrender at Kavieng and again after we had been evacuated to Rabaul', a verbal order from Lieutenant Mori was passed to him by Warrant Officer Jutaro Takata 'that if Allied investigators should enquire into the disappearance of the foreigners, I was to say that they had been sent to Rabaul. I was given more detailed instructions what to say but I have forgotten those.'

A summary of Jitsukawa's evidence was duly typed up in Japanese, corrected, signed by Jitsukawa, then translated into English and again signed by Jitsukawa and Captain Klestadt.[5] Later this was transformed into an affidavit in a form suitable for presentation to a military court.

Kinjiro Jitsukawa had supplied the names of numerous officers and non-commissioned officers who had been involved in the crime and the cover-up, including Lieutenant Mori, Ensign Suzuki, Warrant Officer Takato and all the crew members of the two barges. He had thoroughly spilled the beans to an elated Albert Klestadt, who quickly passed on the news to Lieutenant Colonel Goslett and Major Williams.

That night a celebratory party was held in the Meiji Building, attended by many of the staff of Allied war crimes and military units in the building. Klestadt was the hero of the hour, a man who under intense pressure had finally delivered success for 2 Australian War Crimes Section in the Kavieng case. One of those who attended the party was a 26-year-old American woman, Edna Price, who had come to Tokyo in 1946 from her home in California for duty as an archivist with the Allied Legal Section. They were not to know it on that night in June 1947 when they first met, but within a year Albert and Edna would enter a long and loving relationship as husband and wife which would last for almost sixty years.[6]

Two days later, on 26 June 1947, Goslett sent a signal to Melbourne summarising Klestadt's interview with Jitsukawa, observing that although the crewman's statement was 'fragmentary' it was believed to 'be substantially correct and consistent with the circumstantial evidence surrounding the internees' disappearance'. Goslett concluded by advising Melbourne that arrest warrants were being prepared to have more of the 14th Naval Base Force and 83rd Naval Garrison Unit officers and men brought back to Tokyo for re-interrogation, including Kyoji Mori, Shozo Yoshino and Ryukichi Tamura. Finally, the ex-Rear Admiral was going to be brought face to face with Albert Klestadt.

chapter 22

The prisoners of Sugamo

Sugamo Prison was built at Ikebukuro, near Tokyo, to house political prisoners and 'troublemakers' twenty years before the Pacific war started.[1] Like other famous Asian prisons associated with the war, Changi Prison and Outram Road Gaol in Singapore, and Stanley Prison in Hong Kong, when hostilities ceased the function of Sugamo Prison reversed. Instead of the inmates being enemies of Japan, the prison became populated with thousands of suspected and convicted Japanese war criminals, now controlled by the Allied occupation forces.

Despite the heavy bomb damage inflicted on Tokyo by American B-29 Superfortress aircraft in 1944 and 1945, Sugamo had been almost untouched, and when American occupation forces took over the prison in December 1945 they doubled its size to cover nearly 5 hectares. The US Eighth Army operated the prison until 1952, with a guard of about 500 soldiers at any time, and Sugamo was to eventually house about 2000 war criminals during this term of operation.[2]

By 1947 the most notable residents of Sugamo were about thirty 'Class A' war criminals, the most prominent being General Hideki Eiki Tojo, Prime Minister and War Minister of Japan from 1941 to 1944 as leader of the *gunbatsu* military clique, who spent the last three years of his life in Sugamo. It was Tojo who would become the surviving Japanese wartime leader most closely associated with the wartime excesses. Among many other reprehensible decisions, he had personally approved the Field Service Code issued to the military in early 1941, which contained the orders and exhortations for sailors and soldiers to behave so brutally and suicidally in the name of the Emperor. Other 'Class A' prisoners in Sugamo included former premiers, foreign ministers, war ministers, navy ministers, generals and admirals, ambassadors and bureaucrats. These gentlemen had been the architects of Japan's disastrous war, and the International Military Tribunal had thrown the book at them. They were accused of:

> promoting a scheme of conquest that contemplated murdering, maiming and ill-treating prisoners of war and civilian internees, forcing them to labor under inhumane conditions, plundering public and private property, wantonly destroying cities, towns and villages beyond any justification of military necessity, perpetrating mass murder, rape, pillage, brigandage, torture and other barbaric cruelties upon the helpless civilian population of the over-run countries.[3]

Because of their primary role in this self-inflicted national disaster, they had caused between 3 and 4 per cent of Japan's 1941 population of 75 million to lose their lives—nearly two million servicemen and about one million civilians. Millions more were, by 1945, seriously injured, sick or starving. Approximately one-quarter to one-third of Japan's infrastructure had been destroyed during the war, including nearly all of its merchant and naval shipping, about one-third of all industrial machine tools, and almost a quarter of all railway locomotives and rolling stock, and motor vehicles. Sixty-six major Japanese cities had been heavily bombed, leaving about 30 per cent of the population homeless. The food-supply problems originally caused by wartime military actions would cause hundreds of thousands of Japanese citizens to die of starvation after 1945.[4] Millions of people throughout the Asia-Pacific region had also lost their lives to the Co-Prosperity Sphere through starvation, maltreatment and murder, including tens of thousands of European prisoners of war and civilian internees. Hundreds of thousands of Allied servicemen had been killed in battle when sent to face the Japanese, the first in actions in 1941–42 to contain the spread of Japan, and many more to then defeat it. Acting in the name of the Emperor Hirohito, the Japanese military had left a swathe of destruction and death wherever they had been. This short three years and eight months period in Japan's previously long and noble history, unselfconsciously conducted with never a thought for the country's future reputation, had shocked and disgusted the world, and by 1945 Japan had become a pariah among nations.

Japan was extraordinarily lucky to have been defeated by the Allies, however, and fortunate that the international situation would so quickly change to its advantage after 1945. Despite the deprivations and difficulties within postwar Japan, the paternalistic occupation forces under General MacArthur would prove to be friendly, helpful, and generally sympathetic, especially when reconciliation and economic revitalisation became imperatives.[5] The individual fates of most (but not all) of the prisoners in Sugamo would later reflect the generosity and humanity of the Occupation forces. It would not take long before they realised they were much better off, even as prisoners of the Allies in a free Japan, than they had been as warriors of Emperor Hirohito's totalitarian government.

By the standards of Japanese-controlled wartime prisons, including the internment camp at Kavieng, Sugamo under American management was not such a bad place to be. All categories of prisoners ate normal Japanese foods prepared by Japanese cooks and served by the prisoners themselves. They regularly shaved, bathed, and received laundered clothing and bedding. They were given plenty of freedom within the prison walls, which they put to good use debating the injustice of it all, conspiring and writing. Later, seen as celebrities themselves, they would be entertained in the prison by Japan's postwar celebrity entertainers.[6] Besides, and although the prisoners did not yet know it was going to happen, the lucky majority would be free men in just a few years' time.

In mid-1947, Sugamo was to become home for the ringleaders of the Kavieng murders and conspiracy. Immediately following Albert Klestadt's successful interrogation of the barge mechanic Jitsukawa, Lieutenant Colonel Goslett set in motion proceedings to have the leading officers and non-commissioned officers of 14 Naval Base Force and 83 Naval Garrison Unit arrested and imprisoned in Sugamo as suspected war criminals. There was no question of releasing them after interrogation, as had been done so often before. From now on they were to be confined under guard, and their movements and fates tightly controlled by 2 Australian War Crimes Section.

From their intimate knowledge of the workings of the old Imperial Japanese Navy, the staff of 2 War Crimes Section knew that nothing had ever occurred without the explicit direction or approval of senior officers. They anticipated that as the Kavieng enquiry widened, practically every participant in the crime would most likely plead that they had carried out an unavoidable order and could not be held personally responsible for what had happened. The investigators estimated that up to 70 ex-servicemen had been involved, most of them from the lower ranks. Unless it could be ascertained that men from the lower ranks had acted alone, it was decided to concentrate the weight of investigation and prosecution on the officers. Accordingly, Goslett requested the immediate arrest of former Rear Admiral Ryukichi Tamura, former Commander Shozo Yoshino, former Lieutenant Commander Kyoji Mori, former Lieutenant Soichi Ichinose, former Sub-Lieutenant Hichitaro Mochizuki, former Ensign Shozo Suzuki, former Chief Petty Officer Haruo Miyamoto and former Chief Petty Officer Riohei Kambe. Very soon all these men were behind bars in Sugamo, with the exception of ex-Admiral Tamura, who was still too ill, and Mochizuki, who also was ill—both were sent under guard to a US hospital.

While these arrests took place, Captain Klestadt continued with his interrogation of men like Jitsukawa who were believed to have been on the fringes of the crime, and who were more likely to be prepared to talk. On 3 July 1947, Klestadt found himself seated opposite Jutaro Takata, who had been second in command of the Sea Defence Department of 83 Naval Garrison Unit, and immediate subordinate to the then Lieutenant Mori. It was Takata who had been instructed by Mori to urgently prepare the barges, wire and sinkers, and dispatch the vessels to the South Wharf. Takata told Klestadt how 'a day or two [sic] after the four-hour naval shelling of Kavieng which occurred some time after the heavy air raids on Kavieng in February 1944' he had made these arrangements, who the barge crews were, and how after sending the barges around to the South Wharf he had remained in his barracks.

Takata then filled in a number of the gaps in Jitsukawa's account of the subsequent murders. Although he had not personally been involved, the following morning he had requested a report from the barge crews on the previous night's activities. He was told that:

> the internees had been killed by sailors from the Land Defence Department on the beach and their bodies loaded on the two barges. An officer of the Land Defence Department and his sailors also boarded the barges. The officer then asked the barge captain to take him to a place where the water was deep. The barges proceeded to the deep water and when it was reached the bodies of the internees were thrown overboard, fastened with rope and wire to the cement sinkers.[7]

Takata then told how after the surrender of Japan in 1945 he had been called to a meeting with the officers Yoshino, Mori and Suzuki at the headquarters of 83 Naval Garrison Unit in the jungle east of the Kavieng airfield. The meeting discussed what to do if Allied investigators asked about the disappearance of the internees, and it was decided that the explanation would be that after a heavy air raid on Kavieng in February 1944 the internees had been sent in a barge to board a large steamer. It was at this meeting that Takata had learned that Ensign Suzuki had been in charge of the execution and disposal of the bodies. Takata then signed the record of his interview.

From this, Klestadt now had a much better appreciation of when the murders might have occurred. It looked as though it had not been in mid-February 1944, after a 'particularly heavy air raid', but possibly a month later, around the time of a hitherto unmentioned heavy American naval shelling of Kavieng. He immediately sent off a signal to Melbourne to seek clarification of this point:

MURDER OF 32 INTERNEES IN KAVIENG. PLEASE SIGNAL EARLIEST FOLLOWING INFORMATION. DATE OF HEAVIEST NAVAL BOMBARDMENT OF KAVIENG APPROX FEB OR MAR 44 WHICH LASTED APPROX FOUR HOURS.[8]

The following day, 4 July 1944, Klestadt went to Sugamo Prison and had the ex-Commander Shozo Yoshino brought before him for re-interrogation. Reckoning that Yoshino was probably another who had been on the fringes of the murders and quite likely to be talkative, Klestadt started the interview. From the outset Yoshino, who had had plenty of time to think things over, gave all the signs of someone who was going to be very helpful, and the reason became quickly apparent. In his account of events, he immediately claimed that 'at the time of the heavy air raids and naval shellings in February and March 1944', the then Lieutenant Kyoji Mori, who was in charge of the internees, 'requested two or three times' that Yoshino issue him with orders to dispose of the internees by either 'sending them to Rabaul or taking other action'. Yoshino said that he had transmitted Mori's request to then Captain Tamura, who instructed that the internees be sent to Rabaul, but that it was impossible for Yoshino to carry out this instruction. Then in March 1944 Tamura gave Yoshino verbal orders that 'if the expected Allied landings should materialise, the internees at Kavieng should be killed'. Shortly afterwards, Yoshino transmitted Tamura's order to Mori.

Then, in response to Klestadt's questioning, came Yoshino's wartime Japanese-logic explanation for the killings: 'We all expected to lose our lives in the event of an Allied landing and as it would be impossible under operational conditions to protect the internees, it was thought better to kill them'.

So far, Yoshino was saying that he had just acted as a go-between, carrying Mori's request to Tamura, and carrying Tamura's order back to Mori. He had just been an innocent and dutiful message-carrier.

He went on to place himself completely out of the line of fire. Yoshino explained how on 18 March 1944 he had travelled away from Kavieng to Namatanai for his liaison visit to General Takeo Ito's headquarters; how he had met with Major Sato; how he had stayed at Namatanai at 89 Naval Garrison Unit with Commander Takeda; and returned to Kavieng on 21 March 1944. Back in Kavieng he discovered that there had been a heavy bombardment by the American navy, that there were rumours that the Americans had already landed, and that, to his surprise and consternation, all the internees had been killed:

> During my absence, that is between 18 and 21 March, the thirty-two foreign internees had been killed, and Lieutenant Mori had implemented the order. I was too perturbed at the time to speak to Mori about the matter but I heard the full story of the killing of the foreigners bit by bit later on. I did not report the fact of the killing of the foreigners to Captain Tamura as I was absent when it took place.[9]

Finally, Yoshino described how he had travelled to Rabaul after the surrender, his meeting with Captain Sanagi and Lieutenant Commander Matsumoto, how Sanagi had 'instructed him' to use the story about the *Kowa Maru*, and how he had returned to Kavieng and submitted the alibi to Tamura, who had 'decided the adopt this fiction'. Of course, Yoshino had not personally been involved in inventing the *Kowa Maru* story, but had simply taken Sanagi's instruction and dutifully carried it to Tamura, who had made the decision and issued the order for the cover-up. To conclude, Yoshino admitted that the statement he had provided Klestadt on 20 January 1947 had been a lie, and signed a new record of interview.

Yoshino had been a very senior career officer of the Imperial Japanese Navy with the naval rank equivalent to an army colonel. He enlisted in the navy in 1922, was commissioned in 1927, and had served in various commands, including aboard the venerable aircraft carrier *Shokaku* of Pearl Harbor, Kavieng and Midway fame. In Kavieng he had been the second most senior officer at 14 Naval Base Force. He had been interrogated by Klestadt the previous January, and given a sworn statement which was false. Now, with his new buckpassing sworn testimony, he had squarely implicated his old commanding officer and all his fellow senior officers from Rabaul and Kavieng in both the murders and the conspiracy to conceal them. He had also helped Klestadt fix the probable date of the murders to the time of a US naval bombardment on 20 March 1944.

With his three successive interrogations between 24 June and 4 July 1947 of ex-barge mechanic Jitsukawa, ex-Petty Officer Takata, and now ex-Commander Yoshino, Klestadt had broken the Kavieng case wide open, and demolished the 'fabulous lie'. After nearly two years of frustration, delay and dead ends in this major investigation, he had suddenly solved the puzzle.

On 8 July 1947, Klestadt received a reply from Melbourne in response to his initial request for information about the heavy American naval bombardment. Confusingly, the message only contained details of bombardments by American destroyers on the night of 18–19 February, on 22 February, 24 February and 25 February 1944. There was no mention of anything having happened in March.

Klestadt pressed on with his interrogations. On 9 July it was the turn of Unoharu Yamao, who as a leading seaman in 1944 had been Chief Engineer on No. 2 Barge, and Jitsukawa's immediate boss. He had already been before Klestadt just the month before and given false testimony. Back in the Meiji Building again, and confronted with all the evidence, he now decided to tell the truth. It turned out he was the first person to be interrogated by Klestadt who had witnessed the actual blindfolding and strangling of the internees, and the dumping of their bodies onto his barge from the wharf, although he claimed not to have seen the bodies later being thrown into the sea, despite being on the barge at the time. He named Ensign Suzuki, Warrant Officer Jutaro Takato and Petty Officer Yoshio Horiguchi as having been the ringleaders throughout the night. He fixed the time of the murders as being after the naval shelling of Kavieng, but was vague about the month. He, too, signed a new record of interview.

The interrogations by the indefatigable Albert Klestadt followed one after another in quick succession. On 21 July he interviewed ex-Petty Officer Yashichi Mori, engineer on No. 1 Barge, which had been the second vessel to be loaded with bodies on the night of the murders. Mori also said that the incident had occurred after the naval shelling of Kavieng 'in February 1944', and he had witnessed every one of the murders, including 'that of a boy aged 15 or 16, and we all felt it was pitiful to kill him'. Mori added that when he returned to the Central Wharf later that night, 'I did not return to quarters immediately but remember that I and others of the crew washed down the deck of the barge as there was a lot of blood about'. Finally, he too confirmed the story of the cover-up, how he had been ordered to say that the internees had been sent to Rabaul.

On 26 July 1947, now thoroughly confused about when the heavy naval shelling of Kavieng had occurred, Klestadt sent another signal to Melbourne.

> MURDER OF 32 INTERNEES EX KAVIENG. JAP INTERROGATED STATE THAT IN ADDITION TO FEB SHELLINGS BY DESTROYERS ANOTHER MUCH HEAVIER BOMBARDMENT OF KAVIENG INCLUDING CRUISERS AND OR BATTLESHIPS OCCURRED APPROXIMATELY BETWEEN 18 AND 21 MARCH 1944. PLEASE RECHECK WITH NAVY AS THESE DATES OF UTMOST IMPORTANCE IN ESTABLISHING EXACT DATE OF MASSACRE.[10]

A few days later, back came the reply:

> Naval Historical Research advises heavy bombardment of KAVIENG by battleships and cruisers coincided with landing by marines on EMIRAU Island at 0830 hours on 20 March 1944.[11]

So there he had it, the true story. The shelling of Kavieng by the American ships had triggered a chain of events that had led to a war crime being committed on or about 20 March 1944. In August 1945 all the perpetrators had entered into a conspiracy to conceal this fact. The internees had been killed by their captors because the Japanese anticipated their own imminent deaths. When they were not in fact killed in the expected battle, the Japanese had elaborately concealed their embarrassing mistake.

By early August 1947, Lieutenant Colonel Goslett was in a position to report in detail to Army Headquarters in Melbourne. He described the sequence of events that led to the murders, the names and actions of each of the main actors, and provided a probable date of between 18 and 21 March 1944 (without mentioning the US bombardment). He also mentioned that ex-Lieutenant Soichi Ichinose, ex-Ensign Shozo Suzuki and ex-Petty Officer Haruo Miyamoto had refused to give information when interrogated in Sugamo Prison, but 'were expected to talk at a later date'. He added that Riohei Kambe, a barge captain, had not been located; and that both ex-Sub-Lieutenant Mochizuki and ex-Rear Admiral Tamura were under guard in a US hospital and had yet to be interrogated. Goslett concluded by observing that it had now clearly been established that a war crime had been committed.

By a strange and inexplicable twist in these proceedings, Soichi Ichinose did not 'talk at a later date', and he was neither implicated nor accused. Ichinose had been a direct link in the chain of command of 83 Naval Garrison Unit at the time Tamura's order was transmitted, and was directly implicated in responsibility for the murders. However, alone among the group of key officers involved he had resolutely resisted Klestadt's interrogations and had continued to refuse to make any statement at all. For some unknown reason, neither Ichinose's immediate superior, ex-Lieutenant Commander Mori, nor his immediate subordinate, ex-Lieutenant Mochizuki, implicated him when they were interrogated. When the charges were eventually drawn up, Ichinose's name was not among the accused, making it appear that he had been bypassed in the chain of command. This oversight was later pointed out to Army Headquarters, and separate legal proceedings were contemplated against him in 1948.[12]

Albert Klestadt continued his interrogations and re-interrogations all through August 1947 and into early September. On 14 August he finally came face to face with Rear Admiral Tamura, who by this stage had been blamed by practically every one of his subordinates for having made the verbal order to kill the internees and later to conceal the crime. The upwards chain of command stopped with Tamura. Of all the officers who had been involved in both crime and cover-up, he was by far the most senior. Still stricken with tuberculosis, Tamura knew the game was over even before the interview started. He had

had plenty of opportunities to be briefed about Klestadt's aggressive investigation by his co-conspirators, and knew there was no point in lying. He freely admitted to Klestadt that in March 1944 he had ordered that the murders be carried out, and that after the Japanese surrender in 1945 he had ordered that the *Kowa Maru* story be used to mislead investigators. He admitted that he had provided false statements in Rabaul in 1945 and 1946.[13]

His explanation for ordering the murders was simple. It had been an act of strict military necessity, made 'in the middle of a grave situation of battle' when an Allied landing was expected at any moment. He and all members of his unit fully expected to die in the defence of Kavieng, and there could be no question of permitting the internees to survive. He regretted that it had happened, but in his view he simply had no choice under the circumstances of his command at the time.

On 17 September 1947 Lieutenant Colonel Goslett signalled to Melbourne that the case was ready for trial. It had been decided to use an Australian Military Court which was shortly to be established in Hong Kong to deal with a number of outstanding cases, and Goslett now requested authority from Army Headquarters for the transfer of the six accused from Sugamo Prison to Stanley Prison in Hong Kong, advising that shipping had been made available in late September for this

---

ABSTRACT OF EVIDENCE

ON THE CHARGE: COMMITTING A WAR CRIME in that they at or near KAVIENG in NEW IRELAND in or about the month of March 1944 were, in violation of the laws and usages of war, together concerned in the MASSACRE of approximately twenty-three Australian civilian internees, then held in the custody of the Japanese Armed Forces.

AGAINST: TAMURA   Ryukichi   former Rear Admiral
          YOSHINO   Shozo   former Commander
          MORI   Kyoji   former Lt-Commander
          MOCHIZUKI Hichitaro   former Lieutenant
          SUZUKI   Shozo   former Lieutenant
          HORIGUCHI Yoshio   former Chief Petty Officer

All previously members of the Imperial Japanese Navy[14]

purpose. At the same time Goslett began arrangements for the transfer of trial documents to counterparts at 1 Australian War Crimes Section in Hong Kong, including seventeen sworn statements recently obtained by Albert Klestadt, and an Abstract of Evidence. Because the trial would be conducted under the provisions of the *Australian War Crimes Act*, it would concern only the murder of the Australians; and because Soichi Ichinose had still not implicated himself or been directly implicated by others, only six rather than seven Japanese now stood accused.

The Abstract included five foolscap pages detailing the whole tragic tale, including Admiral Tamura's order of March 1944 to Commander Yoshino—'In the event of a landing by the enemy, you will have the foreign internees held at Kavieng executed'—and all the terrible details of the murders.

At this point, someone at 2 War Crimes Section had the bright idea of preparing a press release about the forthcoming trial, and a little anti-Japanese boasting for consumption by the Australian popular press. A long (four foolscap pages) account of the incident, cover-up and investigation, and announcement of the forthcoming trial, was drafted and on 12 November 1947 sent to Army Headquarters in Melbourne for approval. It contained statements like: 'the trial will bring to light the details of one more inhuman atrocity to be added to the black record of Japan's short and inglorious occupation of South-West Pacific islands'; 'investigations soon revealed the true pattern of this war crime and uncovered more fiendishly brutal details of this atrocity perpetrated by order of the once proud and arrogant Imperial Japanese Navy'; and 'the ostensible reason given for the execution order throws a revealing beam of light on the perverse and warped reasoning of the Japanese war lords'.

Surely such amazing language would be prejudicial to a fair trial? Someone at Army Headquarters certainly thought so, and when conditional approval for the release was wired to Tokyo it came with instructions to drastically tone down the language:

> PRESS RELEASE AT TIME OF ACCUSED BEING BROUGHT TO TRIAL APPROVED PROVIDED FOLLOWING PRINCIPLES OBSERVED (A) NAMES OF VICTIMS AND INFORMANTS OTHER THAN ACCUSED ARE EXCLUDED (B) RELEASE WORDED TO SHOW THAT ANY STATEMENTS OF FACT SHOULD BE PREFACE BY QUOTE ALLEGED UNQUOTE OR SIMILAR WORD (C) CANNOT BE CONSTRUED AS PREJUDICING FAIR TRIAL.[15]

The draft also contained a curious statement. Despite the investigation having discovered that the *Kowa Maru* had been sunk by American B-25 bombers, one sentence read: 'It was discovered that the American submarine which had torpedoed *Kowa Maru* had also picked up a number of Japanese survivors'. After such an exhaustive investigation to determine the complex truth of the Kavieng saga, why would Tokyo now want to say that? In the event, good sense prevailed, and the account was not released to the news media.

It would not be until 18 October 1947 that Tamura, Yoshino, Mori, Mochizuki, Suzuki and Horiguchi were removed from Sugamo Prison and embarked under a guard escort of ten Australian soldiers on the British ship HMT *Devonshire* bound for Hong Kong. Travelling with them were seventeen other former Japanese naval officers who were to be tried before the same Australian Military Court for a war crime committed at a prison camp on Hainan Island, off the south China coast.

The six former Japanese naval officers from Kavieng had all confessed to their crime and to the conspiracy which concealed it. The fabulous lie they had concocted had finally collapsed in the face of Albert Klestadt's persistent enquiry, the truth had come out, and now they would face an Australian Military Court with the power to hand down the death sentence. They were finally about to start pleading for their lives and liberty.

chapter 23

The trial

The Chinese island of Hong Kong on the south China coast had been attacked by Japan on the very first day of the Pacific war, 8 December 1941. The rapid capitulation of this British colony, on Christmas Day, was followed by a period of bloody massacre and mayhem by the occupying troops of the 38th Division, Imperial Japanese Army. Within days the invaders plunged into an orgy of mass murder, rape and looting of the sort practised on the men, women and children of another Chinese city, Nanking, in 1937. Those European civilians who survived this awful time were rounded up and imprisoned in an internment camp in and around the former British prison, Stanley Gaol, on the Stanley Peninsula in the south of Hong Kong Island. For the next forty months these unfortunate people were subject to terrible abuse and starvation. The Chinese population of Hong Kong was treated even more viciously.[1]

It was only natural that, following the Japanese surrender in 1945, Hong Kong would become a centre for war crimes investigations and trials, and Stanley Gaol a major prison for suspected Japanese war criminals and the site of many of the trials. Commencing in March 1946 and continuing for the next two years, British military courts in Hong Kong convicted scores of Japanese war criminals, many of whom would be hung on the well-used gallows at the gaol.

The Australian government would also use the British facilities in Hong Kong to conduct a Military Court between November 1947 and November 1948. The first of the Australian trials would be of the six Japanese officers responsible for the Kavieng massacre, commencing on 24 November 1947. There would be another twelve trials in Hong Kong over the next year until the Australian government moved its war crimes apparatus to Manus Island in the Bismarck Sea for a final series of trials in 1950 and 1951. The move to Manus, an isolated island completely under Australian control, was necessitated by Australia's persistence with prosecutions long after the United States and Britain had lost interest and ceased cooperating.[2]

One of the features of the trials was the vast gulf in time and circumstances between the ordered, sombre, postwar military courtrooms and the madness and brutality of the incidents being considered. It was as if a court constituted under humane laws and comprised of civilised human beings was placing on trial for inhumane conduct previously wild, malevolent, incomprehensible creatures from another planet. Notions of truth and responsibility vary from culture to culture and from time to time, and actions perfectly acceptable in one culture at a particular time can be reprehensible in another. The Australian Military Court in Hong Kong was conducted under the *Australian War Crimes Act* of 1945, and was an expression of Australian moral values of the time. Australia believed that prisoners of war and civilian detainees were protected under international law, and could not be maltreated in any way. During the war Australia had gone to extraordinary lengths to ensure that enemy prisoners under its control were treated appropriately and humanely (even though Japanese prisoners often interpreted acts of kindness and care toward them as Australian 'weakness'[3]), and had fully expected that Japan would care for Australian prisoners in the same way. But between 1941 and 1945 Japan was far from being a civil society which protected even the most basic rights of its own citizens and other persons under its jurisdiction. The Japanese government had been a violent military dictatorship which, with the leadership and approval of the Emperor Hirohito, had ordered the Japanese military to act in decidedly uncivil ways. Under this government, by the late 1930s it was normal and acceptable in Japanese society to despise non-Japanese, particularly Europeans and Chinese; and normal within the ranks of the Japanese military to routinely maltreat prisoners of any age, gender or race, but particularly Europeans and Chinese, and to abuse, torture and kill them with impunity.[4]

For anyone passionately interested in the moral and legal issues of putting on trial six Japanese naval officers, nearly four years after the event and under Australian law, for doing exactly what was expected of them under the prevailing Japanese military code of 1944, the case

Photograph taken in Hong Kong in January 1948 when the Australian Military Court was hearing the Hainan trial, immediately following conclusion of the Kavieng trial in December 1947. The bench comprises Lieutenant Colonel H.G. Guinn (second from right), Lieutenant Colonel J.T. Brock (third from right), Major N. McLeod (far right) and Lieutenant R. Carter (far left, who assisted the defence during the Kavieng trial). AUSTRALIAN WAR MEMORIAL NEGATIVE NUMBER AWM P02654.006

was full of contradictions. These men had admitted to committing an outrageous act by Australian moral and legal standards, and had clearly breached international law, but could they really be held responsible for their actions? In November 1947 the already long-running showcase trial in Tokyo before the International Military Tribunal Far East of Japan's wartime political leaders was seriously considering these matters of wartime responsibility. It would be another year before the bench of that Tribunal would hand down its judgements, in November 1948, and the grave reservations of some of the eleven judges started to become public knowledge. In particular, the Australian President of the Tribunal, Justice Webb, turned out to have been deeply concerned all along that all trials of Japanese 'war criminals' had taken place since 1945 without there having been any indictment of the one person ultimately responsible for overseeing Japan's wartime carnage, the Emperor Hirohito.[5] Thousands of obvious atrocities had been carried out in his name since Japan's invasion of Manchuria in 1931, and particularly following the invasion

Lieutenant Colonel Henry Guinn DSO, President of the Australian Military Court, Hong Kong, for the Kavieng trial. Photograph taken in Changi, Singapore, in October 1945 at the 2nd Australian Prisoner of War Reception Group, where Guinn was Commanding Officer of the 6th Australian Prisoner of War Reception Camp and Rear Headquarters of the Group. AUSTRALIAN WAR MEMORIAL NEGATIVE NUMBER AWM 122339

of China in 1937 and the start of the Pacific war in 1941. How was it possible to hold his subordinates responsible for these acts, when Hirohito himself refused to admit any responsibility, and since 1945 had been manifestly protected by General MacArthur and the US authorities from prosecution? Other judges of the tribunal, as well as eminent observers, would later consider the Tokyo trial to have been full of hypocrisy, double standards and 'victor's justice'. It would, in the end, be seen as a trial with many questionable and inconclusive outcomes, even though portrayed by the United States as a 'new dawn' for world justice and peace.

Had the six Japanese ex-naval officers on trial for the Kavieng massacre wished to raise matters of hypocrisy, double standards and 'victor's justice' they would have found little interest or sympathy in the Hong Kong courtroom, however. They would be arguing their cases before three practical Australian army officers who were highly unlikely to be passionately interested in abstract notions of philosophy and morality, and who naturally had no way of foreseeing Justice Webb's later opinions and doubts. The members of the Court were all senior Australian army officers with substantial battlefield experience during the Second World War. For the Kavieng trial the court's President would be Lieutenant Colonel Henry Guinn DSO, assisted by Lieutenant Colonel John Brock and Major Norman McLeod. Another officer, Major Alexander Mackay of the Australian Army Legal Corps, who was also a barrister of the Supreme Court of Western Australia, acted as prosecutor. Captain Albert Klestadt travelled to Hong Kong to act as a witness for the prosecution, and for this purpose was attached to 1 Australian War Crimes Section and accommodated at the Australian officers' mess on Stanley Hill. The six accused were defended by Isso Konishiike, a barrister of the Tokyo High Court, who was assisted by Lieutenant R. Carter, a lawyer serving with the Australian Infantry.

A Victorian, Lieutenant Colonel Henry Guinn had enlisted as a youth in the Australian army in 1918, the last year of World War I, but did not serve overseas. He continued his military interests in the peacetime army militia and was commissioned as an officer in 1922. In 1939, at the age of 39 and with the rank of major, he was among the very first to enlist following the outbreak of the war in Europe. After service in Greece, in 1942 he became commanding officer of 2/7 Australian Infantry Battalion of the 6th Australian Division in North Africa, and later served in New Guinea, being awarded the Distinguished Service Order in 1943. Following the Japanese surrender in 1945 he was appointed Commanding Officer of the 6th Australian Prisoner of War Reception Camp in Singapore, and later served on the military court sitting in Rabaul. At the time of the Kavieng trial Guinn was 47 years of age, and following his final year of service with the Australian military court in Hong Kong would leave the army in 1949.

Also a Victorian, and a lawyer, Lieutenant Colonel John Brock had enlisted in the Australian army in 1940. He held various battlefield postings, including with 2/7 Infantry Battalion and 2/24 Infantry Battalion. After the Japanese surrender he was appointed as a legal officer assisting with war crimes trials in New Guinea, and as an Assistant Adjutant-General of the Australian Army at headquarters in Melbourne. From his experiences with many earlier war crimes trials in Rabaul, John Brock was very aware that a trial could easily fail if the court was not conducted within the exacting guidelines established by the Adjutant-General. In Hong Kong he would quickly establish himself as the guiding legal brain of the Kavieng trial, frequently intervening in proceedings to ensure that no mistakes occurred, and writing copious instructions on courtroom procedure for the guidance of prosecution, defence and witnesses.[6] At the time of the Kavieng trial he was 37, and would also leave the army in 1948 shortly after the trial's conclusion.

The youngest member of the Kavieng court at 30 years of age, Major Norman McLeod had enlisted in the army 1942 as a 24-year-old, and passed through officer training at the Royal Military College at Duntroon in Canberra before taking up various staff postings in New Guinea.

From direct personal experience Guinn, Brock and McLeod were very familiar with what the Japanese army and navy had perpetrated in the occupied territories between 1941 and 1945. Guinn had dealt with the surviving Australian POWs of Changi Prison and seen at first hand the human wreckage caused by their years of incarceration. Each of the three had seen at first hand what Japanese servicemen had done to Australian servicemen and civilians in New Guinea. They would sit, as down-to-earth, no-nonsense Australian soldiers, to judge six former naval officers from Kavieng who had admitted to a conspiracy to murder 23 Australian civilians in cold blood and then conceal the crime. On the strength of the evidence accumulated before the trial, for Guinn, Brock and McLeod the case would be not so much about responsibility, guilt or innocence, but about finding punishments to fit an obvious and admitted crime.

In these circumstances Counsel for the Defence Isso Konishiike faced an almost impossible task. The best he could hope for was to mitigate the culpability of the defendants by trying to portray their actions in the best possible light. The strategy he used was to claim that the defendants were as much victims of militarism as the internees; that Admiral Tamura was forced by circumstances beyond his control to issue the execution order; that the other defendants had been obligated to unquestioningly carry out this very disagreeable order; that they had carried it out in a 'humane' way which put their victims minds 'at peace' before they were killed; and that the victims had been respectfully 'buried at sea', and prayers said for their souls.

Despite their pre-trial admissions, each of the accused, quite reasonably (after all, they were possibly on trial for their lives) entered a plea of not guilty, thus guaranteeing much lengthier trial and appeal

Lieutenant Colonel John Brock, Member of the Australian Military Court, Hong Kong, for the Kavieng trial. Photograph taken in Lae, New Guinea, in October 1945 when Brock was Legal Officer attached to Headquarters, 1st Army, and involved in many of the Rabaul war crimes trials. AUSTRALIAN WAR MEMORIAL NEGATIVE NUMBER AWM 097665

proceedings than the overwhelming evidence against them might have warranted. Instead of being concluded within a few days, the entire process would take several weeks, until February 1948. There were still two pieces of vital information missing from the case so painstakingly built by 2 Australian War Crimes Section. Although the interrogations in Tokyo had produced numerous signed and sworn affidavits admitting involvement in the murders and the conspiracy to conceal the crime, neither the Australian prosecutors or the accused Japanese could say with any precision who had been murdered, or exactly when this had occurred. This would turn out to be a mass murder trial in which the admitted perpetrators would deny guilt, the victims would not be properly identified, and the exact date on which the crime was committed would not be fixed.

After all the lying and concealment of the preceding two years, most of the six defendants used the opportunity of being in the the courtroom to be apologetic about their murderous actions. The personal circumstances of these men had changed drastically since March 1944. Since repatriation from Rabaul to Japan in 1946, they had each experienced and witnessed the miserable lives of fellow-citizens of a thoroughly defeated and humiliated nation. Everyday life in postwar Japan was a constant struggle for survival, compounded by a widespread malaise, and grief for so many loved ones killed during a pointless war. There was also a great deal of anger directed at Japan's wartime leaders for deceiving the people, taking the nation to a shameful and catastrophic defeat, and causing such misery. Everything would be blamed on the few wartime military leaders still living, in particular the former War Minister and Prime Minister General Hideki Tojo, who became everyone's scapegoat.[7]

In these dispiriting circumstances the inhumanity, arrogance and self-deceit of the war years had been replaced by guilt, sorrow and, for some, a search for repentance. After so many years of living in a world of make-believe, the Japanese people were finally facing the stark truth, and this enforced truthfulness was remarkably humanising for them. Having cast off their own mad wartime behaviours, now before the Military Court the six defendants from Kavieng could be as humble and as honest as their strategy for defence would allow. But, while openly admitting to what they had done, each of the accused would claim that they could not possibly be held responsible for what had happened, given the circumstances in which they had acted. Consider the statements made during the appeals proceedings.

The first to be cross-examined was Admiral Tamura. He was prepared to take command and moral responsibility for what had happened, apparently fully understanding what the consequences of this admission would be for him:

I, as CO of 14 NBF and 83 NGU, issued the order 'To execute twenty-three Australian detainees secretly', on 17 March 1944 at Kavieng. This order was faithfully carried out by my subordinates, thus depriving twenty-three innocent people of their lives, and furthermore, gave astonishment and deep distress to their families. For this act, I hereby express my sincere regret and sympathy to the souls of the victims and their families. I am not trying to escape responsibility, but I sincerely wish to explain the circumstances at the time and my situation. War is cruel wherever it takes place on earth. The Tamura unit were assigned to carry out the duties of warfare in the middle of a grave situation of battle. The execution of internees, for which I gave the order, was not meant as an act of revenge or mere maltreatment to internees, but merely an act of military necessity. The war situation in the Pacific area had become very unfavourable to Japan, and an Allied landing at Kavieng was expected at any moment. I and all members of my unit had decided to defend Kavieng until glorious death. In this solemn moment I issued the order of execution as an operational order to comply with the necessity of the situation at that time. Although my conscience suffered acutely and my mind was in a state of dilemma, confused by two issues: one my duty towards the strict military discipline under which I had been trained, and the other my duty towards humanity.[8]

The other five defendants sheltered behind Tamura's admissions, all arguing that because Tamura had given the order they were unable to object or disobey. His immediate subordinate in Kavieng, the former Commander Yoshino, continued to deny any command responsibility whatsoever, while piously appearing to be carrying a great moral burden:

On the 17th March 1944, when accused Tamura issued the order of execution, I simply transferred the order to accused Mori in the manner of an orderly. I was shocked when I came to know the content of the order, and I am deeply regretful for not having made any refusal or protest against it. As I was a senior staff officer and an assistant to the commander Tamura, I should have advised him not to issue the order, but I could not voice any complaint because I fully understood the difficulty of the situation and sympathised with his position. I was never consulted by Tamura regarding the execution of the internees prior to my receiving the actual order. I made constant efforts concerning the internees' safety, and communicated with headquarters in Rabaul regarding their transference to other places of safety. My personal opinion was absolutely against the execution of the internees, yet I had not enough courage to refuse the order or make any protest. I feel immensely responsible. I, myself, intended to commit suicide or make a clean breast [sic] but had no courage to do so.[9]

The former Lieutenant Kyoji Mori, who had so enthusiastically pursued the matter of the internees' 'disposal' with Yoshino in 1944, would take no responsibility at all for his actions:

It was my responsibility to carry out the order, therefore I transmitted it to my subordinate and issued instructions regarding the details of the execution such as method, the date, the time, and the place. When the accused Tamura initiated the execution, I did not participate in any consultation concerning the matter, nor did I make any suggestion for it. When I received the order I was shocked [however] I was trained with the moral education of the Japanese forces which indicate that an order of a superior was imperative and must be obeyed whether the order was unlawful or against humanity. The one who carried out his duty faithfully in this fashion was considered a loyal warrior, and had I disobeyed I would have been severely punished. I carried out the order of my superior faithfully and that was all, but because of it I became a victim of that unreasonable moral education of the Japanese forces. I have no words to atone for the deceased and the bereaved families.[10]

The former Sub-Lieutenant Mochizuki Hichitaro, who had commanded the security detachment of 83 NGU ordered to conduct the executions, stated in his defence:

When I received the execution order I was shocked and moved to tears. I could not refuse or disobey the order. I was not consulted. I simply obeyed the superior's order and carried out my duty faithfully.[11]

In turn, former Ensign Shozo Suzuki, who had lied to the internees to obtain their cooperation to be moved from camp to wharf, and who had directly supervised the executions, stated:

> I now feel quite sorry that we executed the Australian internees even though the war situation made it unavoidable. In the Japanese military personal opinion of a subordinate is not considered or respected. When an order is issued by a superior officer, the subordinates are compelled to obey absolutely, even though the order be unreasonable or unlawful.[12]

Finally, former Petty Officer Yoshio Horiguchi, who had blindfolded and led the internees to their deaths at the wharf, told the court:

> Having heard the execution order I was entirely shocked and felt quite regretful for this misfortune. My conscience told me I should not obey this miserable order, but I knew I would be punished severely if I disobeyed it.[13]

Thus, the not-guilty pleas of these six former Japanese officers were based on a claim that, at the time in March 1944 when they arranged the killings, each was obeying an unavoidable obligation of duty, or order. What they said was, within the culture of the wartime Japanese military, perfectly true. But it was not going to cut much ice with an Australian military court whose members came from another world entirely.

As well as portraying their acts as unavoidable obligations, the defendants who had been directly involved in the killings attempted the difficult task of creating an impression that the murders had been conducted 'humanely'. During cross-examination by prosecutor Major MacKay and defence counsel Isso Konishiike they repeatedly stated that the killings were conducted without any physical violence, none of the victims had resisted or reacted, and all went to their deaths without uttering a sound.[14] They described how the bodies had been reverently and gently lowered by four sailors onto the deck of the barge, how they had been all been 'buried at sea' in accordance with Imperial Japanese Navy regulations[15], and how prayers had been said for the victims. Major MacKay was quick to point out that observations by other eyewitnesses contained in the sworn statements gathered in Tokyo flatly contradicted this version. According to those witnesses the killings had been violent and bloody, conducted with great force, and with some of the victims resisting violently. The bodies had been dumped into the barges, and tossed into the sea. In the haste to get the deed completed on that black night there had been no reverential burial at sea with prayers for the dead.

For the court, the problem of victim identification partly originated in the haphazard, disinterested way Japan had recorded, stored and communicated the names and personal details of scores of thousands of their prisoners and internees during the war years, and in particular the failure to properly identify persons who had been killed or had died while in Japanese custody. Throughout much of the war with Japan, the Australian government had assumed that their counterpart government in Tokyo was conscientiously recording this information as assiduously as Australia believed it was itself recording Japanese prisoners held in Australian camps, and particularly, Japanese who died while in Australian custody. When the war ended and Australian investigations began in Japan and throughout the formerly occupied territories, it was quickly discovered that reciprocal Japanese record-keeping had been extraordinarily deficient. It was only in rare instances that accurate records were discovered to have been kept, for example the *Montevideo Maru* passenger list which Major Harold Williams had been able to quickly locate from a shipping company in Tokyo in September 1945.

Ironically, it was belatedly discovered that Australian identification of Japanese held in Australian camps was also inaccurate, although this was the result of the prisoners habitually supplying false identities and invented backgrounds to their Australian captors, and to each other. So great was the shame of capture that Japanese POWs routinely concealed their true identities from everyone to avoid later condemnation by the military and shame for their families, another of the behaviours fostered by the Japanese military code of conduct.[16]

Of course, it is highly likely that even had the Japanese in Kavieng bothered to record details of their victims the documents would not have survived the war. Apart from the deliberate destruction of the internees' personal effects immediately after the murders, and the accidental destruction of Tamura's administrative apparatus by Allied bombing and shelling, at war's end the Japanese knew that it was not in their interests to preserve anything which might be of value or use to their former opponents. Even if, by chance, 14 Naval Base Force or 83 Naval Garrison Unit at Kavieng had preserved the names of the civilian internees, it was most unlikely those documents would have survived the wholesale destruction of records and equipment which occurred during August and September 1945. Between the Emperor's capitulation announcement in

Tokyo in August and the formal surrender of the Japanese force on New Ireland in September, large quantities of military equipment and stores were destroyed, damaged, or looted in Kavieng, Namatanai and other places to avoid their 'falling into the hands of the enemy'. The plot to conceal the murders would most certainly have also led to obliteration of any surviving internee records at the same time.

Despite attempts before the trial to obtain an accurate list of the names of the Australian victims from both Australian and Japanese sources, no progress had been made. During the trial none of the accused knew the names of all the men they had murdered, or could even remember their faces, although some remembered Bill Attwood and Jim Naughton, who had worked for the Japanese in Attwood's garage during much of the period of internment. They remembered the teenage David Topal, although they did not remember his name. In the end, the Court officially recorded that 'approximately twenty-three Australians' had been killed, without providing names. The best list of names, which was created long after the event, and which appears in Appendix A of this account, is based on Australian Department of External Territories' records developed between 1945 and 1947, and used by that department as the basis for correspondence with the families. It was also the list eventually supplied to the Commonwealth War Graves Commission in London in an official notification.

The problem of fixing the exact date of the Kavieng murders appears to have been caused by the confused or suppressed memories of Japanese and local civilian witnesses of the series of tumultuous events which occurred in the area in February and March 1944 immediately before the incident. As the US build-up for the subsequently cancelled Operation Forearm went ahead from mid-February, the Japanese garrison and airfields at Kavieng, and Japanese shipping on the surrounding waters, came under unprecedented heavy attack by the USAAF and US Navy, culminating in the final air raid on the night of Sunday 19 March and the massive naval bombardment on Monday 20 March. When Shozo Yoshino finally began telling the truth to Albert Klestadt in 1947 he fixed the date of the executions to that day and the great bombardment. According to Yoshino, before he went to Namatanai on Saturday 18 March the internees were still alive, and when he returned to Kavieng on Tuesday 21 March they had been killed. Many other Japanese witnesses also connected the incident to the bombardment, but could not be sure if it was in February or March 1944. Many local civilian witnesses in Kavieng also reported the internees' disappearance from the internment camp as having occurred immediately following a heavy naval bombardment[17], but their opinions also varied as to whether this had occurred in February or March.[18]

The Abstract of Evidence stated that 'some time during the month of March 1944 after a particularly heavy air raid' Tamura had issued the fateful order, and that 'subsequently, still in the month of March 1944, the accused Mori, deeming that an Allied landing was imminent in view of the heavy air and naval bombardment of Kavieng at that time', had carried out the order. Under cross-examination by Major Mackay during the trial, Tamura asserted that his verbal order had been given to Yoshino on Friday 17 March. In his evidence Lieutenant Commander Mori gave the impression that he had carried out the order that very day, but this was contradicted by information in numerous sworn statements provided to Albert Klestadt in Tokyo by other Japanese who had been in Kavieng and tendered to the court. Although often in disagreement about many details of the affair, most statements confirmed that the murders were associated with a heavy shelling of Kavieng by the US Navy, and this could have only been on 20 March 1944.

Despite Klestadt's earlier research, it is quite possibly the Court did not have access to the detailed records of US navy and USAAF operations in the Kavieng area in March 1944[19], nor that it regarded fixing the exact date as being of such material importance to the case as to warrant a detailed investigation. The fact is that after the cancellation of Operation Forearm by the US Joint Chiefs of Staff on 12 March 1944, there was only one significant USAAF bombing raid on Kavieng, that of 19 March, on the eve of the great bombardment. Another raid on Kavieng which had been planned for Friday 17 March was diverted because of bad weather to attack the Japanese army base further south at Namatanai. The records show there was no 'particularly heavy air raid' immediately before Tamura issued the order, and that following the two American air and naval attacks on 19 and 20 March, US military activity in the Kavieng area abruptly ceased, the next recorded air activity being on 8 April 1944.[20]

chapter 24

Punishments to fit the crime

The Military Court sat in Hong Kong from 24 November until 17 December 1947, a long period in comparison to most other war crimes trials. On the last day Lieutenant Colonel Guinn read the judgement and handed down the sentences. The wartime Japanese-logic defence used by the accused was ignored, while the absence of full victim identification and an exact date for the crime was considered immaterial. The six accused had all freely admitted to their involvement, and their admitted conspiracy to conceal the crime was seen as further self-incrimination. Each of the six not guilty pleas was denied, and stiff punitive sentences were provided.

As the most senior of the former officers, and the person who had ordered the secret executions and the subsequent cover-up, former Admiral Ryukichi Tamura was sentenced by the court to death by hanging. His immediate subordinate, former Commander Shozo Yoshino, who had transmitted the order and later helped develop the *Kowa Maru* fabrication, was sentenced to imprisonment for fifteen years. Former Lieutenant Kyoji Mori, who had so enthusiastically urged Tamura and Yoshino to act against the internees, was given twenty years' imprisonment. Former Lieutenant Hichitaro Mochizuki, who had transmitted the order from Mori to former Lieutenant Shozo Suzuki, was given seven years' imprisonment. For his direct involvement in supervising the actual murders, Suzuki was given twelve years' imprisonment. Finally, the most junior ranking of the accused, former Chief Petty Officer Yoshio Horiguchi, was sentenced to four years' imprisonment.

The accused immediately gave notice to appeal against the verdicts by submitting individual petitions against both findings and sentences.

The appeals process would involve developing the petitions, obtaining character references from relatives and friends in Japan, obtaining a legal opinion from the army's Judge Advocate-General, and then having all this material and the court proceedings examined by the Adjutant-General of the Department of the Army in Melbourne, Major-General Warren Anderson, the confirming authority for all decisions made by Australian Military Courts. Having considered the appeals, and verified that the proceedings of the Court were in accordance with the law, it would then be up to Major-General Anderson to make a final decision about verdicts and sentences and to issue warrants to execute the individual sentences. Once the warrants had been executed, a 'return of warrant' would advise the Adjutant-General, and the case could be concluded.

The appeals process revealed something about the accused which had not hitherto been brought up by the defence. Each man had an extended family back in Japan, and if the verdicts and sentences were confirmed, many people other than the accused would suffer. In late January 1948, a petition on behalf of Admiral Tamura was received by the Adjutant-General, submitted by his eldest daughter, Reiko Oosawa. In four eloquent pages she described aspects of her father's character from the perspective of a close family member:

> I am the eldest daughter of former Rear Admiral Tamura Ryukichi. As I lived with and was loved the longest by my father next to my mother I know his character and actions the best. His mien and character stamp him as a soldier, and yet in many respects it may be more appropriate to call him a kindly father. Ever since I can recollect he was always kind to us, and in his petting [sic, probably a mistranslation] he would teach us manners and etiquette and behaviour towards our fellow men. In this he may have been superior to even our mother. Hence while there was a side of him which was strictly soldierly there was another side to his character which was [softer]. We from early childhood firmly believed that there was not such another father in the whole world and thought that he could do no wrong.[1]

Mrs Oosawa went on to describe Tamura's impeccable record as a naval cadet and officer, and provided numerous examples of his humanity, kindness and strong religious beliefs. She concluded with these words:

My father on returning home from the war used to say that he would devote his remaining life for the betterment of his village and town. After his internment as a war criminal suspect the Tamura family have been plunged into difficulties. I, having been married into another family am in no position to assist my mother and brothers, but there being no source of income and with the main prop in the person of my father being removed, I cannot bear to look on the plight of my family, which is barely maintaining itself by selling its household chattels.

I think that All Merciful God in Heaven would forgive my poor father his misgiving and have pity on the sorrows of our family. If it is within your power I beg you to forgive my father and mitigate his sentence.[2]

In his own petition, Tamura expressed his 'heartfelt remorse and condolences to the innocent Australians who died in the incident', concluding with the plea: 'I hereby beg your Excellency to kindly consider my humble petition and exercise your power to quash the finding or at least mitigate the severe sentence which has been awarded me'.

In his petition, Commander Yoshino stated how he 'sympathized very much with the victims of this incident and their families left behind. I have a wife and three children and am supporting four people of my deceased brother. At present my wife is supporting these families alone'.[3]

Lieutenant Kyoji Mori described how:

I pray to God for the repose of the souls of the deceased and the happiness of the bereaved families. I am a bachelor but I have a mother, a married younger brother, a sister-in-law, and younger brother and sister who are still in schools. Our families are engaged in fishing and farming. My mother takes interest in other people and is respected and loved by the local people. When my family hears the news that I have been sentenced to imprisonment as a war criminal, I am sure they will be very grieved.[4]

Lieutenant Shozo Suzuki revealed:

I have left a wife and four children at home; my dwelling was burnt down by bombing during the war. I am quite afraid that they are suffering from shortages of everything, because we have always been poor, but we have always been very honorouable. I am afraid my family will be unhappy when they learn that I have been sentenced as a war criminal.[5]

The family of Lieutenant Hichitaro Mochizuki was also in a bad way:

At present I am suffering from gangrene and I lost my eldest daughter and second son in recent years, therefore I have spent all my savings for medical expenses. My wife, my eldest son who is eighteen years old, and my third son who is thirteen years old are waiting my return home.[6]

Former Petty Officer Yoshio Horiguchi described how:

[my] father died when I was three years old, and I have been brought up by my mother alone for the past 29 years. My mother, brothers, and sisters are now dwelling in Japan. I think they are suffering with inflated Japanese living costs. I have given much troubles to my old, weak mother, and I want to look after her from now on, but I am now a prisoner. I am very afraid that my mother will mourn very much when she hears this news, and I wish to return to Japan as quickly as possible to look after her and comfort her to the best of my ability.[7]

The Judge Advocate-General of the Australian army was moved to recommend mitigation of two of the sentences. In a minute dated 18 February 1948, and while concurring that Mori and Suzuki had been found guilty as charged, the Judge recommended that their prison sentences be reduced. Mori was recommended to receive the same 15-year sentence as Yoshino, and Suzuki the same seven years as Mochizuki. However, the Director of Prisoners of War and Internees, Lieutenant Colonel J.W. Flannagan, disagreed. He argued that Mori, after Tamura, was easily the most culpable, having been the officer who 'assumed the initiative and responsibility for implementing the order of the Rear Admiral and planning the details of the execution by shooting (subsequently altered to strangulation), should in my opinion receive the full term of imprisonment awarded'. Flannagan also argued that because Suzuki had 'himself supervised the whole of the operation between the place of execution and the debussing point' and for such an active part should receive the full 12-year sentence.

Two days later, on 20 February 1948 all petitions for clemency against the findings and sentences of the Military Court were dismissed, and the original sentences and penalties confirmed by the Adjutant-General. Tamura would be hung, and his fellow officers imprisoned. Major-General Warren Anderson immediately issued warrants for execution of the sentences, addressed to the Officer-in-Charge, Stanley Jail [sic], Hong Kong. The warrant for the condemned Tamura announced the forthcoming termination of his life:

FAR EAST LAND FORCES
MILITARY COURT—WAR CRIMINAL

To the Superintendent/Commander or Officer in Charge Stanley Jail, Hong Kong, or any other Prison to which the prisoner may hereafter be lawfully transferred.

WHEREAS one Rear Admiral TAMURA Ryukichi was on the 17th day of December 1947 convicted by a Military Court at Hong Kong of a war crime and sentenced by such Court to the penalty of death by hanging and WHEREAS as required by law such finding and sentence have come before me for confirmation and after due consideration and in the exercise of the powers conferred upon me, I have confirmed the sentence of death by hanging so imposed,

NOW THEREFORE I hereby order you to execute such sentence forthwith on receipt of warrant of hanging and for so doing this shall be sufficient warrant. Upon execution of the said sentence the return below will be completed and forwarded to AHQ Australian Military Forces.

Dated this twentieth day of February 1948.
W.M. Anderson
Major-General
ADJUTANT-GENERAL
Australian Military Forces
(confirming authority)[8]

Five committal orders were issued also issued on 20 February 1948 over Major General Anderson's signature, commanding the immediate imprisonment of Yoshino, Mori, Mochizuki, Suzuki and Horiguchi at Stanley to serve their long sentences. If these were carried out in full, Yoshino could look forward to release in 1963; Mori in 1968; Suzuki in 1960; Mochizuki in 1955; and Horiguchi in 1952 (less remissions).

A few weeks later, on 16 March 1948 Rear Admiral Tamura was put to death by the Stanley hangman, almost exactly four years after the murders in Kavieng had been carried out under his secret order of 17 March 1944. The death-toll from the Kavieng incident now stood at 33 including Tamura, or 34 including Warrant Officer Kazue Takada, who had committed suicide the previous year. Thirty-four bereaved families, scores of Australian, German and Japanese wives, children and relatives had lost a son, husband, father or brother in this utterly pointless incident.

After the false start the previous November, it was now time for the Australian army to publicly boast for the first time about their success handling the case. A revised press release was prepared by Army Headquarters in Melbourne, headed 'JAPANESE ADMIRAL AND 5 SUBORDINATES SENTENCED FOR MASS MURDER AT KAVIENG'. Based on the much longer account prepared in Tokyo before the trial, it briefly described the case and, without mentioning the names of any of the investigators, claimed:

> This crime is considered as one of the most difficult yet solved by Australian personnel because of the diabolical alibi concocted by the Japanese to explain the disappearance of the internees and to thwart the efforts of Australian investigators to discover the real fate of the victims.[9]

Then, after describing how Admiral Tamura had given the false *Kowa Maru* story when investigations had started immediately after the Japanese surrender, the press release made a startling revelation:

> Investigations disclosed that the *Kowa Maru* had been in the vicinity of Kavieng in February 1944, and had later been sunk by a US submarine, but Tamura's specious story was not believed. It was ordered that the investigations be pursued. Accordingly further enquiries were made which resulted in information being obtained that there were survivors from the *Kowa Maru* who had been rescued by the US submarine, and repatriated to Japan after the war.

Survivors sunk and rescued by a US submarine? There it was again! The *Kowa Maru* had been sunk by American B-25s, and some of the survivors were later rescued by the *Nagaura*, which was in turn sunk a day later by US surface vessels. The two incidents had been compressed into one, and a submarine inserted. Tamura's specious story was not believed? His story was swallowed hook, line and sinker for nearly two years until Harold Williams and Albert Klestadt began to have serious doubts, and certificates of presumed death were issued in 1947 by the Department of External Territories based on the false information Tamura had originally supplied.

The concluding sentence of the press release betrayed the depth of feeling against Japan still harboured in Australia two and a half years after the war had ended: 'This is a typical case of Japanese savagery and cunning but our War Crimes Authorities were up to the task and did a magnificent job in bringing the culprits to justice'.

It is not known to what extent this story was picked up by the Australian press, or if anyone was really interested, but a few days later the Melbourne *Sun* ran a short piece on page one under the heading 'JAP HANGS FOR ISLAND HORROR'.[10] The story paraphrased the army press release, copied its tone, and repeated the US submarine falsehood. Here is a sample:

> For the diabolical murder of 32 civilians, including 23 Australians, at Kavieng, New Ireland, in March 1944, a Japanese rear-admiral has been hanged and five subordinates sentenced to a total of 58 years imprisonment.
> This brings to an end two years of intensive investigation by Australian War Crime authorities who interviewed 70 Japs in a bid to prove the falsity of their alibi.
> The Japs claimed the victims had been in a transport sunk by Allied action, but investigators proved Jap sailors had strangled them in turn with a wire [sic] noose.

So now, with the case concluded, the sentences confirmed and carried out, and the story (albeit an abbreviated and slightly peculiar version) finally made public knowledge, was it time to let the matter rest? Well, not quite: the Australian prosecution was still not finished. Someone had pointed out to Major Alexander Mackay, the prosecutor during the

Hong Kong trial, that sufficient evidence might have emerged during the proceedings to implicate three more Japanese officers.

In July 1948, and apparently somewhat reluctantly, Mackay reopened the Kavieng case and investigation, and in August made recommendations about the new suspects his attention had been drawn to.[11] The first of these was Soichi Ichinose, who in 1947 had refused to cooperate with Albert Klestadt, and who was subsequently believed to have been bypassed in the chain of command when the execution order was transmitted. Major Mackay now proposed that although the evidence against Ichinose was conflicting, it indicated that there was a case against him and he should be immediately re-interrogated. Mackay also realised, however, that if Ichinose was now belatedly put on trial, the recently imprisoned Mori, Mochizuki and Suzuki would need to be called as witnesses for the prosecution. As they had already been tried and sentenced, Mackay believed they would probably be hostile witnesses, although Ichinose's defence counsel should be given an opportunity to cross-examine them.

Mackay's next recommendation concerned a previously unmentioned ex-officer, Seichi Hiratsuka, another of Tamura's senior staff in Kavieng. It had been suggested to Mackay that, from evidence provided during the trial, Hiratsuka knew of the order for the execution, and received and passed on information concerning the massacre. However, following further investigation by Mackay, no evidence emerged to show that Hiratsuka took any part in passing the order, or took any active part in the offence. Mackay decided on the evidence then available that there was no case against him.

Thirdly, Mackay made a recommendation about Captain Sadaru Sanagi, the staff officer from Fleet Headquarters in Rabaul who in August 1945 had helped initiate the cover-up. During the trial Commander Yoshino had provided evidence that Sanagi had known of the murders and had been directly involved in concocting the concealment. Mackay concluded that Yoshino had been the only person to implicate Sanagi, there was no corroboration of this, and that an Australian Military Court would probably not take a very serious view of the offence. He recommended that Sanagi should be re-interrogated to ascertain which other officers at Fleet Headquarters were implicated in the conspiracy.

Mackay concluded his recommendations with an observation:

> This case swarms with accessories after the fact, and in that category could be included all members of the barge crews that disposed of the bodies, all those members of 83 NGU who became parties to the *Kowa Maru* falsehood, Sanagi, Matsumoto, and other officers at Fleet Headquarters Rabaul. If it is intended to prosecute all of them the case would never end.[12]

Mackay was saying 'enough is enough'; he was supported in this viewpoint by Lieutenant Colonel Goslett at 2 Australian War Crimes Section in Tokyo. Providing his own written opinion about Ichinose, Hiratsuka and Sanagi on 17 August 1948, Goslett concluded by saying that 'subject to any instructions to the contrary, it is not proposed to take action against any of the other accessories referred to above'.

And so a war crime committed in Kavieng in March 1944 was finally brought to a conclusion four and a half years later in August 1948. Of the scores of Japanese naval officers and sailors who had directly participated, including the extraordinarily lucky Seichi Ichinose, only six of the leaders were tried, convicted, sentenced and punished (well, sort of punished, as it would turn out). Albert Klestadt's persistent and clever investigation from November 1946 until September 1947 had produced a magnificent result, but a great number of the Japanese men he knew were guilty had escaped punishment, and were able to get on with their lives.

The investigation and trial had also been concluded just in time. Five days after Tamura's execution at Stanley Prison, the British government began warning the Australians that they would need to soon vacate the Hong Kong military court premises, ostensibly because of a 'shortage of accommodation'.[13] By August 1948, when Major Mackay was finally wrapping up the Kavieng case, the US government was bluntly pressuring Australia to end the persecution of war criminals, and in 1949 all assistance was completely withdrawn.[14]

chapter 25

And then what happened?

In January 1948, with the Kavieng case almost at an end, Albert Klestadt left the army and returned to Australia to settle in Melbourne, where he resumed his peacetime occupation as an import and export trader.[1] He married Edna Price, the American beauty he had met at the celebration party in the Meiji Building the previous June, on the day he cracked the Kavieng case. In Melbourne they started a family, having two sons, and Klestadt later took up his old weekend hobby of sailing, now on a 26-foot yacht in Port Phillip Bay.[2]

With his expert knowledge of Asia, and particularly Japan, it wasn't long before he was involved in the growing commercial trade between Australia and Japan, which included travel to Tokyo. One day in the early 1950s he was in the Imperial Arcade in Tokyo, sitting outside a barber shop waiting his turn for a haircut, when he was greeted by a Japanese gentleman. As Sir Paul Hasluck tells the story:

> Klestadt was momentarily at a loss. Where had they met before? The Japanese, bowing low, murmured his name—Mori—and a few other catchwords—enough to link himself with the trial. Mori expressed his thanks to Klestadt for the kindly and courteous way in which the investigation had been carried out. He would be honored to have Klestadt dine with him at his home.[3]

Stunned, Klestadt refused the invitation, responding, 'Mori, it was you who should have been hung, not Tamura.' Here was the primary organiser of the Kavieng massacre out on the street, when he had been given twenty years' imprisonment in Hong Kong only a few years ago. He was not due for release until 1968 at least. What was going on?

What was going on was that by the early 1950s Japanese war criminals were being released in their droves by a government recently emancipated from the years of American postwar occupation. In 1951 the United States, now thoroughly preoccupied in Korea with the first big hot war of the Cold War, had worked out a peace treaty with Japan which went into effect in early 1952. The provisions of the treaty handed back governance of all aspects of Japan to the Japanese, and America became a 'paying guest' in the country, although still entrusted with Japan's defence. America also granted complete amnesty to every Japanese war criminal who was not then serving a term of imprisonment, and did not object when released Japanese war criminals entered parliament or government employment.[4]

There had been a strong public debate raging in Japan about the fate of the thousands of convicted 'Class B' and 'Class C' war criminals imprisoned in Sugamo and other jails, some with long or life sentences, and public opinion was for their release. These were the men like Yoshino, Mori, Mochizuki, Suzuki and Horiguchi who had ended up being convicted by Allied courts for having obeyed unavoidable orders issued in the name of the Emperor Hirohito, who himself continued to resolutely deny any responsibility, and was now feted around Japan as a leader of world peace for his heavily publicised effort to end the war in 1945. The proponents of release, mainly already-released and still-serving war criminals and their families, banded together as the 'Sugamo Peace Movement'. They vigorously argued, and not unreasonably, that those still in gaol were the victims of 'victor's justice', and were still being punished for having committed acts which they themselves had no control over at the time.

Using exactly the same argument put by Admiral Tamura and his fellow ex-officers during the Hong Kong trial, the convicted Class B and Class C war criminals characterised themselves as just as much victims of Japan's wartime government as the Allied prisoners and civilians they had maltreated. The wartime Japanese-logic defence, which in Hong Kong had been rejected by the Australian military court, was fully understood and attracted a great deal of sympathy in postwar Japan. It was considered unfair that so many 'innocents' were still incarcerated long after the war had ended and when many of the prominent wartime leaders, the Class A criminals who had caused all the trouble and had to take the blame, had either already been executed or punished in other ways.⁵

In 1952, as part of the peace treaty with the United States, control of Sugamo was handed back to Japan. With the keys to the prison now out of American hands, Class B and Class C prisoners were declared 'rehabilitated', and began to be quietly 'paroled' to return to their homes and occupations. It is assumed that Mori and his Kavieng comrades Yoshino, Mochizuki and Suzuki were all released at this time. Horiguchi was due for release in 1952 anyway, so it is quite likely that he and the unlucky Admiral Tamura were the only officers convicted for the Kavieng massacre who actually had their sentences carried out in full.⁶

What of the 28 Class A war criminals, the ultimate leaders of wartime Japan, who had been incarcerated in Sugamo while the International Military Tribunal Far East conducted the Tokyo trials and considered their fates? These were the men who had been universally blamed for dragging Japan into an unwinnable war, and whose stubbornness had caused death, destruction and misery for millions of innocent men, women and children. These were the men who could not stand the loss of face of admitting, beginning as early as mid-1942, that they had made a terrible miscalculation, and because of their refusal to admit that mistake protracted the war long after they should have sensibly brought it to an end. By their actions they had also permanently damaged the international reputation of their nation. Two died of natural causes during the trial. One had a mental breakdown on the first day, was sent to a psychiatric ward and released in 1948 a free man. Twenty-five were found guilty, many of multiple counts. Just seven were sentenced to death by hanging; sixteen others to life imprisonment, and two to lesser terms. All seven of those sentenced to death were found to be guilty of inciting or otherwise implicated in mass-scale atrocities, among other counts.

Just after midnight on 23 December 1948, the prisoners sentenced to death, including Tojo, were hanged one after another at Sugamo Prison. Their remains were taken under guard to Yokohama Municipal Crematorium, and after cremation were supposed to have been 'scattered to the winds'. In fact, much later they turned up in the Yasukuni Shrine, the controversial Shinto shrine in Tokyo dedicated to the souls of nearly two and a half million soldiers and others who died fighting on behalf of the Japanese emperor, including over 1000 convicted war criminals.

Canberra, ACT, 1954. Meeting of official Australian War Memorial war historians. Back row, from left to right: Douglas Gillison, Lionel Wigmore, George Hermon Gill, Dr Allan S. Walker, Chester Wilmot. Centre, from left to right: Paul Hasluck, Professor S.J. Butlin, George Odgers, Squadron Leader John Herington, David Dexter. Front row, from left to right: John Balfour, Dr D.P. Mellor, Gavin Long, Dudley McCarthy.
AUSTRALIAN WAR MEMORIAL NEGATIVE NUMBER AWM 044512

Three of the sixteen Class A criminals sentenced to life imprisonment died in Sugamo in 1949 and 1950. The remaining thirteen were paroled between 1954 and 1958, having served less than eight years for their crimes, one of them later to become Prime Minister of Japan. Two former ambassadors were sentenced to seven and twenty years in prison respectively. One died in 1950 in Sugamo; the other was paroled in 1950, and appointed Foreign Minister. Another nineteen unindicted Class A accused were quietly released from Sugamo in late 1948, without facing trial.[7]

In many ways, the proceedings and consequences of the Hong Kong trial of the Kavieng six were a microcosm of the hundreds of war crimes trials conducted after 1945. Scores of unlucky criminals like Tamura, who were convicted and sentenced to death, or like Horiguchi sentenced to relatively short terms of imprisonment, had their sentences carried out in full. But the vast numbers sentenced to life or to long imprisonment for very serious misdemeanors never served their full sentences. In the cases of Mori, Yoshino, Mochizuki and Suzuki, the sentences handed down by the Australian military court in 1947 were quite quickly rendered inconsequential by later events. Although the legal apparatus of the Australian army had almost complete control over the investigation, the trial and the immediate consequences, it ended up having no influence over the ultimate disposition of the majority of those convicted.

But something good did come from the trial. For the first time ever, Tamura, Yoshino, Mori, Mochizuki, Suzuki and Horiguchi had publicly and profusely apologised for the killings in Kavieng, and apologised to the Australian families for whom they had caused so much anguish for so long. There is every reason to believe that these apologies, especially those of Admiral Tamura, were heartfelt and genuine. In the circumstances, this was a courageous and unusual thing for these men to have done, for in postwar Japan scarcely a thought was given to the foreign victims of wartime atrocities. During the years immediately following war's end, the Japanese people were fully preoccupied with their own regrets and miserable circumstances, and full of grief for their own millions of war dead. They saw themselves as the victims of the war, not the victimisers. No leader or public figure in immediate postwar Japan, especially not Emperor Hirohito, uttered a word of official concern or apology to the countless foreign victims of the rampage. Many years after the war concluded official apologies and acknowledgements of guilt have come from Japan's modern leaders, although not everyone in Japan agrees this is necessary.[8] More than sixty years after those awful events, and despite every encouragement and solicitation, many of the victims and some countries at least are still patiently awaiting unequivocal official acknowledgement. At a personal level, the six Japanese officers from Kavieng were able to do this, and should be appreciated for having done so.

Many other ordinary Japanese people not preoccupied with the vanities of high-level face-saving, or totally absorbed in the miseries of defeat, were sensitive to the victims of the war and the need for gestures of contrition and apology. Their compassion and regrets were beautifully expressed in the works of some postwar writers and film makers, although these messages of sympathy and empathy were not translated and widely disseminated throughout the formerly occupied territories as they should have been. Commended among these works are three moving novels, Michio Takeyama's *Harp of Burma*, Shohei Ooka's *Fires on the Plain* and Shusaku Endo's *The Sea and Poison*.[9] Japan has demonstrated through numerous impressive deeds over the ensuing years that the horrors perpetrated by its sailors and soldiers in those few short years of war must have been an aberration, not an expression of the enduring underlying Japanese character.

Regrettably, there is no evidence that the apologies and prayers of Tamura, Yoshino, Mori, Mochizuki, Suzuki and Horiguchi were ever passed on to the Australian families concerned. The evidence suggests that those who cared about the internees' fate knew nothing about the long investigation and trial, nor about the messages directed specifically to them by these six men. Their explanations, apologies and prayers for the families are contained in trial documents which have lain buried in government archives since shortly after they were spoken.

What of the families who had put up with so much grief and loss since 1941? It could have been expected that with the conclusion of the trial in Hong Kong, and the March 1948 publicity surrounding Admiral Tamura's execution, the families of the Kavieng victims would have been thoroughly aware of what had actually happened to their men. It might also have been expected that after the trial the Australian Department of External Territories would have formally communicated to all the families involved a revised version of events surrounding the disappearances. It might also have been the case that the Kavieng family networks shared the news with each other, beginning in 1948. Perhaps publication in the 1960s of Mary Murray's books[10] or the brief account in Sir Paul Hasluck's official history[11] might have helped them connect the dots.

None of these things seems to have happened. Despite the long and eventually successful official investigation from 1945, the military court trial in 1947, and confirmed convictions in 1948, the families were never formally or officially advised by the Department of External Territories or any other government agency of the correct story. We know this because the postwar experiences of at least three of the families are remarkably similar.

Gwendoline, the young wife of Vivian Ives, returned to New Ireland after the war and commenced an unsuccessful search for her husband. Moya Chadderton, Claude's only daughter, did the same. Through 1946 and 1947, even while Albert Klestadt was concluding his successful investigation in Tokyo and the military court was being conducted in Hong Kong, Gwen and Moya continued their separate lonely searches on New Ireland, talking to anyone who might have seen something, following up leads and sightings, never aware that the Australian government had already uncovered the truth. Gwen first learnt the true story in 1950 from a Melbourne newspaper report. Moya was to discover that truth many years later in the 1970s, when the Australian historian Timothy Hall contacted her in the course of researching his book *New Guinea 1942–44*.

For the rest of their lives, Jack Griffin's mother, brother and sisters remained only vaguely aware of what had happened to him during the war.[12] Research for this detailed account began in 1994, the year after Jack's last surviving sibling, Ruth Griffin, died in Sydney, and the story has ended up being a belated explanation to the Griffin family's heirs and successors.

When Jack Griffin moved to Rabaul in 1935 he completed a long and gentle process of estrangement from his parents which had begun when he left their home at the age of nineteen in 1929 and embarked on a life of distant adventures. The only member of his family with whom he appears to have retained constant contact until his internment in Kavieng in 1942 was his middle sister Alison ('Pat'), who lived in Sydney and worked in the city in insurance. They shared a number of common interests, including a love of the arts and classical music, and Jack apparently always named her as his next of kin. After his internment and disappearance, Alison represented him in dealings with the Department of External Territories, and that department's correspondence is all addressed to her.

Alison was diagnosed with cancer some time in late 1947, about the time of the trial in Hong Kong. She was to die in Sydney on 7 March 1948, at the age of 41, after much suffering. This was about a week before Admiral Tamura was executed at Stanley Prison, although the family would have known nothing about that. The death of their much-loved and popular Pat was a time of great sorrow for the remaining Griffins, her mother Ethel, sisters Ruth and Marjorie and brother Gerald. Family archival materials of this time are full of sad references to the event. Poor Ethel was still mourning the death two years earlier of her husband George, her partner of 44 years; and still getting over Jack's disappearance, when she was hit with Alison's death. March 1948 was

Alison Griffin, snapped by a Sydney street photographer in September 1941. She is with her uncle, Vic Barker, Ethel Griffin's brother.

not a good time for the Griffin family to also be confronted with the gory details of the Kavieng massacre.

It is highly likely that Alison's passing removed the one point of contact and one person who felt a particular responsibility to pursue the memory of Jack Griffin. It is also highly likely that, had she been alive a few weeks later and seen the brief press release about Kavieng when it appeared in newspapers, she might have been the only person among the Griffins able to immediately understand its significance.

That press release appears to be the only official and public communication about the Kavieng affair that would ever be made by the Australian government after the trial. Although Secretary Halligan of the Department of External Territories had been continuously informed about progress with the successful investigation from mid-1947, had received the Abstract of Evidence at the time of the trial, and had been provided with the full Court Proceedings in 1949, there is no evidence of further communication about the matter from him to the Griffins or any other family. The only official advice Alison Griffin ever received from the Australian government is Halligan's letter of October 1946, which essentially repeated Tamura's lie, and the letter and Certificate of Presumed Death he issued in April 1947, with the date of presumed death still based on Tamura's original story. The volume of archival material about Kavieng held by the department tapers to nothing after 1948, and there is no sign of any further correspondence with any of the families.

Another obstacle to full disclosure of the true facts, in an age when the Australian government was far more paternalistic than it is today, was the secrecy and sensitivity in government circles about anything that had happened during the war, particularly if revelations were potentially embarrassing to wartime leaders, government officials or the military. The Kavieng massacre had a number of aspects which might have fallen into this category. There was the failure of Australia to properly appreciate the danger to which its citizens in New Guinea were exposed by late 1941; its failure to evacuate all citizens from that danger, or protect or rescue those left behind; its inability to obtain accurate information about who might have been stranded on New Ireland; its inability after the war to quickly identify who had disappeared and discover what had happened to them; the fact that Tamura's lie had been accepted and made the official explanation for the internees' disappearance, even after the truth emerged in mid-1947; and finally the fact that the Hong Kong trial, about which the army had so enthusiastically banged the drum, had proceeded from start to finish with no accurate knowledge of who had been killed or exactly when this had occurred (even though the Department of External Territories had already made its deductions and issued death certificates). Add to all that the fact that by the early 1950s five of the supposedly heavily punished perpetrators were out of jail, four of them long before their sentences had been served. These are enough reasons why Australian officials of the time might have been more than usually coy about the affair, and not wish too much to become public knowledge.

In this regard it is interesting to note that the only official historical account of the Kavieng massacre was never made public. In the 1950s the Australian War Memorial commissioned a number of Australian historians to prepare 22 substantial volumes forming the official history of Australia during the 1939–45 war. The historian, politician and later Governor-General of Australia, Sir Paul Hasluck, was commissioned to write two of these volumes, *The Government and the People 1939–41* (published in 1952), and *The Government and the People 1942–45* (published in 1970). Having access to official archival material unavailable to the public, for the second volume he went to the trouble of preparing a detailed 14-page account of the Kavieng massacre based on transcripts of the trial, which included a long description of the murders and their aftermath. Interestingly, Hasluck describes Albert Klestadt as 'a Nemesis in Australian uniform'. This account was to have been published as an appendix to the second volume, intended to expand the very brief version contained in the full text.[13] However, the account was rejected for publication, and has lain in the archives at the War Memorial ever since. Why was it rejected by the editors? Was it because Hasluck's faithful description of the massacre was too confronting? Was it because the Kavieng incident was seen as unimportant in the overall historical context? Or was it simply in order not to publicly reveal the details of a particularly unpleasant and sensitive matter which reflected poorly on wartime and subsequent governments?

The appalling and nowadays widely accepted truth is that the Australian government secretly abandoned its male citizens and token military forces in New Guinea after December 1941 because it was incapable of withdrawing or protecting them.[14] Australia's greatest wartime disaster at sea, the sinking of the *Montevideo Maru* in 1942, was a direct result of this incapacity, as were the Kavieng, *Akikaze* and numerous other lesser atrocities in the areas of New Guinea which Japanese forces had occupied. Although there is no evidence that the Australian government deliberately concealed the facts surrounding the Kavieng massacre, there is plenty of evidence which suggests that little was done to publicly reveal those facts, even to the families directly affected.

The main reason this information is now more easily disclosed is that over sixty years after the event, in an age of openness and access, and presumably because it doesn't really matter any more, the Australian government and other governments do not mind sharing it with their citizens. Following enactment of the *Australian Freedom of Information Act 1982* and its companion *Australian Archives Act 1983*, original government records about the Kavieng event are now readily available from the National Archives of Australia. Information about Kavieng is also nowadays available in the Australian War Memorial, from American and British war museums and archives, and from the vast number of good books and journal articles that have been published about the Pacific war since 1945. There are also numerous internet sites specialising in revealing the truth about the Pacific war.

Nothing good came out of that war, and the pointless murder of the planters and priests at Kavieng was a perfect example of its inane cruelty. To reiterate through the prism of history, at a time in late 1941 when the Australian government had secretly abandoned Australian male nationals living in eastern New Guinea, Jack Griffin was sent from Rabaul by Burns Philp & Co. to assume management of Lemus Island Plantation, near Kavieng on New Ireland. Within a month the Japanese invaded and Jack and the other Australian planters hid at plantations on the east and west coasts of New Ireland where they turned down offers to escape to Australia in small boats, some of which later and miraculously made it to freedom. Eventually interned in Kavieng with a number of stranded German priests, the men survived for another twenty months. In March 1944 the US Navy conducted a massive diversionary bombardment of Kavieng which the Japanese occupiers took to be the prelude to an invasion they could not survive. In compliance with their prevailing military code, Japanese sailors were immediately instructed to secretly kill the internees and destroy all evidence of their existence. No invasion of New Ireland occurred, and when the war ended seventeen months later with Japan's defeat, the Japanese navy concocted a clever lie to explain the internees' disappearance. This lie fooled Australian government investigators for nearly another two years, until a particularly unusual and persistent investigator uncovered the truth in Tokyo. A war crimes trial followed in Hong Kong, resulting in a death sentence for the admiral who claimed he was compelled to order the secret killings, and stiff prison sentences for five of his senior officers, four of whom were later prematurely released from prison under a postwar amnesty. Although the six Japanese officers apologised to the victims' families during the trial, there is no evidence this apology was ever reported or passed on. In fact, the families continued to know very little about what had happened to their men, and the official record of the date and circumstances of the 32 deaths remains to this day based on the false information originally supplied in 1945 to the Australian government by the Japanese admiral.

What of Albert Klestadt, that particularly unusual and persistent investigator who uncovered the truth about Kavieng in 1947? He would live a very active life to a very old age. After the war, as well as starting a family and his highly successful import-export business in Melbourne, he continued his interest in army affairs as an officer in the Citizens' Military Forces. He remained a keen and regular sailor, eventually becoming Commodore of the Royal Yacht Club of Victoria. He became a most active and respected member of the Melbourne Club. Well into his eighties he enjoyed robust health, and remained a man of action, inveterate traveller and yachtsman, and avid reader and writer. In 2005, at the grand age of 91, Albert was suddenly beset by a series of strokes. To him this was initially just a temporary setback, but in October of that year he was admitted to hospital for what would turn out to be the last time.

In Melbourne on Good Friday, 14 April 2006, having successfully evaded the grim reaper so many times, and especially during his years in Asia between 1935 and 1945, Albert finally surrendered his life at the age of 92.

And what of Kavieng today, long after the war? After 1945 it rapidly reverted to its pre-war obscurity and unimportance, and to a plantation economy largely based on growing coconuts. For a while an active temporary industry recovered scrap metal from the expensive war machines manufactured far away in Japan and the United States, painstakingly brought all the way to the town by Japanese and American forces, and then violently destroyed. Sixty years later Kavieng remains small, unimportant and difficult to reach, but a brand-new marine tourism industry has been established because of the area's still-pristine islands and coral reefs. Scuba divers come from all over the world to dive in the beautiful seas and examine the swarming marine life. They also dive on still-surviving underwater relics of the mad war, the sunken Japanese ships and float-planes. Down in the depths there are also many wrecked American planes, nearly all shot down in the violent months of February and March 1944 when the American attacks were approaching their crescendo with the great bombardment of 20 March

1944. If those divers could dive slightly further south, down to the underwater coral sands of the deep channels in the Eickstedt Passage, in the middle of a triangle formed by Nago, Edmago and Usien islands, about 2 kilometres off Cape Sivisat, they might find two clusters of about 30 large Japanese concrete sinkers, perhaps with some old rusting steel cables still attached. These are the gravestones of Australian and German men, and this is their cemetery.

Appendix A

Lists of the Kavieng victims

This appendix contains two Kavieng victim lists, the first based on 1947 Australian government information; the second a list of the Kavieng victims taken from a longer list of Civilian War Dead in Papua New Guinea maintained by the Commonwealth War Graves Commission in London.

1. List compiled from Australian sources

The following list of the Australians at the Kulangit camp and Germans at Panapai near Kavieng on New Ireland is reconstructed from various lists compiled after the war by the Department of External Territories, in particular in April 1947 when that department was preparing to issue Certificates of Presumed Death (see Australian Archives Series MP742/1 File number 336/1/1601 which contains a number of separate but cross-correlating lists). Earlier External Territories lists were presumably the basis for lists compiled by the Prisoners' Welfare Section in Sydney, and published by *Pacific Islands Monthly* in September 1945. Ridges (2002) also lists civilian casualties on New Ireland, including the executed Kavieng internees, and provides some of their personal details.

In the list the background information which could be obtained for each victim has been added. This includes additional details from Ridges (2002); the Prisoners' Welfare Section list published in *Pacific Islands Monthly* in September 1945; from Australian War Memorial military service records from the 1914–18 war; and information provided by surviving family members. The ages of the internees are those at the time of internment in 1942.

Kulangit camp

At the Kulangit camp for 'European Enemy Aliens', all internees were Australians (although then classified as British citizens) except for Vivian Ives, an Englishman, and the two Ostroms who were of Finnish-Russian descent. The inmates of the Kulangit camp were believed to be:

Attwood, William, 'Bill' Australian, aged 30, unmarried, a mechanic and garage owner from Kavieng. Attwood was in the 'Saunders' escape party in five boats which departed from Kavieng on 21 January 1942 after the air raid. Along with the others he was captured by invading Japanese at Albatross Passage and returned to Kavieng jail. Because of his special skills he was not sent to Rabaul with the other men but held in Kavieng and used as a mechanic by the Japanese. He was one of only two internees later remembered by the Japanese as having been in the camp. His next of kin was listed as Miss B.M Bestmann, of Riverview Apiary at Caboolture, Queensland. In October 1944 Harry Spanner told Eric Feldt that Attwood had been captured by the Japanese (NAA B6121/3/98).

Bell, John William Australian, originally from Herberton, Queensland, aged 62. He was the owner of Soubu and Penipol Plantations, adjoining estates located on the mid east coast of New Ireland. It appears almost certain John Bell served in the Australian army during the 1914–18 war. He was the husband of Ethel Harriett Victoria and father of Les, Lincoln, Stan and Don. His next of kin was listed in 1945 as Mrs E.H.V. Bell, his wife, of Kangaroo Point, in Brisbane. In October 1944 Harry Spanner told Eric Feldt that Bell had been captured by the Japanese (NAA B6121/3/98).

Chadderton, Claude Garfield Australian, aged 51, originally from Lindfield, Sydney, NSW, and from the early 1920s owner of firstly Kapsu Plantation (on the north-east coast, which was acquired, cleared and planted in the early 1920s); secondly Lamerika Plantation (at Lamerika point on the mid east coast, which was acquired, cleared and planted in the mid-1920s); and Darlum Plantation (near Lamerika, acquired, cleared and planted in the early 1930s) on New Ireland. Because of chest complaints, between 1914 and 1918 he was refused seven times for enlistment in the AIF but was eventually accepted in June 1918, too late for overseas service. He was the husband of May Fitzgerald Chadderton (who was sent from New Ireland to Sydney in 1941), and father of Moya. Moya Chadderton grew up in New Ireland, attended boarding school in Australia, and later studied medicine at Sydney University. During the Pacific war Moya discontinued her studies to find income-generating employment in order to look after her invalid mother. Shortly after the war May Chadderton died, never knowing what happened to Claude. Moya returned to New Ireland with her husband to assume management of the plantations and conduct a fruitless search for her father, including petitions to the Australian government, the Red Cross and the Vatican. She eventually learnt what had happened to Claude during the early 1970s when contacted by the Australian writer Timothy Hall, who was preparing his book *New Guinea 1942–1945*. Claude was posthumously awarded the Civilian Service Medal in 2005 for services as a coastwatcher. In 1945 his next of kin was listed as Mrs M. Chadderton, his wife, then living at Dulwich Hill, an inner Sydney suburb. In October 1944 Harry Spanner told Eric Feldt that Chadderton had been captured by the Japanese (NAA B6121/3/98).

Consterdine, Cedric Royston, 'Frank' Australian, aged 48, manager for W.R. Carpenter & Co. of Koka Plantation on the mid west coast of New Ireland. He was the husband of Mabel Olive. He is listed as 'F.C. Consterdine' in the Prisoners' Welfare Section list. His next of kin was listed as Mrs. M. Consterdine, his wife, of Mosman, a northern harbourside suburb of Sydney.

Davies, Edward Lonsdale, 'Lon' Australian, aged 35, unmarried, originally from Roseville in Sydney, and manager of Ungan Island Plantation in the Nusa Channel, not far from Kavieng. At the time of the Japanese invasion in January 1942 he had started to escape from Kavieng with Harry Murray, but on 5 February decided to stay at Panaras Plantation on the west coast. He is believed to have been a member of the New Guinea Volunteer Rifles. His next of kin was listed as Mrs L. Davies, Roseville, on Sydney's North Shore.

Furlong, Robert Barry, 'Bob' Australian, aged 40, manager of Lamussong Plantation on the east coast of New Ireland. He was the husband of Agnes Marion. In 1945 his next of kin was listed as his wife, Mrs A.M. Furlong, 'Wilton' via Picton, a rural township south-west of Sydney.

Garnett, William Foster Stawell, 'Bill' Australian, aged 59, originally from Armadale, Victoria. Married to May and owner of Kamiraba Plantation on the mid east coast of New Ireland, next to the Chaddertons at Lamerika Plantation. He served from 1916 to 1919 with the 10th Field Ambulance, 1st AIF, 1914–18 war, rising to the rank of Second Lieutenant. He is also believed to have been a member of the New Guinea Volunteer Rifles. In 1945 his next of kin was listed as his wife, Mrs M. Garnett, of Toorak, an eastern suburb of Melbourne, Victoria. In October 1944 Harry Spanner told Eric Feldt that Garnett had been captured by the Japanese (NAA B6121/3/98).

Gordon, Leonard Leslie, 'Les' Australian, aged 51, originally from Kalgoorlie, Western Australia. He was the owner of Bulu-Logon Plantation on the mid east coast of New Ireland. He served from 1915 until 1919, initially with the 28th Battalion and later with the 51st Battalion, 1st AIF, 1914–18 war, rising to the rank of Staff Sergeant. He was the husband of Dorothea Marie. His next of kin was listed in 1945 as Mrs L. Gordon, c/- Mrs Corlass, of Burleigh Heads, Queensland. In October 1944 Harry Spanner told Eric Feldt that Gordon had been captured by the Japanese (NAA B6121/3/98).

Griffin, John Kenneth Vicars, 'Peter', 'Tiny' Australian, aged 32, originally from Tocumwal, New South Wales, and unmarried. He was normally employed by Burns Philp in the New Britain area as a plantation auditor and superintendent, but in December 1941 was appointed temporary manager of Burns Philp's Lemus Island Plantation in the Nusa Channel near Kavieng. His next of kin was listed as Miss Griffin c/- Manufacturers Mutual Insurance Co., Sydney, who was his sister Alison.

Heming (sometimes spelt Hemming), Horace, 'Ray' Australian, aged 56, the manager of Burns Philp's Kolube Plantation on the mid west coast of New Ireland, near Kalili Harbour. He was the husband of Minnie, and father of Gillian and Rob. His next of kin was listed as

Mrs M. Hemming [sic], c/- Dr Stuart Welch, of Manly, a northern beach suburb of Sydney.

Heydon (sometimes spelt Haydon), Walter Australian, originally from Sydney, aged 58, unmarried. He was manager of Put Plantation, Malendok Island, a remote estate in the Tanga Island Group, 75 kilometres to the east of New Ireland. He served from 1916 until 1918 as a private in the 13th Battalion, 1st AIF, 1914–18 war. His next of kin was listed as Miss Haydon, of Chatswood, on Sydney's North Shore.

Ives, Vivian Gervis Lavie Neil British-Australian, aged 47, manager of Burns Philp's Kurumut Plantation on the far south west coast of New Ireland. He had served in the East Yorkshire Regiment of the British army, and also with the Indian army during the 1914–18 war in Egypt, Gallipoli, Belgium, France, Mesopotamia and Kurdistan, rising to the rank of captain. He was twice awarded the Military Cross for gallantry in France and in Mesopotamia. After the war he settled in Australia, then New Ireland. He was the husband of Gwendoline Muriel and father of Patricia. His next of kin was listed in 1945 as his young wife, Mrs G. Ives, of the Melbourne suburb of Carnegie.

Levy, Philip Montague, 'Phil' Australian, aged 50, manager of the large Burns Philp & Co. branch in Kavieng. He was the husband of Mabel, and his next of kin was listed as Mrs M. Levy, of North Adelaide in South Australia, presumably his wife. In October 1944 Harry Spanner told Eric Feldt that Levy had been captured by the Japanese (NAA B6121/3/98).

Lightbody, Harrison Leigh Australian, originally from Warragul, Victoria, aged 49, unmarried. He was the manager of Burns Philp's big Kalili Plantation at Kalili Harbour on the mid west coast of New Ireland. Lightbody died of dysentery in Kavieng on 29 March 1943 and was buried at Lemakot Plantation. He had served from 1915 until 1919 as a sergeant in the 13th Field Ambulance, 1st AIF, in the 1914–18 war. His next of kin was listed as Mrs G. E. Lightbody, of Warragul, a rural town in the Gippsland area of eastern Victoria.

Miller, Ernest Russell, 'Dusty' Australian, originally from Eltham, Victoria, aged 57, unmarried. He was a planter and trader who owned

Tsaliui Plantation on Tsaliui Island, adjacent to New Hanover, about 40 kilometres to the north-west of Kavieng. He is reported to have died in the camp in early 1944, but this is unconfirmed. He served from 1914 until 1918 initially as private in the 4th Battalion, then as a corporal in the Australian Pay Corps in Egypt, 1st AIF, 191418 war. In 1945 no next of kin was listed for him. In October 1944 Harry Spanner told Eric Feldt that Miller had been captured by the Japanese and was 'still in Kavieng' (NAA B6121/3/98).

Moseley, Albert Edward Australian, aged 60, was originally from the Darling Downs, Queensland. He was manager of Belik Plantation on the south-east coast of New Ireland. Serving from 1915 until 1919 in the 1914–18 war Moseley won the Military Cross as a lieutenant in the 14th Australian Light Horse Regiment, 1st AIF. He was the husband of Annie May and his next of kin was listed as his wife, Mrs A. M. Moseley, of Kedron, Queensland.

Naughton, James Forestall, 'Jim' Australian, aged 31, unmarried, an overseer and mechanic at Burns Philp's Kalili Plantation on the west coast. His mechanical skills were also found useful by the Japanese, and because of this he was one of only two internees later remembered by the Japanese as having been in the camp. His next of kin was listed as Mrs M. A. Houghton [sic], of the large rural town of Wagga Wagga, in the Riverina area of southern New South Wales.

Ostrom, Carl, 'Charlie' Finnish-Russian, elderly owner of Lakurafanga Plantation on the north-east coast of New Ireland, about 40 kilometres from Kavieng. He was a long-time resident of the island. In 1945 his next of kin was listed as Mrs R. Cowley, of the southern beach suburb of Maroubra Bay in Sydney.

Ostrom, Maxwell Joseph, 'Max' Finnish-Russian, about 20, son of Carl. His next of kin was also listed as Mrs R. Cowley, of Maroubra Bay in Sydney. (NOTE ABOUT KARL AND MAX OSTROM. This father and son were not later officially regarded as Australian or British citizens because of their non-Australian and non-British antecedents, and presumably for this reasons their names are sometimes omitted from Australian government victim lists.)

Pinnock, Leonard Joseph Australian, aged 54, manager of Ulul-Nono Plantation, about 30 kilometres from Kavieng on the north-east coast of New Ireland. He was the husband of Louise Jane, and his next of kin was listed as his wife, Mrs L.J. Pinnock, c/- A.W. Hicks of Killara, on Sydney's North Shore. In October 1944 Harry Spanner told Eric Feldt that Pinnock had been captured by the Japanese and was in a 'very weak condition' (NAA B6121/3/98).

Topal, Henry James Isaac Australian, from Ashfield, New South Wales, aged 49. Manager of Tereri Plantation on Tabar Island, about 50 kilometres to the east of New Ireland in the Tabar Group. It is reported that he had arrived in New Ireland only two weeks before the Japanese invasion, sent from New Britain at the last minute to manage Tereri. Henry Topal was of Jewish extraction and originally from Stepney Green in London. His military service records list his occupations as 'Dispenser' and 'Hospital Superintendant'. He first enlisted in the 1st AIF in September 1914 as a Private in the Australian Army Medical Corps, and during this first period of enlistment was attached to the 1st Australian Light Horse Brigade. He re-enlisted with the AAMC in June 1917 for service as a corporal with the Australian Naval and Military Expeditionary Force. This Australian unit had originally been formed in 1914 to seize and occupy German possessions in New Guinea. During this second period of service he was briefly stationed in Kavieng. He had no no next of kin listed in the 1945 Prisoners' Welfare Section list.

Topal, David James Australian, aged 12, son of Henry James Isaac.

Whitehead, Boyd Nepean Australian, aged 44, manager for W.R. Carpenter & Co. of Karu Plantation on the mid east coast of New Ireland. He was husband of Eileen Isobel, and father of Elizabeth (Libby) Ann and James Stanley. Whitehead is also believed to have been a member of the New Guinea Volunteer Rifles. His next of kin was listed as Mrs Whitehead, of Glen Iris, a Melbourne suburb.

Williams, Leon Leslie Williams Australian, aged 38, unmarried, area manager for Burns Philp based at Kimadan Plantation on the mid east coast of New Ireland. His next of kin was listed as Mrs D.L. Williams, of Birmingham, England.

Woodhouse, Edmund Samuel Flavelle Australian, originally from South Brisbane, aged 48. He was the manager for W.R. Carpenter & Co. of Katu Plantation on the north-east coast of New Ireland. He enlisted in September 1914 in the 2nd Australian Light Horse Regiment, and later served until 1919 as a lieutenant in the 43rd Australian Battalion, 1914–18 war. He was the husband of Jessie Lily, and his next of kin was listed as Mrs J. Woodhouse, of Maryborough, Queensland.

Woolcott, Leonard George, 'Len' Australian, aged 42, unmarried, manager of Fileba Plantation on the north-east coast of New Ireland. His next of kin was listed as Mr H.G. Woolcott, of Wahroonga, on Sydney's North Shore.

(NOTE ABOUT HAUGHEY, THOMAS FRANCIS, AND MERNIN, T.P. In the Department of External Territories August 1946 list of civilians missing in New Ireland a T.P Mornin [sic] is included. The same department's March 1947 list of Civilian Internees Not Recovered From Enemy Hands includes the names Mernin, T.P. (or Haughey, T.F.) listed as interchangeable. T.P. Mernin appears in the Prisoners' Welfare section list published in the *Pacific Islands Monthly*, with next of kin listed as Mrs N. Dwyer, of Manly, New South Wales. In *People of the Plaque* Jim Ridges lists a T.P Mermin [sic], explaining that he was 'an itinerant plantation manager, possibly at Ulul-Nono just before the war'. Jim also relates a story told to him by a former New Ireland resident that Mermin and Haughey were one and the same person. The Commonwealth War Graves Commission list below includes Thomas Haughey of Aua, Manus Island, as having died at Kavieng on 18 February 1944, the same day stated for all other Kavieng victims. It is believed that Haughey and Mernin are the same person, and that he may also have been in the Kavieng camp in March 1944.)

Panapai camp

At the Panapai camp for 'Neutral European Aliens' were the seven German missionaries. In early 1944 when Allied bombing and shelling of the Kavieng area intensified, the missionaries were moved into the Kulangit camp with the Australians. They were:

Kohlstette, Father Heinrich MSC Komalu Catholic Mission of the Most Sacred Heart of Jesus, on the far south west coast of New Ireland.

Krutzenbichler, Father Josef MSC Tanga Islands Catholic Mission of the Most Sacred Heart of Jesus, in the Tanga Islands group to the east of New Ireland.

Kutscher, Father Paul MSC Lamussong Catholic Mission of the Most Sacred Heart of Jesus, on the east coast of New Ireland near Bob Furlong's plantation.

Lakaff, Father Josef MSC Kavieng Catholic Mission of the Most Sacred Heart of Jesus.

Schluetter, Father Karl MSC Lihir Catholic Mission of the Most Sacred Heart of Jesus, in the Lihir Islands group to the east of New Ireland.

Utsch, Father Franz MSC Lavongai Catholic Mission of the Most Sacred Heart of Jesus, on New Hanover Island, north west of Kavieng.

Zunkley, Brother Heinrich MSC Kavieng Catholic Mission of the Most Sacred Heart of Jesus.

(NOTE ABOUT FATHER HEMIG AND FATHER NEUHAUS. Jim Ridges provides mission records that show that the German priests Father Johannes Hemig of Lemakot Catholic Mission and Father Karl Neuhaus of Namatanai Catholic Mission, whose names appear on the External Affairs list as being still alive in early 1944, had already died before the permanent internments in early September 1942.)

2. Commonwealth War Graves Commission list

During and after World War II, the War Graves Commission was given the task of compiling as complete a list as possible of Commonwealth civilians whose deaths were due to enemy action. The complete roll of some 66 400 names is bound in seven volumes and kept near St George's Chapel in Westminster Abbey, London, where a different page is displayed each day.

Within this larger roll is a list entitled 'Civilian War Dead in Papua New Guinea, WW2' which contains 89 names of Commonwealth citizens, including 23 men and a teenaged boy all described as having died at Kavieng on '18th February 1944'. This list must have been provided to the Commission by the Australian government, and includes the name of Thomas Haughey. It also includes Leigh Lightbody, noting that he died 'at Panapai' on 29th March 1943 (he died at Kulangit). It also states that Ernest Miller was among those who died at Kavieng on 18th February 1944, although Australian sources indicate that he may have died before that date. The ages in this list are those at the date of death.

ATTWOOD, Civilian, WILLIAM, Civilian War Dead. 18 February 1944. Age 32. Of Kavieng, New Ireland. Son of William James and Mary Ann Attwood. Died at Kavieng.

BELL, Civilian, JOHN WILLIAM, Civilian War Dead. 18 February 1944. Age 64. Of Penipol Plantation, New Ireland. Son of George and Mary Ellen Bell; husband of Ethel Harriet Victoria Bell. Died at Kavieng, New Ireland.

CHADDERTON, Civilian, CLAUDE GARFIELD, Civilian War Dead. 18 February 1944. Age 53. Of Lamerika Plantation, New Ireland. Son of Harry and Fanny Sutton Chadderton; husband of May Fitzgerald Chadderton. Died at Kavieng, New Ireland.

CONSTERDINE, Civilian, CEDRIC ROYSTON, Civilian War Dead. 18 February 1944. Age 50. Of Koko Plantation, New Ireland. Son of Arthur Robert and Alice Jane Consterdine; husband of Mabel Olive Consterdine. Died at Kavieng, New Ireland.

CRAIG, Civilian, Civilian War Dead. 18 February 1944. Died at Kavieng, New Ireland.

DAVIES, Civilian, EDWARD LONSDALE, Civilian War Dead. 18 February 1944. Age 37. Of Ungan Plantation, New Ireland. Son of Evan Augustus and Monica Mary Davies. Died at Kavieng, New Ireland.

FURLONG, Civilian, ROBERT BARRY, Civilian War Dead. 18 February 1944. Age 42. Of Lamussong Plantation, New Ireland, Son of Joseph and Margaret Furlong; husband of Agnes Marion Furlong. Died at Kavieng, New Ireland.

GARNETT, Civilian, WILLIAM FOSTER STAWELL, Civilian War Dead. 18 February 1944. Age 61. Of Kamiraba Plantation, New Ireland. Son of Wade Shenton and Josephine Mary Garnett; husband of May Garnett. Died at Kavieng, New Ireland.

GORDON, Civilian, LEONARD LESLIE, Civilian War Dead. 18 February 1944. Of Kavieng, New Ireland. Son of John Barrie and Charlotte Gordon; husband of Dorothea Marie Gordon. Died at Kavieng, New Ireland.

GRIFFIN, Civilian, JOHN KENNETH VICARS, Civilian War Dead. 18 February 1944. Age 36. Of Rabaul, New Britain. Son of George Thomas and Ethel Beatrice Griffin. Died at Kavieng, New Ireland.

HAUGHEY, Civilian, THOMAS FRANCIS, Civilian War Dead. 18 February 1944. Age 44. Of Aua, Manus. Son of Charles and Bridget Haughey. Died at Kavieng, New Ireland.

HEMING, Civilian, HORACE RAY, Civilian War Dead. 18 February 1944. Age 58. Of Kolube Plantation, New Ireland. Son of William and Sarah Heming; husband of Minnie Heming. Died at Kavieng, New Ireland.

HEYDON, Civilian, WALTER, Civilian War Dead. 18 February 1944. Age 60. Of Put Plantation, Tanga Islands. Son of William and Amy Heydon. Died at Kavieng, New Ireland.

IVES, Civilian, VIVIAN GERVIS LAVIE NIEL, Civilian War Dead. 18 February 1944. Age 49. Of Kurumut Plantation, New Ireland. Son of Edwin Robert and Lucy Ada Ives; husband of Gwendoline Muriel Ives. Died at Kavieng, New Ireland.

LEVY, Civilian, PHILIP MONTAGUE, Civilian War Dead. 18 February 1944. Age 52. Of Kavieng, New Ireland. Son of Montague and Catherine Levy; husband of Mabel Levy. Died at Kavieng, New Ireland.

MILLER, Civilian, ERNEST RUSSELL, Civilian War Dead. 18 February 1944. Age 59. Of Tsalui Plantation, New Ireland. Son of George Alexander and Rhoda Miller. Died at Kavieng, New Ireland.

MOSELEY, Civilian, ALBERT EDWARD, Civilian War Dead. 18 February 1944. Age 62. Of Belik Plantation, New Ireland. Son of Edward Thomas and Mary Jane Moseley; husband of Annie May Moseley. Died at Kavieng, New Ireland.

NAUGHTON, Civilian, JAMES FORRESTALL, Civilian War Dead. 18 February 1944. Age 33. Of Kalili, New Ireland. Son of James Forrestall and Margaret Amy Naughton. Died at Kavieng, New Ireland.

PINNOCK, Civilian, LEONARD JOSEPH, Civilian War Dead. 18 February 1944. Age 56. Of Ululnono Plantation, New Ireland. Son of Charles Heath and Helen Louise Pinnock; husband of Louisa Jane Pinnock. Died at Kavieng, New Ieland.

TOPAL, Civilian, DAVID JAMES, Civilian War Dead. 18 February 1944. Age 14. Of Koka Plantation, New Ireland. Son of Henry James Topal. Died at Kavieng, New Ireland.

TOPAL, Civilian, HENRY JAMES, Civilian War Dead. 18 February 1944. Age 51. Of Koka Plantation, New Ireland. Died at Kavieng, New Ireland.

WHITEHEAD, Civilian, BOYD NEPEAN, Civilian War Dead. 18 February 1944. Age 46. Of Karu Plantation, New Ireland. Son of Edward Stanley and Cecilia Whitehead; husband of Eileen Isobel Whitehead. Died at Kavieng, New Ireland.

WILLIAMS, Civilian, LEON LESLIE, Civilian War Dead. 18 February 1944. Age 40. Of Kimadan Plantation, New Ireland. Son of David James and Florence Annie Williams. Died at Kavieng, New Ireland.

WOODHOUSE, Civilian, EDMUND SAMUEL FLAVELLE, Civilian War Dead. 18 February 1944. Age 50. Of Katu Plantation, New Ireland. Son of Joseph and Elizabeth Ann Woodhouse; husband of Jessie Lily Woodhouse. Died at Kavieng, New Ireland.

WOOLCOTT, Civilian, LEONARD GEORGE, Civilian War Dead. 18 February 1944. Age 44. Of Fileba Plantation, New Ireland. Son of Harry Leonard and Bernice Ina Jeanette Woolcott. Died at Kavieng, New Ireland.

Other British citizens listed by the CWGC as having died in the Kavieng area:

LIGHTBODY, Civilian, HARRISON LEIGH, Civilian War Dead. 29 March 1943. Age 51. Of Kalili Plantation, New Ireland. Son of James and Rachel Bruce Lightbody. Died at Panapai, New Ireland.

MURPHY, Civilian, THE REVD MICHAEL, Civilian War Dead. 30 November 1942. Age 31. Of Tabar Island. Died at Kavieng, New Ireland.

TALMAGE, Civilian, JOHN SAMUEL, Civilian War Dead. 30 November 1942. Age 67. Of Tomalabat Plantation, Tatau Island. Son of John and Agnes Talmage. Died at Kavieng, New Ireland.

(NOTE ON CRAIG, listed by the CWGC as having died in Kavieng on 18 February 1944 with the other victims of the Kavieng massacre. Nothing further is known about this person and his name does not appear in any Australian government lists. The entry 'Craig?—New Ireland' appears in the Prisoners' Welfare Section list of missing persons published in the September 1945 edition of the *Pacific Islands Monthly*.)

Appendix B

The civilian and missionary victims of the sinking of the *Montevideo Maru*

The two lists which follow are taken from National Archives of Australia, Series A7030 Item 11, 'New Guinea Civilians and New Guinea Missionaries Previously Reported Missing, Now Lost At Sea'. Both lists were developed by the Department of External Territories in 1945 and 1946 following the discovery in Tokyo in September 1945 of the nominal passenger list of the *Montevideo Maru*'s final voyage from Rabaul in June 1942. The first is a list of 166 male civilian internees, mainly from New Britain and some from New Ireland, who had been held in the Japanese internment camp at Rabaul from early 1942. The second is a list of sixteen Methodist, Catholic and Seventh Day Adventist male missionaries and mission employees who were also on the *Montevideo Maru*.

Apart from the lists reproduced on these pages a number of different *Montevideo Maru* victim lists were compiled by various authors after the war, and there are inconsistencies between these lists. For example, in his 1982 book *Rabaul 1942*, Douglas Aplin included the names of most of the Kavieng victims in his list of civilians on the *Montevideo Maru*, which we now know was incorrect. In addition, according to Gillian Nikakis (2005) the names of thirty additional men also believed to have been on the ship, including her father Bill Spensley from Rabaul, do not appear on the official *Montevideo Maru* list. A longer list published in her book is based on a nominal role compiled in 1942 by survivors of the Rabaul internment camp. Many of these inconsistencies can probably be explained by errors and omissions in the Japanese embarkation roll discovered after the war, partly because of Japanese inefficiency or disinterest in maintaining perfect records of POWs and internees, and sometimes because of a deliberate intention to mislead by including names of men who in fact died elsewhere. As can be seen in the chapters of this book, the Japanese used the loss of Japanese ships sunk by the Allies to conceal wrongdoing committed elsewhere and at different times.

The 24 names on the first list and three on the second list which have been set in SMALL CAPITALS and annotated by the author are persons who originated from New Ireland and outlying islands, and were captured by the Japanese trying to escape by boat after the invasion in January 1942, or who were subsequently apprehended and transferred to the Rabaul internment camp. In the cases of Ashby, Cobb, Edwards, Hay, Kelly, Livingstone, Rand and Savage, it is not entirely clear how these men ended up transferring from New Ireland to Rabaul on New Britain, or when this occurred. It is also not clear why they were transferred to Rabaul by the Japanese when so many other stranded New Ireland male residents were not, including all of the victims of Kavieng South Wharf.

Annotations are partly based on information provided in Ridges (2002) and also include information gathered from other sources including the Prisoners' Welfare Section lists published in *Pacific Islands Monthly* from September 1945.

1. New Guinea Civilians Previously Reported Missing Now Reported Lost at Sea

ADAMS, H.A., Planter. Harry Adams owned Patlangat Plantation on the west coast of New Ireland, was married, and was a Member of the Legislative Council for the Territory of New Guinea.
Allen, A.G., Planter
Allen, W.E., Police Officer, Administration
Ash, N.E., Police Officer, Administration
ASHBY, S.A., Planter. Stan Ashby, married, owned Kanam Plantation and managed Maramakas Plantation on the east coast of New Ireland. He evacuated to Panaras plantation on the west coast in early 1942 following the Japanese invasion. It is not known how or when he transferred to Rabaul and ended up on the *Montevideo Maru*.
Atherton, J.M., Dispenser, Administration

Atkinson, W., Planter

Banks, E., Hotel Manager

Barnes, C.W., Printer, Rabaul Printing Works

Bath, V.G., Labour Overseer, W.R. Carpenter & Co.

Beck, N.R., Labour Overseer, Administration

BELL, D.J., 'Don', was the married son of John Bell of Soubi/Penipol Plantation, one of the victims at Kavieng Wharf. He is listed as being a Plantation Manager for W.R. Carpenter & Co. However, there is doubt about this as he had just been discharged from the Australian army at the time of the Japanese invasion.

Berman, R.A., Plantation Manager, W.R. Carpenter & Co

Bowman, H., Medical Assistant, Administration

BOX, W.C., Planter. 'Bill' Box owned Meteinge Plantation on New Hanover Island. He had joined the 'Saunders' escape party from Kavieng immediately after the air raids, was apprehended at sea by the Japanese, and subsequently moved to Rabaul. In October 1944 Harry Spanner told Eric Feldt that Box had been captured by the Japanese 'and sent away in a ship which was sunk' (NAA B6121/3/98).

Brett, G.L., Mine Employee, Papua

Brinston, H.G.W., Clerk, Administration

Brown, R.A.L., Mechanic, Administration

Brown, T.G., Police Officer, Administration

Bruckshaw, A.F., Clerk, Administration

Bunny, J., Plantation Inspector, W.R. Carpenter & Co.

Burke, J.D., Clerk, Administration

Bye, E.C., Ship's Captain, W.R. Carpenter & Co.

Cameron, A., Mechanic, Administration (did not embark)

Campbell, C.J., Visitor

Cannon, C.F., Ship's Officer, W.R. Carpenter & Co.

Carlysle, L., Plantation Overseer, W.R. Carpenter & Co.

Carr, L.A.A., Road Overseer, Administration

CARSON, L., Plantation Manager. Lewis Carson, married, was the owner of Fead Island Plantation in the Nuguria Islands group off the far south coast of New Ireland.

Clark, I., Medical Assistant, Administration

Clark, R.L., Company Manager

Clunn, C., Storeman, Burns Philp & Co

Cobb, F., Plantation Manager. Forbes Cobb managed Panaras Plantation on the west coast of New Ireland for W.R. Carpenter & Co.
Coe, P.E.R., Clerk, Administration
Considine, L.A., Clerk, Administration
Cook, R.E., Accountant, W.R. Carpenter & Co.
Coomber, A., Medical Assistant, Administration
Cooper, Dr R.W., Medical Officer, Administration
Coote, P., Company Manager, Burns Philp & Co.
Crocker, M.C., Agricultural Inspector, Administration
Cruise, J.B., Dispenser, Administration
Davies, R., X-ray Technician, Administration
Daymond, J.E., Assistant District Officer, Administration
Dockrill, W., Poultry Farmer
Dodd, H., Clerk, Custodian's Office
Doyle, H.G., Plantation Manager. Harry 'Tiki' Doyle, married, managed Selapiu Island Plantation in the Steffen Strait close to Kavieng, and was a member of the 'Saunders' escape party captured at sea by the Japanese shortly after the invasion of Kavieng, and then moved to the Rabaul internment camp.
Doyle, N., Manufacturer
Downs, J., Timber Worker
Drane, C.T., Manager, Vacuum Oil Company
Duus, W.L., Telephone Technician, PMG's Department
Earl, R.B., Planter
Edwards, J.H., Labour Overseer, Burns Philp & Co
Edwards, M.S., Murray, Patrol Officer, Administration. Murray Edwards, married, was in Kavieng at the time of the Japanese invasion and escaped to Kaut Harbour. There are conflicting stories about his death, including one that he was publicly executed by the Japanese in Kavieng. The official version is that he was transferred from Kavieng to the Rabaul internment camp, and was on the *Montevideo Maru*.
Eglinton, A.M., Storeman, Administration
Einsiedel, E.R., Clerk, Burns Philp & Co.
Evans, T.E., Medical Assistant, Administration
Field, C.R., Director of Public Works, Administration
Filan, S.H., Clerk, Administration
Florance, V.A., Solicitor
Forsyth, R.H., Clerk, Administration

Fulton, H., Clerk, Burns Philp & Co.
Garrett, T., Planter
Gascoigne, C.J., Auctioneer
Gascoigne, I.N., Clerk
GOAD, J.C., Medical Assistant, Administration. John Goad, married, was the senior medical assistant at Kavieng hospital and also owner of Kaut Plantation on the west coast of New Ireland at Kaut Harbour. He was probably a member of the unsuccessful Saunders escape party, and was later transferred to the Rabaul internment camp.
Gray, K.M., Medical Assistant, Administration
Green, A.S., Plantation Manager, Burns Philp & Co.
Green, E.C.D., Agricultural Superintendant, Administration
Greenwood, F.O., Planter
Greenwood, W., Plantation Manager, W.R. Carpenter & Co.
Gregory, H.A., District Officer, Administration
Hamilton, J.E., Store Manager, W.R. Carpenter & Co.
HAMILTON, L., Planter. Latham Hamilton owned Sumuna Plantation on Djaul Island, off the north-west coast of New Ireland. He may have been escaping from Kaut Harbour with 1 Independent Company when the *Induna Star* was captured at sea by the Japanese.
Hawnt, E.M., Telephone Foreman, Administration
HAY, DR A., Medical Officer, Administration. Dr. Arthur Hay, married, was the government medical officer in Kavieng.
Herket, T.H., Agricultural Inspector
Heron, W.L., Planter
Herron, A.G., Bank Official, Commonwealth Bank
Hogan, G., Crown Law Officer, Administration
Holden, H., Timber Worker
Holland, H.D., Manager, Amalgamated Wireless Australasia Ltd
Hoogerwweff, J., Manager, Rabaul Printing Works
Hosking, Dr H.C., Medical Officer, Administration
Houghton, C.W., Plantation Manager
JERVIS, C.C., Planter. Charles Jervis was a planter and coastwatcher on Nissan Island, in the Green Islands south-east of New Ireland.
KELLY, E.T.C., Agricultural Inspector, Administration. Edward Kelly was the government copra inspector in Kavieng. He was with other civilians from Kavieng at Kaut Harbour after the invasion, but remained on New Ireland.
King, A.J., Audit Clerk, Commonwealth Government

LIVINGSTONE, W.J., Police Officer, Administration. Police Seargeant Bill Livingstone, married, was the most senior policeman in Kavieng, and was present in the town on the night of the Japanese invasion. He may have been captured by the Japanese while attempting to escape from Kaut Harbour on the *Induna Star*.

Lockhart, J., Health Inspector, Administration

McCheane, G., Butcher, Rabaul Freezer

McDougall, D., Police Officer, Administration

McEvoy, J.T., Planter

MACKELLAR, C., Planter. Colin Mackellar was a married ex-serviceman who moved to New Ireland in the 1920s to work for the Expropriation Board, and later acquired Pigibut Plantation in the Tabar Islands group. He is believed to have been a member of the unsuccessful Saunders escape party, and was subsequently transferred from Kavieng to the Rabaul internment camp. In October 1944 Harry Spanner told Eric Feldt that Mackellar had been captured by the Japanese 'attempting to escape by launch'. Spanner also reported that Mackellar had subsequently been 'sent away on a ship which was sunk' (NAA B6121/3/98).

McLaren, T.W., Baker, Rabaul

Maclean, C.H.R., Manager, W.R. Carpenter & Co.

MACPHERSON, R., Accountant, FV Saunders. Roy Macpherson had worked as a school teacher in Kavieng before becoming an employee of Frank Saunders. He was apprehended at sea by the Japanese while attempting to escape with Saunders, and transferred to Rabaul shortly afterwards.

Mantle, F.W., District Officer, Administration

Mater, C.S.P., Clerk, Administration

Millington, B., Ship's Officer, W.R. Carpenter & Co.

Mitchell, E.H.F., Patrol Officer, Administration

Moore, R.K.P., Planter

Muggleton, H.A., Planter

Mulligan, E.W.C., Baker

Mulvey, N., Engineer, Administration

Murray, G.H., Director of Agriculture, Administration

Naulty, P.G., Police Officer, Administration

Nunan, A.C., Sawmiller, W.R. Carpenter & Co.

Oaten, F.E., Plantation Manager, Burns Philp & Co.

O'Dwyer, N., Planter

ORMOND, J.L., Plantation Manager, HL Cameron. James Ormond, married, was an elderly plantation manager on Djaul Island, off the north-west coast of New Ireland. He may have been escaping with 1 Independent Company from Kaut Harbour when the *Induna Star* was captured at sea by the Japanese.

Page, H.H., Government Secretary and Deputy Administrator, Administration

Parry, A.R., Senior Medical Assistant, Administration

Perrett, A., Mechanic, Administration

Pickering, M.B., Clerk, Administration

Pinching, E., Plantation Manager, W.R. Carpenter & Co.

Pines, C.M., Senior Medical Assistant, Administration. Cedric Pines was a senior medical assistant at the Taskul Leprosy Rehabilitation Centre on the east coast of New Hanover Island, and was a member of the unsuccessful Saunders escape party.

Plunkett, T.M., Telephone Technician, PMG's Dept

Raff, G.S., Bank Officer, Commonwealth Bank

RAND, D., Plantation Manager, Burns Philp & Co. Dixon Rand, married, was manager of Maritsoan Plantation near Namatanai on the south-east coast of New Ireland, and had earlier managed Kurumut Plantation.

Rankin, D.J., Storeman, Administration

Reed, A.R., Dairy Farmer

Renton, A., Plumber

Reynolds, J.A., Clerk, Administration

ROBERTS, D.L., Teacher, Administration. Dudley Roberts, married, was a teacher at Maiom Native School very close to Kavieng. He was a member of the unsuccessful Saunders escape party. In October 1944 Harry Spanner told Eric Feldt that Roberts had been captured by the Japanese 'and shot' (NAA B6121/3/98).

Robinson, H.E., Accountant, Administration

Robinson, W., Plantation Overseer

Ryan, W.J., Departmental Manager, Burns Philp & Co.

SAUNDERS, F.V., Planter and shipowner. Frank Saunders, married, was a wealthy planter, ship owner, and wharf operator in Kavieng. He arranged the attempted escape from Kavieng in five vessels shortly after the air raids, but was captured at sea and later transferred to the Rabaul internment camp. In October 1944 Harry Spanner told

Eric Feldt that Saunders had been captured by the Japanese 'and died after a flogging' (NAA B6121/3/98).

SAVAGE, S.K., Clerk, Administration. Stuart Savage, married, was a government clerk in the Kavieng district administration office. After the Japanese invasion he had escaped from Kavieng as far as Patlangat Plantation, but on 5 February 1942 decided to proceed no further.

SAWKINS, A., Plantation Manager, Burns Philp & Co. Alfred Sawkins, married, was the manager of Panapai Plantation near Kavieng, and a recent arrival from the United Kingdom at the time of the Japanese invasion. He was probably a member of the unsuccessful Saunders escape party.

SCHMIDT, A., Head Teacher, Administration

Scott, H., Plantation Manager, Roberts & Cooper

Sedgers, J.C., Plantation Inspector, W.R. Carpenter & Co.

Setchell, W.P., Plantation Manager, W.R. Carpenter & Co.

Shebler, A., Chemist

Smith, D. M.c.D., Foreman Carpenter, Administration

Smith, J.O., Overseer Native Labour, Administration

Smith, J., Postmaster, Administration

Snook, S., Police Officer, Administration

Solomon, E.E., Mechanic, Administration

Solomons, R.L., Clerk, Administration

Squires, R.T., Senior Medical Assistant, Administration

Staley, W.G., Road Overseer, Administration

Stephen, R.J., Departmental Manager, W.R. Carpenter & Co.

Stevens, R.H., Clerk, Administration

Stewart, J., Overseer, Administration

Strathearn, A.J., Clerk, Administration

Symes, H.H.C., Plantation Manager

Thomas, C., Police Officer, Administration

Thompson, L.C., Medical Assistant, Administration

Tichener, J., Agricultural Inspector, Administration

Townsend, H.O., Treasurer, Administration

Tritton, A.J., Bank Officer, Commonwealth Bank

Turnbull, H.F., Telephone Technician, PMG's Dept

Tynan, J., Merchant Seaman, Herstein

Voss, G.H.D., Teacher, Administration

Walker, T., Police Officer, Administration

Wallace, T.V., Journalist and Trader
Walsh, T.R., Telephone Techician, Administration
Washington, H.J., Planter
Wayne, R.N., Interpreter, Administration
Whiteman, A.K., Senior Clerk, Administration
WILKIN, W.M., Planter. William Wilkin, was a former district officer who owned Lungatan Plantation on New Hanover Island. He was probably a member of the unsuccessful Saunders escape party.
Wilmot, P., Plantation Manager, W.R. Carpenter & Co.
Youlden, R., Clerk, Administration

NOTE ON MORELL, J., who is not on the official *Montevideo Maru* list, but is believed to have been on board. Before the war John Morell, married, worked as a plantation manager on Djaul Island, off the north-west coast of New Ireland, directly south of Kaut Harbour. He enlisted in the Australian army for service in World War II, but was invalided out of service and returned to New Ireland. While escaping at the time of the Japanese invasion he joined the evacuating 1 Independent Company at Kaut Harbour and embarked on the *Induna Star*, and following its capture by the Japanese was transferred to the Rabaul internment camp.

NOTE ON SPENSLEY, W., who is also not on the official *Montevideo Maru* list, but is also believed to have been on board. William 'Bill' Spensely is the subject of a 2005 book entitled *He's Not Coming Home*, written by his daughter Gillian Nikakis. Spenseley was a senior manager in Rabaul for the New Zealand trading and shipping company Colyer Watson & Co., who in 1935 married 'Tick' Cox, a Rabaul nurse. Although Gillian Nikakis' book has few references to the expatriate community on New Ireland, it contains a wealth of detail about the pre-war life of the Australian islanders on New Britain, which is where Jack Griffin commenced his life in New Guinea.

2. New Guinea Missionaries Previously Reported Missing Now Reported Lost at Sea

Abbot, Pastor E.M., Seventh Day Adventist Mission
Alley, Rev D.C., Methodist Missionary Society of New Zealand

Beazley, Mr S.C., Methodist Missionary Society of Australasia

Brennan, Rev Brother C.A., Catholic Mission of the Most Sacred Heart of Jesus

COLLETT, MR TREVOR, Seventh Day Adventist Mission. Trevor Collett, married, operated the SDA sawmill on Emirau Island. He escaped with others from Emirau in a small boat at the time of the Japanese invasion, but was forced ashore on the east coast of New Britain and interned in Rabaul.

Hennessy, Rev Father J., Marist Mission Society

Linggood, Rev W.L.I., Methodist Missionary Society of Australasia

McArthur, Rev L.A., Methodist Missionary Society of Australasia

McCullagh, Rev Father D., Catholic Mission of the Most Sacred Heart of Jesus

OAKES, REV W.D., Methodist Missionary Society of Australasia. William Oakes was, with his wife, a missionary at Pinikindu Methodist Mission on the mid east coast of New Ireland, where he had worked since 1935, mainly improving the standard of public health.

Pearce, Mr E.W., Methodist Missionary Society of Australasia

Pearson, Rev H.J., Methodist Missionary Society of Australasia

Poole, Rev J.W., Methodist Missionary Society of Australasia

Shelton, Rev H.B., Methodist Missionary Society of Australasia

SIMPSON, REV T.N., Methodist Missionary Society of Australasia. Tom Simpson, married, arrived on New Ireland in 1936 and built the first Methodist mission on New Hanover Island, mainly to minister to leprosy patients, including the Anelaua Island leprosy colony. Tom Simpson is the subject of his daughter Margaret Henderson's 2000 book, *Yours Sincerely, Tom: A Lost Child of the Empire*.

Trevitt, Rev J.W., Methodist Missionary Society of Australasia

Endnotes

Prologue

1. In 1946 Eddie Ward was the Labor member for East Sydney in the Australian Federal Parliament, and also concurrently the Minister for Transport and the Minister for External Territories. For much of the Pacific war he had also been Minister for External Territories, with responsibility for New Guinea.
2. For a detailed account of the Brisbane Line controversy see Burns (1998).
3. The then Country Party federal Member for Richmond, northern New South Wales, and father of a future Deputy Prime Minister of Australia, John 'Doug' Anthony.
4. *Commonwealth of Australia Parliamentary Debates* 10 Geo VI, Vol. 187.
5. The July 1946 edition of *Pacific Islands Monthly* carried an extensive report of the parliamentary debate of 27–28 June 1946, with pointed inferences about Eddie Ward's performance.

Chapter 1

1. The eighteenth century saw most of the south-west Pacific explored and mapped by the English navigators Dampier, Carteret, Wallis and Cook, and their French rival Bougainville.
2. At the same time as Carteret and HMS *Swallow* were in the New Britain area, the great French navigator Louis-Antoine de Bougainville in the fast frigate *La Boudeuse* was naming and charting some of the Solomon Islands immediately to the south. On their return journey to Europe, Bougainville followed in Carteret's wake to the Atlantic, overtook him, and arrived back in France while Carteret was still slowly sailing back to England.
3. Since the seventeenth century ownership of the large island of Papua had been contested by a number of colonial powers including Holland, Germany, Great Britain and Australia, Japan and Indonesia, and this has resulted in a number of different names being given to its various parts. The western half has been

variously named New Holland, Hollandia, Irian Jaya, West Papua and Papua. Parts of the eastern half have been named New Guinea and Papua.

4 Billy Hughes had argued vociferously at the Paris conference in 1919 for New Guinea to be ceded to Australian control. Although eventually successful, he was strongly opposed by the US government, which wanted New Guinea to be ceded to Japan.

5 It was a common practice for Burns Philp & Co. and W.R. Carpenter & Co. to use ex-servicemen as 'dummy' buyers of low-cost but highly valuable expropriated property, which could end up being legally owned by the companies after a few years. Burns Philp and Carpenter's secretly funded many ex-servicemen for the purchase of plantations, and many ex-servicemen who were managers of company plantations were in fact the original legal owners.

6 About 85 to 380 hectares.

7 The most commonly recurring tropical diseases were malaria and skin complaints.

8 There were small Overseas Chinese communities throughout the islands of New Guinea and in the Solomon Islands. China was attacked and invaded by Japan in 1937, and after 1941 became a major partner of the US-led allies in the war against Japan. Because of this Overseas Chinese became particular targets for Japanese repression.

9 Impressions and descriptions of life in pre-war Kavieng in this chapter have been drawn from a number of sources, particularly Mary Murray (1965 and 1967), Margaret Reeson (2000), Gillian Nikakis (2005), the private correspondence of Jack Griffin, from Jim Ridges' historical notes, and from Paul Hasluck (1962).

10 The Caroline Islands were another former German colonial possession which the Treaty of Versailles had ceded to Japan in 1921, Japan having been on the side of the victorious Allies during the First World War.

Chapter 2

1 More details about Francis 'Frank' Falkiner and his family's pioneering grazing activities in western New South Wales can be found in Falkiner (1981).

2 Some of these nineteenth century hardbound editions are still preserved by various members of the Griffin family, including the author, who also enjoyed them as a child.

3 Information about Jack Griffin's career with the Bank of NSW between April 1927 and November 1939 comes from archival materials provided by the Westpac Banking Corporation in a letter to the author dated 28 August 2000.

4 Original held by the author.

5 The people in China for whom the funds were being raised were refugees from a particularly vicious war which had been instigated by the 1937 invasion of eastern China by Japan.

6 Original held by the author.

7. Information about Jack Griffin's career with Burns Philp & Co. Ltd. between 1939 and 1942 comes from company archival materials provided to the author in October 1994.
8. Original held by the author.
9. Interviewed in August 2006, Mrs Gwen Diercke, the widow of Vivian Ives, manager of Burns Philp's Kurumut Plantation, remembered 'Peter' Griffin as a frequent visitor to Kurumut, who nearly always walked to the plantation, usually accompanied by his companionable German Shepherd dog.

Chapter 3

1. There are numerous accounts of Australia's indecisiveness regarding the Japanese threat and the 1941 deployment of piecemeal forces to eastern New Guinea. See Aplin, Hasluck, Long, McNab and Reeson, among others.
2. Just twenty 1 Independent Company troops under a lieutenant were stationed on Buka Island to 'defend' the newly-constructed airfield.
3. Original held by the author.
4. The secret abandoning of eastern New Guinea immediately prior to the Japanese invasion is well documented. The Australian Government decided that the military units deployed in 1941 'must be regarded as hostages to fortune; they will not be reinforced, withdrawn or re-equipped'. (See Stone 1995, Nikakis 2005, and also the memoir of David Smith, a lieutenant in 2/22 Battalion at *Lost Lives* website.)
5. The Tol and Waitavalo mass murders were carried out under the orders of Colonel Masao Kusunose of the 3rd Battalion of the 144th Infantry Regiment of the Imperial Japanese Army. The postwar whereabouts of Colonel Kusunose was eventually established by Australian investigators in December 1946, when it was discovered that he had recently committed suicide by starving himself to death with a nine-day fast.
6. For a full account of the collapse of resistance in Ambon and imprisonment of 'Gull Force', see Beaumont (1988) and Harrison (1988).
7. For a full account of 'Sparrow Force' see Henning (1995).
8. See Hank Nelson (1985)

Chapter 4

1. For more detailed accounts of the evacuations see Reeson (2000) and also the PNG Association at <http://www.pngaa.net/Articles/articles_JohnsonH_Xmas_2001.htm>, particularly the reminiscences of Patricia Murray, who was one of the evacuees from Namatanai.
2. According to Fuchida (1951) who was there on the day, the Japanese air attacks on Rabaul and Kavieng on 21 January 1942 were conducted using aircraft from *Akagi* and *Soryu*, two of Vice Admiral Nagumo's four carriers. Aircraft from the

two other carriers in 'Nagumo Force', *Zuikaku* and *Sokaku*, attacked the airfields at Lae and Salamaua on the same day. The following month this carrier force conducted the first raids on Port Darwin in northern Australia.
3 See Mary Murray (1965).
4 See Alexander McNab (1998).

Chapter 5

1 There is a very small number of published accounts of such attempted escapes. Parkin (1960) describes an unsuccessful attempt to sail a jury-rigged lifeboat from the Sunda Straits in Indonesia to Australia after the sinking of HMAS *Perth* in early 1942. Harrison (1988) and Beaumont (1988) both describe successful ocean escapes to northern Australia from Ambon in 1942 of survivors of 2/21 Battalion AIF. Klestadt (1959) describes his successful escape from the southern Philippines to Arnhem Land later that year.
2 Frank Saunders had been head of the Expropriation Board on new Ireland, and ended up owning six of the plantations put up for auction by that organisation. He later owned various businesses in Kavieng including a wharf and coastal vessels.
3 See Annex B.
4 See Mary Murray (1965)
5 This account of the Chambers escape from Emirau has been related by Hasluck (1962) and Feldt (1975). Jim Ridges believes the story has been confused with the Atkins-Cook-Collet escape made from Mussau Island at the same time, and this is quite conceivably the case.
6 Pastor Atkins died of disease on 13 March 1942 at Vunapope Catholic Mission on New Britain.
7 Trevor Collett died on 1 July 1942 on the *Montevideo Maru*.
8 See Jim Ridges (2002), and endnote 3 above.
9 Lieutenant A.F. Kyle, DSC, RAN; Sub-Lieutenant G.M. Benham, DSC, RAN. Alan Kyle had served as a sapper in 1916 and 1917 in the 4th Australian Division. Immediately before the war the Australian navy had established a network of 'coastwatchers' throughout the islands of eastern New Guinea and the Solomons. When war broke out this secret network was expanded and strengthened and provided valuable early warnings of subsequent Japanese military activities. See Feldt (1946).
10 This story comes from various sources, including Murray (1965) and Hasluck (1962).
11 Murray and McDonald were interviewed at length after their arrival, and provided the first comprehensive account of the fall of New Ireland and a list of 25 Australian males they knew had been trapped and believed to 'still remain on their plantations without guards and apparently very little interference from the Japanese', including 'P. Griffin'. See AWM, '*New Ireland–interview with evacuees…*'.

12 Mary Murray (1965) provides a detailed account of the Murray-McDonald escape, related to her by Harry Murray.
13 Sub-Lieutenant C.L. Page, MID, RAN.
14 Jack Talmage was an elderly ex-soldier who supported Con Page in his secret coastwatching activities, but who was not commissioned into the navy as Page had been.
15 Of this group, Harry Murray escaped to Australia. Bill Livingstone was interned, sent to Rabaul, and died on the *Montevideo Maru*. Murray Edwards is also believed to have drowned on that ship, although there are conflicting reports about this. Major Wilson was imprisoned in Rabaul with other POWs, and later sent to Japan with the remaining officers of 2/22 Battalion.
16 The account on these pages of Jack Griffin's escape from Kavieng is reconstructed from numerous separate references to it in Murray (1965), from Jack's own correspondence, and from Jim Ridges' notes. In Murray's account, Jack is always referred to as 'Peter'.
17 Leon Williams was caught by the Japanese on the east coast in about June 1942 and imprisoned at Pinikidu Methodist Mission, and two months later was transferred to Kavieng.
18 John Bell's sons were Donald (drowned on the *Montevideo Maru*), Les, Stan and Lincoln. Stan and Lincoln were both coastwatchers, Lincoln being killed as a result of his coastwatching activities (see references to Sub-Lieutenant S.G.V. Bell and Lieutenant L.J. Bell in Feldt, 1946). Les survived the war.
19 After the war Claude Chadderton's daughter was told by The Woo You, a local Overseas Chinese, that Claude had been caught by the Japanese in the bush on the Lelet Plateau, after they had tracked him 'using dogs'.
20 For further personal details of these men, see Annex A.
21 Drowned on the *Montevideo Maru*, 1 July 1942 (Ridges, 2002)
22 It is not known how Stan Ashby ended up interned in Rabaul, but he is also listed amongst those drowned on the *Montevideo Maru*, 1 July 1942. Ashby was owner of Kanam Plantation, and had also managed Maramakas Plantation for another well-known New Ireland planter, Alf Lussick (see Annex B).
23 Ibid.
24 Dorothy Maye was later sent to Japan and was one of the few Australian prisoners from New Ireland to eventually survive the war.
25 Japanese civil administration of southern New Ireland from Namatanai was established in May 1942.
26 Original held by the author.
27 The envelope which contained Jack Griffin's last letter from New Ireland is in the author's possession. He had typewritten Alison Griffin's office address on the front, and the back is marked in pencil, presumably in Harry Murray's handwriting, 'H.J. Murray, Room 431, Hotel Sydney'.
28 Murray's Silver Star citation reads: 'For conspicuous gallantry and intrepidity during operations against the enemy. By his grim determination, brilliant leadership and daring aggressiveness, Captain Murray overcame almost insurmountable difficulties and contributed materially to our operations in the South Pacific Area'.

Chapter 6

1. Harry Murray carried copies of these proclamations with him during his escape. Written in good English, presumably long before the invasion of New Ireland, they provide very detailed instructions from the Japanese to citizens of the island. See AWM *'New Ireland–interview with evacuees…'*.
2. Phil Levy was caught by the Japanese in June 1942 on the east coast of New Ireland and imprisoned for two months at the Methodist Mission at Pinikidu, before being transferred to Kavieng.
3. We know that Jack was ordered to Bopire Plantation in July 1942 because this information appears in a 1951 statutory declaration by Rudolph Carl Diercke, who was at the time managing Komalu Plantation, about 20 kilometres down the coast from Kalili Plantation to which Jack had fled in February. In a signed 6-page Statutory Declaration at Rabaul dated 26 February 1951, Diercke stated: 'At that time I was working on the Komalu Plantation and was occupying the plantation house with my grandmother Mrs. Phebe Parkinson, who was aged 78. Mr. Ives of Kurumut was also putting up with me at the time and the Japanese permitted us to remain on in the guard of 3 Japanese stationed at the Mission House about 400 yards from my bungalow. Mr. Ives was permitted to stay on with me till he was ordered to shift to Bopiri with Mr. Peter Griffin in July 1942.' Rudolph Diercke provided the statutory declaration in connection with an investigation of the crash of a USAAF B-17 on Komalu reef in May 1943. A further reference to Mr Diercke appears in Chapter 16. This information is provided by Jim Ridges.
4. There are numerous sources which describe the Japanese navy's failure at Pearl Harbor. Hoyt (1986) provides a very detailed account of Admiral Yamamoto's private reaction to Vice Admiral Nagumo's timidity. See also Macksey (1998).
5. A number of good sources are available describing Allied successes in breaking Japanese naval and diplomatic codes before and during the Pacific war. See especially Rusbridger et al. (1991), Smith (2000) and Stripp (1989). The fact that the Allies were so successful at this has raised many questions about their possible secret knowledge of the disposition of allied POWs and internees, and suspicions that far more may have been known about the location, movements and eventual disposal of the Kavieng and *Akikaze* internees, who were the subject of signals by the Japanese navy. However, codebreaking secrets were tightly protected by the Allies during the war and for years afterwards, and it is unlikely if such suspicions can ever be confirmed.
6. An interesting first-person description of the Doolittle Raid originally written in 1943 is provided by one of the pilots, Ted Lawson (2004), who describes the preparations, raid, his crash landing in China, rescue by Chinese civilians and amputation of a leg, his eventual evacuation to the United States, and an account of reprisals against Chinese civilians by the Japanese.
7. See Millot (1974) and Hoyt (1986), among numerous other accounts of the Coral Sea battle.

8   An interesting first-person account of Midway is that provided by Fuchida et al. (2002). This includes Fuchida's own observations about the timidity of Vice Admiral Nagumo.
9   There are numerous sources dealing with the *Montevideo Maru* tragedy, including Aplin, Hasluck, Reeson, and a complete website containing numerous original sources, <www.montevideomaru.info/Montevideo/htm/Montevideo%20Maru.htm>, maintained by Rod Miller.
10 There is a report that when the planters began to be rounded up in mid-1942, at least some of them may have tried to hide in the mountainous interior of New Ireland. Claude Chadderton's daughter Moya, who unsuccessfully searched for him after the war, was told that he had hidden on the Lelet Plateau, and was eventually tracked down by Japanese using dogs.
11 The abbreviation Kenpeitai is derived from *Nihon Kenpei Seishi*, and is frequently also spelt as *Kenpetai*, *Kempeitai* or *Kempetai* in source materials used to research this book.
12 Among the many first-person accounts of Kenpeitai treatment of prisoners, that of an Australian army lieutenant, Penrod Dean (1998), provides detailed descriptions of his torture by Kenpeitai officers in Singapore (and his two years in Outram Road Gaol). See also the first-person account of Eric Lomax (1996), who attempted to escape from the Burma railway, was caught by the Kenpeitai, and also ended up in Outram Road Gaol.
13 In NAA B6121/3/98 *An Intelligence Report on New Ireland*, Lt. J. Mollison RAN describes how when Australians first arrived at Kavieng in October 1945 to assume control of administration, because of the presence of large numbers of Japanese still in the area the natives were reluctant to speak openly to Australian officers, 'and had considerable difficulty in not using common Japanese expressions during conversations'. Mollison observed that even with the war over and hostilities ceased, 'it was noticed that when staff cars carrying [Japanese] officers passed along a road, all native men, women, and children would stop and bow from the waist'.
14 See Feldt (1946).
15 There were a number of postwar reports of these executions. See accounts in Chapter 16.
16 The wartime experiences of the nuns were obtained in 1945 by the first Australians to return to New Ireland. The only written account possessed by the author is that described in November 1948 to an investigating officer, Lieutenant W.A. Doddridge, by the elderly Sister M. Brigitta of the Sacred Heart Mission. See AWM, *Statement by Rev. Sister M. Brigitta*. Jim Ridges has provided a number of corrections to this account.
17 Popularly known as the Sacred Heart Mission, and founded in France in the nineteenth century by Jules Chevalier, the mission had been active in the Pacific islands since the early twentieth century.
18 Interviewed in September 1946, local eyewitness Anton de Silva confirmed that the Kulangit camp comprised three houses. NAA MP375/14 WC43.
19 Information about the exact geographical location of the two camps comes from Jim Ridges. However, postwar documentary and witness reports frequently confuse

the two locations, often placing the Australians at Panapai and missionaries at Kulangit.
20   There are numerous brief postwar eyewitness accounts of the September 1942 internment of the Australians at Kulangit; see Chapter 16. Sister M. Brigitta claimed that this was on 7 August 1942. Part of the confusion appears to have been caused by the temporary indecisiveness of the Japanese, who initially interned all the civilians at Panapai Plantation in August, then released them after a week with the requirement that they each report to the Japanese authorities every month, but then a few weeks later arranged for their permanent internment.
21   This service may have been with the Kavieng Volunteer Rifles.
22   ibid.
23   Information about Henry Topal's visit to Kavieng in 1917 comes from Ridges (2002).
24   Lightbody's burial service at Lemakot was conducted by Father Peekel of the Lemakot Mission, and four of the internees were permitted to attend. Of these Father Peekel identified Ray Heming but did not know the other three. Quite possibly they were Lightbody's three other close Burns Philp colleagues, Phil Levy, Lon Williams and Jack Griffin.

Chapter 7

1   The Japanese Prisoner of War Information Bureau (PWIB) was later described by Major H.S. Williams as 'a Bureau for the dissemination of false information'.
2   Conflicting versions exist about Warrant Officer Funayama's duration of duty as supervisor of the internees. Tomoichi Iwaoka testified that Funayama had ceased these duties in December 1943, but at the trial in 1947 Ensign Shozo Suzuki testified that Funayama was still in charge in March 1944. What is definitely known is that Funayama committed suicide in Kavieng in March or April 1944, allegedly because he had been accused of minor corruption.
3   NAA MP742/1/336/1/1444. Iwaoka was interrogated by Albert Klestadt in Tokyo on 19 August 1947 and provided a statement in which he described his duties at Kulangit, his relationships with the Australians, and the state of their health and general wellbeing at the time he last saw them in December 1943. Interestingly, in this statement he says, 'I also remember Mr. Naughton. I believe he was a plantation manager, and was about 60 years of age. He occupied the position of camp leader and I spoke with him frequently on camp matters'. In fact, Jim Naughton was in his thirties, and was a plantation mechanic. Iwaoka may have confused him with Albert Moseley, who was aged 60, was a plantation manager, and was most likely prominent in camp leadership.
4   See note 2 above.
5   There are numerous accounts available describing the brutal hierarchy and unconditional obedience in the Imperial Japanese Navy. These were discussed at length during the Kavieng trial in 1947 by the six Japanese officers involved (see Chapters 23 and 24).

Endnotes

6 The suicidal behaviours of Japanese soldiers and sailors have been widely discussed and analysed since 1945. In particular see Gilmore (1998) and Hoyt (2001).

7 Not much appears to be known about the social impact of such a large number of young Japanese males on the local female population of New Ireland. At Rabaul, local Chinese women and girls were initially used as 'comfort women' until their numbers were supplemented by Koreans and young women kidnapped from other places in Asia. Hicks (1994) says that the Japanese were normally averse to Melanesian women because of their 'smell' and fear of contagious skin diseases.

8 It appears that help was provided to the internees from time to time by some Melanesian Christian church workers, by some local Overseas Chinese, and by some local people of mixed race. Melanesian sanitary workers were also permitted to enter the camp to collect nightsoil. Through these visitors the internees were able to maintain limited contact with the outside world, although at no small risk to the visitors.

9 Since 1945, thousands of accounts have been published describing living conditions in the POW and civilian internment camps. Just as a small selection, for general descriptions see Beaumont (1988), Nelson (1985) and McKernan (2001). For first-person accounts see Braddon (1952), Bradley (1984), Dean (1998), Lomax (1996) and Wright-Nooth (1994).

10 Although there is no direct evidence, and because of the overwhelming importance to the Japanese of maintaining food supply, the author has assumed that this must have occurred. Given the high mortality rates in other camps in the Asia-Pacific area where occupants were mainly dependent on the Japanese for food, it is highly unlikely that so many of the Kavieng internees would have survived for so long had they not been useful themselves as food-producers.

11 In her analysis of survival rates at the Sandakan POW camps in British North Borneo, Silver (1998) determined that, in general, Australian POWs from a rural background had been more likely to survive for longer than those originating from urban areas.

12 These rituals and abuses were commonly practised by the Japanese in POW and civilian camps throughout the occupied territories and are well documented. I have assumed that the Kavieng camp was no different.

13 The bacteria, viruses and parasites referred to were present in Kavieng before the war, but the pre-war European population had access to some kinds of preventive medicine, and certainly used physical protection, mainly mosquito netting. Ironically, the Pacific war was to produce huge advances in tropical medicine for the Allies, particularly the prevention and cure of malaria, but these new drugs were not available to either the Japanese or internees.

14 In his statement contained in NAA MP742/1/336/1/1444, Iwaoka told Albert Klestadt that 'I saw the Australian internees for the last time in December 1943. All 23 or 24 appeared to be quite well then, and I heard that the German missionaries were also all quite well in their separate internment camp'.

15 In statements tendered to the trial in 1947, and when Japanese defendants familiar with the internment camp were repeatedly questioned on this point by

the prosecutor, all stated that the internees were well behaved and were never a cause for Japanese concern.
16 The *Akikaze* massacre became the subject of a war crimes investigation from 1945. See NAA MP742/1/336/1/1444, also later chapters of this book, and also Tanaka (1996).

Chapter 8

1 Much of the material in this and subsequent chapters describing the history of Allied strategy in the south-west Pacific, key decisions made, and the early targeting of Kavieng, comes from two official American histories, those of Miller (1959), a history of US army operations, and Morison (1950), a history of US naval operations.
2 This coastwatcher was Captain Martin Clemens, and the airfield he observed under construction was subsequently captured by US forces and named 'Henderson Field' after Loftus Henderson, a US aviator killed during the Battle for Midway.
3 The actual cost of Guadalcanal in lives lost was about 1600 Americans, but the Japanese lost nearly 15 000 killed, and 9000 died as a result of disease. See Miller (1959).
4 ibid.
5 Throughout the war Japanese leaders were fond of using the figure of 'one hundred million', even though the population was actually about 75 million.
6 Hoyt (1986) provides from original sources some very detailed descriptions of the Japanese government's suicidal intentions for its population after 1943.
7 Much fragmentary evidence exists regarding these orders, and it certainly appears that from 1943 local-area Japanese commanders throughout the Asia-Pacific area were given the clear impression there was an expectation that POWs and civilian internees in their control should be exterminated should the military situation deteriorate. The frequency of these orders increased as the war progressed. See, for example, Silver (1998), pages 181 and 218.
8 The Australian government's abandoning of eastern New Guinea in 1941 was replicated just a few years later by the Japanese, with numerous Japanese garrisons themselves becoming 'hostages to fortune'.
9 See Miller (1959).

Chapter 9

1 See Morison (1950).
2 See *Chronology of USAAF Operations in World War II*.
3 These attacks on the *Kokai Maru* and *Kowa Maru*, and on the *Naguara*, were later examined in great detail by 2 Australian War Crimes Section in Tokyo (see later chapters).
4 See *Chronology of US Naval Operations in World War II*.

5   One American Catalina pilot, Nathan Gordon, later received the Congressional Medal of Honor for having, during a single flight in February 1944, made four separate ocean rescues of downed bomber crews, all under the guns of the Kavieng Japanese.
6   Jim Ridges believes that by this time the missionaries had also been moved into the Kulangit camp with the Australians. The close proximity of the Panapai camp to the nearby Japanese Number 2 airfield may have made it untenable as a camp for 'Neutral European Aliens'.

Chapter 10

1   The events described in this chapter are reconstructed from material later provided in 1947 by the Japanese officers to 2 Australian War Crimes Section in Tokyo, as a result of their re-interrogations, and is contained in the many sworn affidavits eventually extracted from them.
2   Information about Tamura's career in the Imperial Japanese Navy comes from the website *Imperial Japanese Navy*, maintained by Hiroshi Nishida, which contains chronologies of the careers of many senior IJN officers.
3   The dates of the first key meetings between Yoshino and Tamura about the internees were revealed during the trial. See NAA B4175/0/13, *Proceedings of a Military Court*.
4   The exact date of Tamura's verbal order was not revealed until December 1947 in his testimony to the Australian Military Court in Hong Kong. Even after the Japanese had earlier begun telling the truth about the murders, a great deal of vagueness surrounded the exact day on which Tamura had given the execution order to Yoshino, and the exact time Yoshino relayed it to Mori.
5   Hoyt (1986) describes the origins of all of these suicidal behaviours in great detail.

Chapter 11

1   Events in this chapter regarding US decision-making, and the bypass debate, are again taken from Miller (1959) and Morison (1950).
2   The endless acrimonious debates and rivalry between senior officers of the US Army and US Navy over the direction of the south-west Pacific campaigns was an expression of a general rivalry between the two arms. However, unlike in the European theatre of operations in World War II, the army and navy were forced to work closely together throughout the Pacific campaign, thus exacerbating the problem. The Imperial Japanese Army and Imperial Japanese Navy suffered from a similar inter-service rivalry.
3   Locked up in the camp at Kavieng, Jack Griffin could not have possibly even dreamed that a namesake was an admiral of the US navy, and that another Griffin was about to lead a naval action at Kavieng which would ultimately lead to his death.

4   The old US battleships sunk at their Pearl Harbor moorings by the Japanese in December 1941 were all of the same First World War vintage, and their loss was in fact not such a great blow to the Americans as the Japanese imagined.
5   Detailed descriptions and battle histories of each of the main American ships which participated in the Kavieng action were obtained from the US Navy Historical Centre.
6   This description of the bombardment of Kavieng is largely drawn from a detailed account in the US Navy Historical Center's battle history of BB43 USS *Tennessee*.
7   Morison (1950) provides the exact numbers–1079 14-inch shells and 12 281 5-inch shells–and adds that according to the Allied Translator and Interpreter Service (ATIS), which presumably had been eavesdropping for Japanese radio reaction, the Kavieng garrison was 'demoralized' by the attack.
8   Ironically, Fuchida (1951), who led the Japanese air raids on Kavieng in January 1942, wrote that in his view the use by Admiral Nagumo of all aircraft from two of his carriers to attack Kavieng and Rabaul at that time was wasteful and extravagant: 'If ever a sledgehammer had been used to crack an egg, this was the time'.

Chapter 12

1   From the evidence which came out at the trial, it is not clear exactly when Mori first began discussing the killing of the Europeans with his subordinates. However, it is safe to assume that this had become a hot topic of discussion among the sailors long before mid-March 1944. Through the gossip grapevine, the non-commissioned officers and sailors would have been well aware of what had happened to Japanese defending other places invaded by the Americans, and would by now have been aware that it would be extremely difficult to escape from New Ireland alive. After the heavy American raids began in February, the attention of the lower ranks would have automatically been drawn to the Europeans, but mainly as objects for angry reprisal, not for the reason of 'military necessity' provided by Tamura. During the trial Tamura was asked why he had not simply released the internees when it had become apparent that their continued presence in the camp was an embarrassment. The very first reason he gave for not releasing them was that 'his men would not have been happy with that solution'.
2   These discussions were eventually reported to 2 Australian War Crimes Section in 1947, and are contained in the sworn affidavits.
3   According to Jim Ridges, there were up to five wharves at Kavieng during the Japanese occupation. The northernmost was the privately-owned Saunder's Wharf. Two hundred metres south was a disintegrating breakwater, and 300 metres south of this was the central or government wharf, which the Japanese called 'Kavieng Central Wharf'. Another 300 metres south was the hospital wharf, and 300 metres south of this was the main and largest wharf in Kavieng. This southernmost wharf was called 'Kavieng South Wharf' by the Japanese.

4   The times of all meetings and actions on the day of the murders were established during various cross examinations at the trial. See NAA B4175/0/13, *Proceedings of a Military Court.*
5   The passing of responsibility for carrying out the murders all the way down the chain of command of commissioned officers was typical of the Imperial Japanese Navy when atrocities were being actioned. The long relay of the order from Captain Tamura to Commander Yoshino, then to Lieutenant Mori and on to Lieutenant Ichinose, then to Sub-Lieutenant Mochizuki and finally, to Ensign Suzuki, the most junior of all, was peculiarly elaborate.
6   See cross examination of Suzuki in NAA B4175/0/13, *Proceedings of a Military Court.*
7   During the trial Suzuki described his final visit to the camp, and the methods he used to get the internees to move quickly to the trucks. NAA B4175/0/13, *Proceedings of a Military Court.*

Chapter 13

1   Events described in this chapter are reconstructed from information contained in Affidavits of Evidence prepared for the trial, and from the trial proceedings.
2   The roster of crews for Numbers 1 and 2 Barges on 20 March 1944 eventually became of intense interest to 2 Australian War Crimes Section in 1947, and I have deliberately included the names of the crew members because of this.
3   This incident came out during the trial and was related to the author in 2000 by Albert Klestadt.
4   The washing down of at least one of the barges was described by barge crewmen in their affidavits.

Chapter 14

1   In September 1946 de Silva was interviewed by Patrol Officer K.W. Jones as part of the still-ongoing investigation. He reported that the morning after the US naval bombardment he went to the Australian internment camp to discover that it was deserted. NAA MP375/14 WC43.
2   The existence of this bloodstain was interpreted by investigators to mean that force may have been used by the Japanese to remove at least some of the Australians from the camp. Although that is possible, it is also possible that with so much shrapnel flying about during the naval shelling one or more of the internees had been wounded.
3   The description of Yoshino's trip to Namatanai was provided in elaborate detail by him when he started telling the truth to Albert Klestadt in 1947, presumably as an attempt to create an alibi for himself.
4   Hirohito's pre-recorded radio broadcast was an unprecedented experience for his subjects, who had never before even heard his voice.

5   Tamura's surrender was taken on the beach at Fangelawa Bay because it had been discovered that the sea approaches to Kavieng still contained many Japanese and American anti-shipping mines (see Murray, 1967).

6   In the understandable confusion immediately following Hirohito's entirely unexpected broadcast, it took some time for Japanese officers in isolated areas to fully comprehend they had lost the war. Much discussion and radio-signalling occurred to obtain confirmation, and in the meantime wholesale destruction of military materials occurred to prevent their 'capture by the enemy'.

7   This account of Yoshino's journey to Rabaul was provided by him in 1947 to Albert Klestadt. In his account, and at the trial, he attempted to characterise Captain Sanagi as the initiator of the cover-up, and that he, Yoshino, had been ordered to participate in it.

8   An account of the Allied bombing of the POW camp at Ambon is contained in Beaumont (1988), and of many camps in British North Borneo in Silver (1998).

9   Shortly after this attack *Tang* was sunk by one of its own torpedoes.

10 The *Rokyu Maru* sinking is an interesting story, but far too long to relate here. Another of the author's uncles, then Sergeant Ross Dunbar of 2/15 Field Regiment AIF, was on the ship, and after spending two days abandoned in the sea by his Japanese guards was recaptured with many of his POW companions by a Japanese destroyer. They all ended up working as slaves in the dangerous coalmines of Japan. However, a number of the POWs from *Rokyu Maru* were picked up by the American submarines and eventually returned to Australia, where they were able to report the vile conditions in the POW camps (see McKernan, 2001 for a detailed account of this incident).

11 A very detail account of scores of US friendly-fire incidents during World War II can be found at the Friendly Fire website, <http://www.ww2pacific.com/friendly.html>.

12 In late 1945 Japan was required to provide a detailed list showing what had happened to hundreds of POWs and civilian internees who had been in the care of the Japanese Navy during the war. This list was eventually produced (see NAA MP375/14 WC43, *The List of Prisoners of War and Civilian Internees Under the Protection and Care of the Imperial Japanese Navy*) and quite unselfconsciously includes the falsehood that 116 US servicemen and Australian civilians from Rabaul were 'sent by *Kokai Maru* on February 20 1944', with a footnote that after the ship was attacked 'a few passengers were rescued by our side and the rest are presumed to have died'. The list does not include the names of the Kavieng internees, nor is the *Kowa Maru* mentioned.

13 For detailed accounts of the many deceitful methods used by the Japanese to lure Asian women into becoming 'comfort women', see Hicks (1994).

14 Hoyt (1986) provides numerous details from original Japanese sources of the official self-deception increasingly practised, particularly during the desperate years from 1943.

15 See Hoyt (1986).

16 An extremely detailed and scholarly account of the activities of FELO and PWB appears in Gilmore (1998).

17 The well-known saying, 'Truth is the first casualty of war', is ascribed to Benito Mussolini.

Chapter 15

1. Detailed accounts of the management of information about Australian prisoners by the Australian government are in McKernan (2001).
2. This included Overseas Chinese.
3. Background information in this chapter about the *Australian War Crimes Act* and statistical information about Australian war crimes trials mainly comes from Sissons (1997).
4. This was related to the author by Albert Klestadt in 2000.
5. In later chapters it will be seen how rumour and gossip seriously impeded investigation of the Kavieng massacre.
6. See Gilmore (1998).
7. A very detailed account of Hirohito's 'public conversion' is in Dower (1999).
8. Many accounts are available describing the gradual loss of interest by the United States in continuing the pursuit of war criminals. See Dower (1999), Hoyt (1986) and Ward (1996).

Chapter 16

1. The *Pacific Islands Monthly* was so authoritative it was popularly known as the 'planters' bible'.
2. *Pacific Islands Monthly*, Volume XVI, No. 2, September 1945
3. After the war Williams would move with his family back to Japan, successfully re-establish his business, and continue his avid collecting of Japanese artefacts.
4. See Annex B for the names of all New Guinea civilians believed in 1945 by the Department of External Territories to have been on the ship. This list is based on the nominal roll prepared by the Japanese army in Rabaul before handing over the POWs and civilian internees to the Japanese navy for transhipment to Hainan on the *Montevideo Maru*.
5. See AWM 54, 417/1/4. There are good accounts of Williams' *Montevideo Maru* investigation in Reeson (2000) and at Rod Miller's *Montevideo Maru* website.
6. *Pacific Islands Monthly*, Volume XVII, No. 1, January 1946
7. Accounts of the interviews with Hermann, Lundin and Diercke appear in Department of External Territories reports (NAA MP742/1 File 336/1/1601). An impression is given that these men were embarrassed by their lucky survival, and annoyed by suspicions that they might have cooperated with the Japanese to obtain it.
8. Rudolp Diercke was at Komalu Plantation on the west coast when Jack Griffin was, in July 1942, ordered by the Japanese to Bopire Plantation on the east coast, one of the first steps towards his eventual permanent internment in Kavieng.
9. Harry Murray was at the forefront of these grave searches (see Murray 1967).
10. NAA MP742/1 File No. 336/1/1601. The use of an interpreter by Havilland would have again made it much easier for Tamura to be evasive in answering these questions. Neither Havilland nor his interpreter, Tom Hi-oma Amaki, appear to have had any suspicions whatsoever that the courteous Tamura was thoroughly fooling them.

11 NAA B6121/3/98, *H.P. Spanner: escapee from Kavieng*. Harry Spanner provided Eric Feldt with a lot of quite amazing information about 22 Australian civilians who had been stranded on New Ireland, including eight of the internees. In some instances his information later turned out to be incorrect (for example, he reported that Sister Dorothy Maye had been shot when she in fact survived the war), but with the test of time most of what Spanner reported turned out to be true.
12 NAA B6121/3/98, *An Intelligence Report on New Ireland*.

Chapter 17

1 The account of Klestadt's life to 1945 in this chapter is largely a summary of his 1959 book *The Sea Was Kind*, to which has been added considerable detail provided by him in 2000 and 2005.
2 Klestadt was a very short and slight man, by any standards.
3 After the confiscation by the Nazi government of his business and property and the failure of his marriage, Klestadt's father emigrated from Germany to America, and his sons lost contact with him.
4 By his own admission, as a sailing master Klestadt was in nearly the same league as Captain Bligh, and he insisted on the highest standards of behaviour and hygiene during the voyage from the Philippines. To his much more casual Moro crewmen, Klestadt's behaviour was inexplicable and irritating, to the extent they seriously considered doing away with him and returning to the Philippines.
5 The broad outline of Klestadt's Australian army record comes from the AWM collections database, including three 1945 photographs.
6 When the author first met him in 2000, Klestadt was very self-effacing about his work with FELO.
7 Eric Klestadt later settled in Australia and became an academic and historian.
8 Although there was an apparently long-established relationship between Harold Williams and Klestadt which had commenced in Kobe in the 1930s, and although Williams' name appears in Klestadt's Australian Army record as his next of kin, in 2005 Klestadt informed the author that Williams was 'quite a bit older and we had nothing in common'. He also revealed that although they worked together in Tokyo on war crimes investigations, 'we never saw eye to eye'.
9 This account of Klestadt's postwar transfer to Japan and recruitment into 2 Australian War Crimes Section was provided by him to the author in May 2005.

Chapter 18

1 This death sentence was apparently never confirmed by the Australian Adjutant-General.
2 See Reeson (2000) for more detail of the approaches by the families to External Territories.
3 In the second half of 1946, when civilians were permitted to return to New Ireland Moya Chadderton returned with her husband Ted Carter. Together they

Endnotes

conducted an extensive search for her father. In the course of this there were provided with many hopeful leads by Melanesians and others who claimed to possess useful information. Moya was not to discover the truth about Claude's disappearance for almost another thirty years.
4   Original held by the author.
5   NAA Series MP742/1 File No. 336/1/1601. Tamura's interview by Backhouse in October 1946 appears to have assisted Tamura much more than it assisted Australian War Crimes Section. Again working through an interpreter, Junso Higiri, Backhouse was at a tremendous disadvantage. By introducing the red herring of the 'mass grave', Backhouse handed the initiative to Tamura, and simultaneously aroused the later interest of both the Directorate of Prisoners of War and Internees and 2 War Crimes Section, who mistook the information about the mass grave to be an established fact.

Chapter 19

1   Because of its close proximity to the Imperial Palace the Meiji Building had been spared destruction by wartime USAAF bombing, and was one of the few modern office buildings still standing in Tokyo at the end of the war.
2   Sometimes he signed as 'D. Beresford Goslett'.
3   As described to the author by Albert Klestadt, 2005.
4   Klestadt describes this in his 1959 book. Reverend Kentish met his end at the hands of the Japanese after the coastal vessel he was travelling in off Arnhem Land was sunk by a Japanese seaplane. The aircraft landed, took Kentish and other survivors on board and returned to its base in the Kei Islands, where Kentish was interrogated, beaten and beheaded. As a result of Australian enquiries the Japanese administrator responsible was traced, tried and eventually hanged.
5   2 Australian War Crimes Section had received reports of numerous actual and presumed executions of civilians, sometimes singly and sometimes in small groups, by the Japanese throughout eastern New Guinea, in Bougainville and in the Solomon Islands.
6   This detailed account of the voyage of the *Kowa Maru* and *Kokai Maru* from Japan to Rabaul and then to their sinking is reconstructed by the author from reports of interrogation of a number of survivors in NAA Series MP742/1 File 336/1/1601.
7   ibid.
8   It is a mystery why these *Kokai Maru* survivors who had been living in Kavieng were not included in the conspiracy. Their presence was either completely overlooked by Tamura and his officers or, as merchant mariners, they could not be entrusted with a navy secret.
9   NAA Series MP742/1 File 336/1/1601.
10 Records of Klestadt's January 1947 interrogations exist in NAAMP 742/1.
11 In 2000 Klestadt informed the author that it was very obvious by early 1947 the Kavieng sailors were lying about the internees.

12   NAA MP742/1/336/1/1444 contains top secret minutes and signals between 2 Australian War Crimes Section, the Directorate of Prisoners of War and Internees in Melbourne, and the Director of Naval Intelligence.

Chapter 20

1   The execution of the German priests appear to have hardly rated a mention in all the Australian enquiries, and they were not included in the eventual charges brought against the Kavieng Japanese. The *Australian War Crimes Act* only related to incidents involving Australian, British or Allied nationals.
2   The author has assumed that this meeting, or meetings, occurred. There is considerable evidence in NAA MP375/14 Item WC41 and in NAA MP742/1/336/1/1444 of much correspondence and cooperation between the Department of External Territories and the Department of the Army.
3   ibid.
4   ibid, NAA MP375/14.
5   ibid.
6   Original held by the author.
7   Copy of the original certificate held by Geraldine Condron.

Chapter 21

1   This information is contained in a memorandum from the Japanese Government Central Liaison Office to the General Headquarters of SCAP in Tokyo. NAA MP742/1 336/1/1444 Kavieng.
2   Jim Ridges has provided information that the English-language interpreter, Masayoshi Oyabu, who was used by the Japanese navy in Kavieng in 1942 and 1943, committed suicide in Japan on 12 September 1948.
3   This detailed account of the interrogation of Jitsukawa was related to the author by Albert Klestadt in 2000.
4   According to Klestadt, these were his exact words.
5   *Summary of Examination of Jitsukawa*, Kinjiro, NAA MP742/1 File 336/1/1601.
6   The account of this meeting was provided to the author by Mrs Edna Klestadt in November 2005.

Chapter 22

1   Many of these 'troublemakers' were leaders of Japan's fledgling Communist movement, who stayed in jail for years until their release after the war, when they became a force in postwar Japanese politics. See Dower (1999).
2   Much of the background information about Sugamo ('Stockade 1' as it was codenamed) comes from a website maintained by US veterans of the Sugamo guard, 1945–52. See website *Sugamo Prison*.

3   *Summary of the Indictment for Class-A War Criminals*, International Military Tribunal for the Far East (IMTFE.)
4   For a detailed assessment of the cost of the war for Japan, see Dower (1999).
5   US procurements of military supplies in Japan for the Korean war saved the Japanese economy and re-established heavy industry.
6   Dower (1999) describes the troupes of famous Japanese comedians, singers, and sports stars who were admitted to Sugamo to 'put at ease' the minds of the war criminals.
7   NAA MP742/1/336/1/1444 *Summary of Examination of Takata, Jutaro*
8   NAA MP742/1/336/1/1444
9   NAA MP742/1/336/1/1444 *Summary of Examination of Yoshino, Shozo*
10 NAA MP742/1/336/1/1444
11 ibid.
12 See Chapter 14.
13 When the author discussed this with him in 2000, Albert Klestadt clearly remembered Tamura's resigned confession of guilt.
14 NAA MP742/1/336/1/1444
15 NAA MP742/1/336/1/1444

Chapter 23

1   For a full account of the Japanese invasion of Hong Kong and aftermath, see Wright-Nooth (1999). George Wright-Nooth was a young British police officer at Hong Kong in 1941, survived internment at Stanley Prison, and went on to become an Assistant Commissioner of Police.
2   The background to this move to Manus, and what transpired there, is described by Ward (1996).
3   In this regard, see the descriptions in Gordon (1978) of the behaviour of Japanese POWs held at the Cowra camp in New South Wales.
4   In terms of Western psychology, the behaviours of Japanese leaders before and during the war can only be described as psychopathological. See Dower (1999: 492–3) for postwar Japanese discussions of this phenomenon.
5   See Dower (1999).
6   See NAA series number B4175/15, *War crimes papers relating to Rabaul and Hong Kong trials (collected by Lt. Colonel John Brock)*. This archive contains extensive background notes about proceedings of the Kavieng trial.
7   Although he had botched his suicide attempt and ended up before the Tokyo War Crimes Tribunal, Tojo became a willing scapegoat, believing that by doing this he could honourably protect Emperor Hirohito by taking all blame for wartime excesses himself.
8   NAA MP742/1 File 336/1/1951.
9   ibid.
10 ibid.
11 ibid.
12 ibid.

13 ibid.
14 Major MacKay asked the question, 'Did any of the internees cry, or scream, or yell out, or make a row at all whilst they were being killed?', to which Horiguchi replied, 'They did not.' NAAB4175/0/13, *Proceedings of a Military Court.*
15 Cross-examined on this point by MacKay, Suzuki stated that he had ordered the barge commanders 'to bury the dead bodies with respect, the way a water funeral is performed by the Japanese Navy which is that after putting the dead bodies into the sea the boat circles three times round the place and during that period everybody on the boat prays'. NAAB4175/0/13, *Proceedings of a Military Court.*
16 A full account of the identity-concealment behaviours of Japanese POWs appears in Gordon (1978).
17 See NAA MP375/14 WC43, statements of Joseph Moni, Anton de Silva and Pusi, made in September 1946 to an Australian Patrol Officer, K.W. Jones.
18 Before the massive bombardment on 20 March 1944, warships of the US Navy had already visited Kavieng three times. On 18 February 23 USN destroyer Squadron bombarded; on 22 February destroyer squadron TG39.4 bombarded; and on 25 February destroyer squadron 12 also delivered a bombardment. However even the firepower of a destroyer squadron using 5-inch guns cannot compare to the firepower or psychological shock of the battleships and aircraft carriers of TF37 on 20 March. The Japanese and local residents, from the perspective of many years later, could easily have mis-remembered that there had been four separate bombardments, and that execution of the internees was associated with the last and greatest.
19 Was this because by late 1947 the US navy was beginning to be uncooperative in providing 2 Australian War Crimes Section with their detailed records?
20 See *Chronology of USAAF Operations*, February-April 1944.

Chapter 24

1 NAA MP742/1 File 336/1/1951.
2 ibid.
3 ibid.
4 ibid.
5 ibid.
6 ibid.
7 ibid.
8 ibid.
9 NAA MP 742/1/336/1/1601 *War Crime Uncovered Twenty Months After War's End*
10 Although there is a copy of this press clipping in the Australian Archives files, the actual newspaper is not identified. The author has assumed it was either the Melbourne *Sun* (or the Melbourne *Herald*), partly because Army Headquarters was in Melbourne, and partly because the *Sun* was particularly active reporting war crimes.

11 Later in 1948 Yoshino, Mori, Mochizuki and Suzuki, were re-interrogated in Stanley Prison regarding the involvement of Ichinose, Hiratsuka and Sanagi, with mixed results. Yoshino alone accused all three of involvement, and twice repeated his claim that Sanagi 'had ordered' him to invent the cover-up. Nothing was ever done with this information.
12 NAA MP 742/1/336/1/1601, where there is considerable correspondence about this matter.
13 At the request of the Australian government, the British eventually extended this occupancy until November 1948. See Ward (1996).
14 ibid.

Chapter 25

1 Klestadt's business, Scrivenor-Klestadt, specialised in the export of Australian minerals, metals and chemicals to Asia.
2 Klestadt became a member of the Royal Yacht Club of Victoria in 1963, and served as Commodore for two years (see Sabey, 2006).
3 See Paul Hasluck's unpublished AWM Series 68, item 3DRL 8052/122 notes. The anecdote was confirmed by Klestadt to the author in 2000, when he furnished additional details.
4 For detailed accounts and impressions of the discreet amnesties arranged for war criminals, see Dower (1999) and Ward (1996).
5 See Dower (1999).
6 NAA records show that in late 1948 Yoshino, Mori, Mochizuki and Suzuki were still being held in Stanley Prison in Hong Kong, controlled by the British government. It is not known if they were released from Stanley or from a Japanese-controlled prison.
7 For details see Dower (1999) and Stuart Stein's *Web Genocide Documentation Centre*.
8 In a speech on the fiftieth anniversary of the Japanese capitulation in 1995, Prime Minister Tomiichi Murayama said that Japan had followed a mistaken national policy of colonial rule and aggression that caused tremendous damage and suffering to the people of many countries, in particular those in Asia. He said, 'In the hope that no such mistake be made in the future, I regard, in a spirit of humanity, these irrefutable facts of history, and express here once again my feelings of deep remorse and state my heartfelt apology.' In a speech before the Asia-Africa summit in Jakarta in April 2005, Prime Minister Junichiro Koizumi said, 'In the past, Japan, through its colonial rule and aggression caused tremendous damage and suffering to the people of many countries, particularly to those of Asian nations. Japan squarely faces these facts of history in a spirit of humility.'
9 Takeyama's novel is set in Burma, Ooka's in the Philippines, and Endo's deals with the frightful activities of wartime Japanese medical experimenters who used living prisoners as 'laboratory materials'.

10 In her 1960s books Mary Murray always referred to Jack as 'Peter'. The author read *Escape a Thousand Miles to Freedom* many years ago, and had no idea he was reading about his own uncle.
11 For a more detailed explanation, see the later description in this chapter and note 11 below.
12 The author remembers as a child his mother telling him that her brother had been 'shot dead by Japanese'. Ruth Griffin believed he had drowned on the *Montevideo Maru*, as for a long time did the author when he discovered from Aplin (1982) there were two Griffins on the ship's passenger list (as it turned out, one was a member of 2/22 Battalion). It was not until 1994 when Tom Hall located J.K.V. Griffin in an NAA Kavieng list that Jack's true story could begin to be told.
13 See AWM Series 68, item 3DRL 8052/122.
14 The two Australian battalions and other forces deployed to Ambon (2/21 Battalion AIF, 'Gull Force') and Dutch Timor (2/40 Battalion AIF, 'Sparrow Force') were abandoned along with 2/22 Battalion ('Lark Force') and 1 Independent Company in eastern New Guinea. Part of Sparrow Force which moved into Portuguese Timor was eventually rescued. For more detail about the Sparrow Force disaster, see Henning (1995).

Abbreviations

AIF	Australian Imperial Forces
ANGAU	Australia-New Guinea Administrative Unit
AWM	Australian War Memorial
CWGC	Commonwealth War Graves Commission
FELO	Far Eastern Liaison Office
HMAS	His Majesty's Australian Ship
HQ	Headquarters
ICRC	International Committee of the Red Cross
IJA	Imperial Japanese Army
IJN	Imperial Japanese Navy
MP	military policeman
NAA	National Archives of Australia
NBF	Naval Base Force (IJN)
NGR	Naval Garrison Unit (IJN)
NGVR	New Guinea Volunteer Rifles
PNG	Papua New Guinea
POW	Prisoner of war
PWB	Psychological Warfare Branch (US Army)
PWS	Prisoners' Welfare Section
RAAF	Royal Australian Air Force
RAN	Royal Australian Navy
USAAF	United States Army Air Force
USMC	United States Marine Corps
USNHC	United States Naval Historical Center
USN	United States Navy

References

Interviews

With Mr Albert Klestadt at the Australian Archives, Melbourne, 20 August 2000. On that occasion an NAA archivist, Andrew Griffin, had retrieved all of the original government archival material about the Kavieng massacre, and the author spent an interesting two hours going through the material with Mr Klestadt, still spritely and trim, although 86 years of age.
With Mrs Moya Carter (nee Chadderton), in Brisbane, 18 August 2006.
By telephone with Mrs Gwen Diercke in Leura, 22 August 2006.

Archival sources

Australian War Memorial Series 54, item 183/5/22, *Interview with Evacuees – JH McDonald, H.J. Murray et al. Evacuated from New Ireland-New Britain-Kavieng, 1942*
Australian War Memorial series 54, item 417/1/4, *Reports from 1 Australian POWs Contact and Enquiry Unit (Includes: missing RAN personnel; Fukuoka, Yokakama, Hokkaido, Konan PW Camps; crashed aircraft in Talaud Sangihe Group; missing Allied PWs, Ambon, Bunka Camp; destruction of records; and Montevideo Maru)*, (Sep-Nov 1945)
Australian War Memorial Series 54, item 1010/4/21, *War Crimes and Trials-Affidavits and Sworn Statements 1945–47*, Statement by Rev. Sister M. Brigitta
Australian War Memorial Series 68, item 3DRL 8052/122, *Part 4, Official History, 1939-45 War: records of Paul Hasluck Volume II, source materials including a rejected appendix titled 'The Executions on Kavieng South Wharf'*
Commonwealth of Australia, *Parliamentary Debates*, 11 April to 23 July 1946, 10 Geo. VI, Vol. 187, pp. 1441–2886, 17th Parliament, 3rd session.
Commonwealth War Graves Commission, *Civilian War Dead in Papua New Guinea WW2*, undated, London.

References

National Archives of Australia, Series A7030 Item 11, *New Guinea Civilians and New Guinea Missionaries previously reported missing, now lost at sea*

National Archives of Australia, series number B4175/13, *Proceedings of a Military Court held at Hong Kong, December 1947*

National Archives of Australia, series number B4175/14, *Part transcript of the trial including command structures*

National Archives of Australia, series number B4175/15, *War crimes papers relating to Rabaul and Hong Kong trials* (collected by Lt. Colonel John Brock)

National Archives of Australia, series number B6121/98, *Japanese operations in the occupation of Kavieng*

National Archives of Australia, series number B6121/3/99, *Kavieng: SOPAC plan for capture*

National Archives of Australia, series number MP375/14, item WC41, *New Ireland—execution of civilians at Kavieng*

National Archives of Australia, series number MP375/14, item WC43, *Missing Civilians and Allied Airmen, Kavieng*

National Archives of Australia, series number MP742/1, item 336/1/1444, *'Akikaze' Massacre – reported killing of civilians 18.3.43 (also murder of internees at Kavieng)*

National Archives of Australia, series number MP742/1, item 336/1/1951, *War Crimes—Rear Adm. Tamura Ryokichi (Massacre of Australian civilians at Kavieng)*

National Archives of Australia, series number MP742/1, item 336/1/1601, *War Crimes—Murder of 32 civilians at Kavieng*

National Archives of Australia, series number PP50/7/WW1957/352, *Kowa Maru crew lists of ships*

Correspondence

Julie Gleaves, archivist, Westpac Banking Corporation, Sydney, 28 August 2000, to the author, Bank of NSW personnel and payroll records of Jack Griffin, 1927-1939

Jack Griffin to Alison Griffin, 1 December 1938

Jack Griffin to Alison Griffin, 6 March 1940

Jack Griffin to Alison Griffin, November 1941

Jack Griffin to Alison Griffin, 14 March 1942

James Halligan, Secretary, Department of External Territories, to Alison Griffin, 17 October 1946

James Halligan, Secretary, Department of External Territories, to Alison Griffin, 16 May 1947

Joan Humphreys, archivist, Burns Philp & Co., Sydney, 24 October 1994, to the author, personnel and payroll records of Jack Griffin, 1939–1942, and other materials

Albert Klestadt, 19 May 2005, in which he provides detailed written answers to eleven questions provided by the author

Journal and newspaper articles

'Australian Government will not enquire into Rabaul', *Pacific Islands Monthly*, Volume XVII, No. 7, July 1946

'Civilians missing—fate unknown', *Pacific Islands Monthly*, Volume XVII, No. 1, January 1946

Beaumont, Joan, 'The Allies and the transport of prisoners-of-war by sea', *Journal of the Australian War Memorial*, Issue No. 2, April 1983

'New Guinea's Missing Civilians: news of nearly 700 people now anxiously awaited', *Pacific Islands Monthly*, Volume XVI, No. 2, September 1945

Sabey, Mike, 'Intrepid sailor who found the sea to be kind: obituary for Albert Klestadt', *The Age*, Melbourne, 15 May 2006

Sissons, David, 'Sources on Australian investigations into Japanese war crimes in the Pacific', *Journal of the Australian War Memorial*, Issue No. 30, April 1997

Special correspondent, 'A thousand miles to freedom', *The Sydney Morning Herald*, 10 November 1945

Maps

Cape St George, New Ireland, Papua New Guinea 1:250,000, Joint Operations Graphic, Sheet SB56-3 (Edition 1), Series 1501, Royal Australian Survey Corps, 1976

Kavieng, Sheet 9092 (Edition 1), Series T601, Papua New Guinea 1:100,000 Topographical Survey, Royal Australian Survey Corps, 1975

Namatanai, New Ireland, Papua New Guinea 1:250,000, Joint Operations Graphic, Sheet SA56-14 (Edition 1), Series 1501, Royal Australian Survey Corps, 1976

Papua New Guinea 1:2,600,000, 2nd Edition, South Pacific Maps (Hema Maps), 1992

Rabaul, Sheet 9389 (Edition 1), Series T601, Papua New Guinea 1:100,000 Topographical Survey, Royal Australian Survey Corps, 1976

General sources

Aplin, Douglas, *Rabaul 1942*, 2/22 Battalion AIF Lark Force Association, Melbourne, 1980

Beaumont, Joan, *Gull Force: Survival and leadership in captivity 1941–1945*, Allen & Unwin, Sydney, 1988

Braddon, Russell, *The Naked Island*, Werner Laurie, London, 1952

Bradley, James, *Towards the Setting Sun*, JML Fuller, Wellington NSW, 1984

Burns, Paul, *The Brisbane Line Controversy: Political opportunism versus national security, 1942-45*, Allen & Unwin, Sydney, 1998

Dean, Penrod V., *Singapore Samurai*, Kangaroo Press, Sydney, 1998

References

Dower, John W., *Embracing Defeat: Japan in the wake of World War II*, Norton & Co., New York, 2000

Endo, Shusaku, *The Sea and Poison*, Tuttle, Tokyo, 1958

Falkiner, Suzanne, *Haddon Rig: The first hundred years*, Valadon, Adelaide, 1981

Feldt, Eric, *The Coast Watchers*, Lloyd O'Neill, Melbourne, 1975

Forbes, Cameron, *Hellfire: The story of Australia, Japan, and the prisoners of war*, Macmillan (Pan Macmillan Australia), Sydney, 2005

Foster, Simon, *Assault on the Empire: Okinawa 1945*, Cassell & Co., London, 1994

Fuchida, Mitsuo and Okumiya, Masatake, *Midway: The Japanese story*, Cassell & Co., London, 2002

Gilmore, Allison B., *You Can't Fight Tanks with Bayonets: Psychological warfare against the Japanese Army in the Southwest Pacific*, University of Nebraska Press, Lincoln, 1998

Goodwin, Michael J., *Shobun: A forgotten war crime in the Pacific*, Stackpole Books, Mechanicsburg PA, 1995

Gordon, Harry, *Die Like the Carp! The story of the greatest prison escape ever*, Cassell Australia, Sydney, 1978

Hall, Timothy, *New Guinea 1942–44*, Methuen Australia, Sydney, 1981

Harrison, Courtney, *Ambon: Island of mist*, Harrison, North Geelong, 1988

Hasluck, Paul, *Australia in the War of 1939–1945, series 4—Civil: The Government and the People 1939–1945*, AWM, Canberra, 1952

Hasluck, Paul, *Australia in the War of 1939–1945, series 4—Civil: The Government and the People 1942–1945*, AWM, Canberra, 1970

Henderson, Margaret L., *Yours Sincerely, Tom: A lost child of the empire*, Openbook Publishers, Adelaide, 2000

Henning, Peter, *Doomed Battalion: Mateship and leadership in war and captivity, the Australian 2/40 Battalion*, Allen & Unwin, Sydney, 1995

Hicks, George, *The Comfort Women*, Norton & Co., New York 1994

Holmes, John, *Smiles of Fortune*, Kangaroo Press, Sydney, 2001

Hoyt, Edwin P., *Japan's War: The great Pacific conflict*, Cooper Square Press, New York, 2001

Klestadt, Albert, *The Sea Was Kind*, Kangaroo Press, Sydney, 1959

Lawson, Ted, *Thirty Seconds Over Tokyo*, Pocket Star Books, New York, 2004

Lomax, Eric, *The Railway Man*, Vintage, London, 1996

Long, Gavin, *The Six Years War: A concise history of Australia in the 1939–45 war*, AWM/AGPS, Canberra, 1973

Long, Gavin, *Australia in the War of 1939–45*, Series 1 Army, Volume VI, The New Guinea Offensives, AWM, Canberra, 1961

Lynch, E.P.F., *Somme Mud* (edited by Will Davies), Random House, Sydney, 2006

Macksey, Kenneth, *Military Errors of World War Two*, Cassell, London, 1998

McKernan, Michael, *The War Never Ends: The pain of separation and return*, University of Queensland Press, Brisbane, 2001

McNab, Alexander, *We Were the First: The unit history of No. 1 Independent Company*, Australian Military History Publications, Loftus, 1998

Miller, John, *United States Army in World War II, the War in the Pacific* (especially the volumes Guadalcanal: The First Offensive, MacArthur and the Admiralties, and

Cartwheel: the Reduction of Rabaul), Office of the Chief of Military History, Department of the Army, Washington DC, 1959

Millot, Bernard, *The Battle of the Coral Sea*, Ian Allan Ltd, London, 1974

Morison, Samuel E., *History of United States Naval Operations in World War II*, Vol. 6, Breaking the Bismarcks Barrier 22 July 1942 to 1 May 1944, Oxford University Press, London, 1950

Murray, Mary, *Escape a Thousand Miles to Freedom*, Rigby, Adelaide, 1965

Murray, Mary, *Hunted: A coastwatcher's story*, Rigby, Adelaide 1967

Nelson, Hank, *Prisoners of War: Australians under Nippon*, ABC Books, Sydney, 1985

Nikakis, Gillian, *He's Not Coming Home*, Lothian Books, South Melbourne, 2005

Ooka, Shohei, *Fires on the Plain*, Tuttle, Tokyo, 1957

Parkin, Ray, *Out of the Smoke*, Hogarth Press, London, 1960

Ramsay Silver, Lynette, *Sandakan: A conspiracy of silence*, Sally Milner Publishing, Bowral, 1998

Reeson, Margaret, *A Very Long War: The families who waited*, Melbourne University Press, Melbourne, 2000

Ridges, Jim, *People of the Plaque*, self-published, Kavieng, 2002

Rusbridger, James, and Nave, Eric, *Betrayal at Pearl Harbor: How Churchill lured Roosevelt into World War II*, Summit Books, New York, 1991

Smith, David (Mick), 'The Japanese Invasion of Rabaul 23rd January 1942', at website *Lost Lives: The Second World War and the Islands of New Guinea*, <www.jje.info/lostlives.html>

Smith, Jim and McConnell, Malcolm, *The Last Mission: The secret history of World War II's final battle*, Bantam Books, London, 2002

Smith, Michael, *The Emperor's Codes: The breaking of Japan's secret ciphers*, Penguin Books, New York, 2000

Stone, Peter, *Hostages to Freedom: The fall of Rabaul*, Oceans Enterprises, Yarram, 1995

Stripp, Alan, *Code Breaker in the Far East*, Oxford University Press, Oxford, 1989

Takeyama, Michio, *Harp of Burma*, Tuttle, Tokyo, 1966

Tamayama, Kazuo, and Nunneley, John, *Tales by Japanese Soldiers*, Cassell, London, 1992

Tanaka, Yuki, *Hidden Horrors: Japanese war crimes in World War II*, Westview Press, Colorado, 1996

US Naval History Center, *Dictionary of American Naval Fighting Ships*, descriptions of USS *New Mexico* (BB40), USS *Mississippi* (BB41), USS *Idaho* (BB42), USS *Tennessee* (BB43), USS *Manila Bay* (CVE61) and USS *Natoma Bay* (CVE62), Office of the Chief of Naval Operations, Naval History Division, Washington DC, [n.d.]

Ward, Ian, *Snaring the Other Tiger*, Media Masters, Singapore, 1996

Whitecross, Roy, *Slaves of the Son of Heaven*, Kangaroo Press, Sydney, 2000

Wigmore, Lionel, *Australia in the War of 1939–1945*, Series One Army, Volume IV: The Japanese Thrust, Australian War Memorial, Canberra, 1957

Wright-Nooth, George, *Prisoner of the Turnip Heads: The fall of Hong Kong and imprisonment by the Japanese*, Cassell, London, 1994

Websites: general sources

The Australian War Memorial website, <http://www.awm.gov.au/>. A comprehensive collection of documents and images about the Second World War in New Guinea.
Lost Lives: the Second World War and the islands of New Guinea, <http://www.jje.info/lostlives/pub/book.html>. Comprehensive site maintained in Australia by Joanne and Jenny Evans.

US military operations chronologies

USAAF <http://www.usaaf.net/chron/44/mar44.htm>. Provides the entire World War II Chronology of Air Operations 1942–45 from the Center for Air Force History, Washington DC, 1991
US Marine Corps <http://www.ibiblio.org/hyperwar/USMC/I/USMC-I-A-B.html>. Chronology of USMC Operations in World War II
US Navy <http://www.ibiblio.org/hyperwar/USN/>. The Official Chronology of the U.S. Navy in World War II, Robert J. Cressman, Contemporary History Branch, Naval Historical Center, Washington DC, 1999

Websites: specific information

FELO, <http://home.st.net.au/~dunn/index.htm> <www.ozatwar.com>. A very comprehensive Australian site about the Second World War which contains text and images about the Far Eastern Liaison Office. Maintained by Peter Dunn.
Friendly Fire website, <http://www.ww2pacific.com/friendly.html>. Chronicles hundreds of mainly US friendly-fire incidents in World War II.
Imperial Japanese Navy, <http://homepage2.nifty.com/nishidah/e/index.htm>. Maintained by Hiroshi Nishida.
Kavieng, <http://www.pacificwrecks.com/>. Pacific Wrecks contains a vast quantity of postwar text and images of wartime locations in the Pacific, including a good section on Kavieng. There are numerous underwater images of WWII wrecks.
Montevideo Maru, <http://www.montevideomaru.info/>. Maintained by Rod Miller.
Papua New Guinea Association of Australia (PNGAA), <http://www.pngaa.net/about.htm>. This site contains a number of interesting historical items and images.
Sugamo Prison, <http://www.geocities.com/sugamo_prison/geobook.html>. Maintained by veterans of the US 35th AAA and 579th AAA, originally assigned to the Prison, later assimilated into the US Eighth Army.
War Crimes <http://www.ess.uwe.ac.uk/genocide/>. This is the Web Genocide Documentation Centre maintained by Dr Stuart Stein of the University of the West of England.
Winterbotham, John, maintains a set of undated web pages relating to the Japanese occupation of New Guinea including a short history and nominal roll of the New Guinea Volunteer Rifles. <http://www.angelfire.com/alt2/prisonersofwar/ngvrnominalroll.html>

Index

In this index of names and subjects illustrations including photos and maps are indicated by *page numbers in italic font*. Standard military abbreviations are used.
'*See*' and '*see also*' references will guide the reader to the preferred heading used.

Abbot, Pastor EM, 261
Adams, HA, 254
Admiralty Islands, 4, 12, 24, 68, 71, 73
air raids, 30, 32–33, 71–76, *78*, 93–94
Akikaze, 64–65, 118, 138, 156, 161, 171, 272
    witness, 168, 177
Albatross Passage, 35, 241
Allen, AG, 254
Allen, WE, 254
Alley, Rev DC, 261
Allied Intelligence Bureau, 120
Allied landings
    island–hopping, 83, 85–86, 112
    rumours, 81, 217
Allied Occupation Forces in Japan, 126, 192, 194
Allied prisoners killed on Japanese ships, 115–116
Ambon, 28, 265, 266, 284
Anderson, Maj Gen W, 219, 222–223
Anthony, HL, xii,263
apologies, Japan, 231–232, 237–238, 283
Ash, NE, 254
Ashby, SA 'Stan', 42, 254, 267
Atherton, JM, 254
Atkins, Pastor A, 35, 37, 266
Atkinson, W, 255
Attwood, W 'Bill', 48, 56, 62, 106, 216, 241, 249

Australia, SE Asia PNG map, *2*
Australia–New Guinea Administrative Unit (ANGAU), 135–138, *139*
Australian Archives Act 1983, 237
Australian Army, 28, 43, 112–114
    1 Independent Company Commandos, 24, 28, 30, 284
    Buka Island airfield, 265
    Namatanai station, 37
    prisoners of war, 33
    retreat from Kavieng, 33, 38, 40
    6th Division, 150, 153
    8th Division surrender, 28
    11th Division, 113, *115*, *155*
    Eighth Military District, Rabaul, 171
    Infantry
        65th Battalion, 151–153
        Battalion 2/21 (Gull Force), 266, 284
        Battalion 2/22 (Lark Force), 24, 28, 33, 37, 267, 284
        Battalion 2/40 (Sparrow Force), 284
        New Guinea Infantry Battalion, *155*
    Papua 1942 land campaigns, 53
Australian Army, Adjutant–General, 126
Australian Army, Directorate of Prisoners of War and Internees, 126, 134–135, 161, 221
    see also Australian War Crimes Section
Australian Army, Headquarters, 171, 223–224

292

Index

Australian Army, Intelligence Corps, 150
Australian Army, Judge Advocate–General, 219, 221–223
Australian Army, Legal Corps, 208
Australian Army Medical Corps, 57
Australian Army nurses, 30, 43–44, 128, 162, 267, 278
Australian Freedom of Information Act 1982, 237
Australian government
  abandons New Guinea, 235–236, 265, 272, 284
  accepts cover–up story, 159, 178–181
  invasion contingency plans, 23
  secrecy, 125, 156, 180–181, 235, 236
Australian Labor Party *see* Labor Party
Australian Mandated Territory of New Guinea, xii, 5, 18–19, 23, 66
Australian Military Courts, 126, 127, 161, 173, 219
  Hong Kong, 201, 204–205, *206*, *207*, 218
Australian *National Security (Inquiries) Regulations*, 126
Australian *National Security (War Deaths) Regulations*, 156, 178, *179*, 180
Australian Naval and Military Expeditionary Force, 5, *9*, 48
Australian Navy
  coastwatch unit, 37, 55, 141
  intelligence gathering, 140–142
Australian Parliament
  Australian War Crimes Act, 126, 151, 174
  parliamentary enquiry, xii–xv
Australian Red Cross, 132
Australian Returned Servicemen's League, 9
Australian servicemen, Pacific campaign, 69
Australian War Crimes Act, 126, 151, 174, 202, 205, 280
  death penalty, 126
  rules of evidence, 126
Australian War Crimes Section, 126–128, 152, 226
  1 Singapore, 126, 208
  1 Hong Kong, 126, 204–205, 208
  2 Tokyo, 126, 133–134, 152, 159–161, 170–171, 176, 178, 226
    arrests and interrogation, 194, 210
    German missionaries, 279
    press release, 202–203
    international pressure, 129–131, 187, 226
    Rabaul Military Court, 127, 154–155, 158
    Wewak, 127

Australian War Memorial historians, *230*, 236–237
Azuma, Eng Hd, 102, 184

Backhouse, Lt J, 158 159, 170, 279
Baia Plantation, 55
Bangka Island, 128, 162
Bank of NSW, Rabaul, 17–20, *18*, *19*
Banks, E, 255
barges, Japanese *see* Japanese Navy, ships, barges
Barnes, CW, 255
Bath, VG, 255
Beazley, SC, 262
Beck, NR, 255
Belik Plantation, 41, 57, 245, 251
Bell, DJ 'Don', 255
Bell, JW, 41, 56–57, 106, 241, 249, 255, 267
Benham, GW, 36, 37, 41, 55, 138
Benson, Lt–Col SJ, *137*
Beresford–Goslett, Lt–Col D *see* Goslett, Lt–Col D
Berman, RA, 255
Bismarck Archipelago, 4, *67*, 68, 88
Bismarck Sea, 4, 12, 64, 70–71, 150, 175, 205
Bo village, 138
Boang Island, 37
'boat people', 34
Bopire Plantation, 49, 268, 277
Bougainville, 24, 37, *40*, 70, 79, 85, 175
Bowman, H, 255
Box, WC 'Bill', 35, 255
Bremerhaven, 10
Brennan, Rev Br CA, 262
Brett, GL, 255
Brigitta, Sr M., 269, 270
Brinston, HGW, 255
'Brisbane Line', xii, xiii, 263
Brock, Lt Col JT, 206, 208–209, *210*
Brown, RAL, 255
Brown, TG, 255
Bruckshaw, AF, 255
Buka Island, 37, 265
Bulu–Logon Plantation, 41, 243
Buna, 37, 70
Bunny, J, 255
Burke, JD, 255

Burns Philp & Co Ltd, vii, 9–10, 25, 38, 56, 237, 264
  plantations, 22, 40–42, 48, 243–244, 246, 257–258, 260
  warehouses, 30, 40, 255
Bye, EC, 255

Cameron, A, 255
Campbell, CJ, 255
Cannon, CF, 255
Cape Metlik, 37
Cape St George, 38
Cape Sivisat, 106, 239
Cape Wom, *152*, *153*
Carlysle, L, 255
Carolina Maru, 10–11
Caroline Islands, 10, 70, 264
Carpenter WR & Co, 10, 30, 40, 255–256
  plantations, 40, 42–43, 137–138, 247, 255–258, 264
Carr, LAA, 255
Carson, L, 255
Carter, Lt R, *206*, 208
Casablanca Conference, 68
Catholic Church, 174
Catholic missionaries, 7, 9–10, 30, 38, 43, 54–56, 58, 135, 174–175, 247–248, 262
  see also German missionaries
censorship, Australian government, 127
Chadderton, CG, *25*, *32*, 41, *49*, 57, 106, 241–242, 249, 267
Chadderton, M, 156, 232–233, 242, 267, 278
Chambers, KW, 35, 266
Changi Prison, 209
Chifley, Rt Hon JB (Ben), xi–xv
China, 23, 51, 54
Chinatown, Kavieng, 10, 20, 56, 177
Chinese, 20, 30, 264
  children executed on *Akikaze*, 64
  killed by Japanese, 54
  on New Ireland, 10, 61
  war crimes trials, 127, 154–155, 171
  witnesses, 177, 267, 271
Choiseul, 85
Christianity, 7
civilians, 30, 49–51, 127, 132, 163, 175
  evacuation plans for, 24–25, 29–30
  house arrest, 54
Clark, I, 255
Clark, RL, 255

Clemens, Capt M, 272
Clunn, C, 255
'Co–Prosperity Sphere', 61, 69, 193
coastwatchers, 35–38, 46, 54–55, 67, 138, 141–142, 242, 257, 266–267, 272
Cobb, F, 42, 256
codebreakers, 50–52, 173, 268
Coe, PER, 256
Collett, T, 35, 37, 262, 266
'comfort women', 271, 276
Commonwealth War Graves Commission, 216, 247, 248
  Civilian War Dead in Papua New Guinea, 249–252
Considine, LA, 256
conspiracy and cover–up, 99–100, 111, 113–121, 171–172, 190–192, 199, 211, 226
Consterdine, CR 'Frank', 43–44, 46, 106, 242, 249
Cook, C, 35, 37
Cook, RE, 256
Coomber, A, 256
Cooper, Dr RW, 256
Coote, P, 256
copra, 5–8, *6*, 10, 26, 30–32, 35
  Japanese requisition, 47
Coral Sea, 12
  Battle of, 51, 53
Corlass, AJ, 177–178
Country Party, xi, 263
Craig (Civilian War Dead), 249, 252
Crocker, MC, 256
Cruise, JB, 256
Curtin, John, xi

Darlam Plantation, 41, 241
Davies, EL 'Lon', 38, 40, 42, 48, 56, 57
  death, 16, 106, 242, 249
Davies, R, 256
Daymond, JE, 256
de Silva, A, 111, 269, 275, 282
death of victims
  Certificate of Presumed Death, 156–158, *157*, 175, 178, 224, 240
  legal and financial issues, 156, 174–175
Department of the Army, 142, 175–176, 219
Department of External Affairs, 178
Department of External Territories, 5, 7, 140, 142, 263
  case closed, 187

Certificates of Presumed Death, 156–158, *157*, 175, 178, 224, 240
enquiries, 132, 155–156, 175–177, 235
evacuations, compulsory, 29
letters to families, 178, *179*
missing civilian internees, 216, 247, 253
relatives seek answers, 132–134, *157*, 174–175, 232–233
secret enquiry, xv
see also Halligan, J
Diercke, R, 137–138, *141*, 268, 277
disinformation, 119, 120–121
District Officers, 29–30, 37, 38, 261
see also patrol officers
Djaul Island, 257, 259
Dockrill, W, 256
Dodd, H, 256
Doi Island, 140, 158, 163
'Doolitttle raid', 51, 91, 129, 268
Downs, J, 256
Doyle, HG 'Harry', 35, 256
Doyle, N, 256
Drane, CT, 256
Dutch East Indies, 5, 28, 128
Duus, WL, 256

Earl, RB, 256
Eather, Maj–Gen K, 113, *115*
Edmago Island, 106
Edwards, JH, 256
Edwards, MS 'Murray', 38, 256, 267
Eglinton, AM, 256
Eickstedt Passage, 106, 239
Einsiedel, ER, 256
Emirau Island, 35, 262, 266
 US occupation, 85, 86–90, 92, 198–199
Emperor of Japan see Hirohito, Emperor
escape attempts, 32, 34–38, 41–42, 44–46, 48, 255–256, 258–261, 266–267
European Enemy Aliens, 56, 241
evacuation, 24–25, 29–33, 38, 237
 exclusions, 30
 women and children, 29–33
Evans, TE, 256
executions, 28, 54–55, 102–107, 118, 138
 Australian army nurses, 128, 162
 Australians executed as spies, 55
 lies and cover-up, 99–100, 114, 116–119
 Tamaru's secret orders, 97–99, 112, 114
 witnesses, 111, 136, 142
 see also Nago Island; Kavieng massacre

Falkiner, FSB, 13, 17
families see relatives
Fangelawa Bay, 113, 116, 276
Far Eastern Liaison Office, 120–121, 129, 150, *151*
Fead Plantation, 255
Feldt, Lt Cdr Eric, 141
Field, CR, 256
Filan, SH, 256
Fileba Plantation, 42, 247, 252
Finschafen, 70
Flannagan, Col JW, 221–221
Florance, VA, 256
Fong, Chin Wah, 177
Forsyth, RH, 256
freedom of movement, 47–48, 54
'friendly–fire myth', 114–116, 276
Fuchida, Cdr M, 30
Fulton, H, 257
Funayama, WO T, 60, 270
Furlong, RB 'Bob', 41, 106, 243, 250

Garnett, WFS 'Bill', 41, 57, 63–64, 106, 243, 250
Garrett, T, 257
Gascoigne, CJ, 257
Gascoigne, IN, 257
German Empire in PNG, 5, 7, 8, 10
German missionaries, 9–10, 38, 55–56, 58, 76, 97, 135, 177, 247–248, 271, 273, 280
 Australian disinterest, 174–175, 280
 execution, 106–107, 174–175, 280
 nuns, 43, 55, 60, 135, 269
 send boats for evacuation, 30
Gnair, 37
Goad, JC 'John', 35, 257
Gordon, LL 'Les', 41, 57, 106, 177, 243, 250
Goslett, Lt Col D, 161, *162*, 168, 173, 187, 191, 194–195, 201, 226
 report on civilians on NI, 168, 171, 200–201
Goulburn Island Methodist Mission, 162
Gray, KM, 257
Greater East Asia Co–Prosperity Sphere, 12
Green, AS, 257
Green, ECD, 257
Green Islands, 68, 71, 73
Greenwood, FO, 257
Greenwood, W, 257
Gregory, HA, 257

Griffin, A 'Pat', 14, *14*, 17, 19–20, 25–26, 44–46, *45*, 132, *157*, 158, 178–*179*, 233–235, *234*, 267
Griffin, Adm RM, *88*, 89, 90, 92, 95–96, 97
Griffin, E, 13–14
Griffin family, *14*, 20, 233, *234*
Griffin, G, 13–14, *14*, 17
Griffin, JKV 'Jack', 13–15, *14*, *16*, *21*, 106
 bank clerk, 17, *18*, 264–265
 Burns Philp, 21–22, 25–27, 237, 265
 capture and internment, 48–49, 56, 63, 268
 death, 106, 243, 250
 death certificate, 178–181, *180*
 escape attempt, 40–42, 44–45, 48–49, 267
 family correspondence, 267
 government correspondence, *157*, 178–180
 in Kavieng, 38, 40
 name change, 18–19, 284
 Pacific Islands Monthly listing, 132
 in PNG, 18, 20
Guadalcanal, 53, 67, 70, 84, 89, 90–91, 166, 272
Guinn, Lt–Col HG, *206*, *207*, 208, 218

Hainan Island, 54, 115, 203, 206
Hall, T, viii, 233, 242
Halligan, J, 142, 156–158, *157*, 174–176, 178, *180*, 235
Halsey, Adm. W, 85–86, *87*, 90–93, 112
Hamilton, JE, 257
Hamilton, L, 257
harbour, Kavieng *see* Kavieng Harbour
Hasluck, Sir Paul, 227, 230, 232, 236
Haughey, TF, 247, 249, 250
Havilland, Lt A, 138–140, 170, 277
Hawnt, EM, 257
Hay, Dr A, 257
Haydon, Walter *see* Heydon, Walter
Hemig, Fr J, 248
Heming, H 'Ray', 42, 48, 106, 243–244, 250, 270
Hemming, Horace *see* Heming, H 'Ray'
Hennessy, Fr J, 262
Herket, TH, 257
Hermann, R, 135–136
Heron, WL, 257
Herron, AG, 257
Herterich 'Sailor', executed, 138
Heydon, Walter, 48, 57, 106, 244, 250
Hichitaro, Sub–Lt M, 98, 117, 213

Hiratsuka, SO, 112, 225–226, 283
Hirohito, Emperor, 24, 47, 61, 112, 119, 187, 275
 protected by US, 129–130, 205–207, 228
HMAS *Kiama*, *139*
HMAS *Swan*, 113, *115*, *139*
HMT *Devonshire*, 203
Hogan, G, 257
Holden, H, 257
Holland, HD, 257
Hong Kong, 126, 204–205, 208
Hoogerwweff, J, 257
Horiguchi, WO Y, 98, 103–104, 198, 214, 218–223, 229, 282
Hosking, Dr HC, 257
'hostages to fortune', 34
Houghton, CW, 257
Hughes Rt Hon WM, 6, 8, 264

Ichinose, Lt S, 98, 117, 172, 195, 200–202, 225–226, 283
Imamura, Gen H, 113, 154
Imperial Japanese Army *see* Japanese Army
Imperial Japanese Navy *see* Japanese Navy
International Committee of the Red Cross, 59
International Military Tribunal Far East, 126, 193, 206, 229, 281
internees, 33, 53–55, 271
 moved from Rabaul, 53–54
 repatriation, 113
 request to transfer from Kavieng, 77
 see also Kavieng internment camps; Rabaul internment camp
'island bypass strategy', 83, 85–86, 112
Ito, Maj–Gen T, 111, 113, *115*, 154, 197, 216
Ives, G (Diercke), 156, 232–233, 256, 265
Ives, VGLN, 48–49, 57, 63, 106, 241, 244, 250
Iwaoka, PO T, 60, 270

Japan, 23–24
 claims New Guinea, *6*, 11, 273
 military intelligence, 11, 12
 suspicion of all foreigners, 54
 trading with New Ireland, 10
 victory at any cost, 70
Japan, post–war, 187, 193–194, 211
 demilitarising and democratising, 129–131

Index

Japanese Army, 24, 33, 70
  3rd Btn 144th Inf Reg, 265
  Army Brigade Group, Namatanai, 44, 111
Japanese Army Air Force, 33, 56, 163
  evacuation from Kavieng, 70, 72
Japanese civil administrators, 48, 267
Japanese civilian contractors, 33
Japanese Field Service Code, 192–193
Japanese forces
  conditions in field, 85, 150
  defeat, 52, 67–68, 70, 79–80
  dishonesty from superiors, 120, 150
  imprisoned following trials, 127
  orders and responsibility, 195, 206–214, 228–229
  repatriation, 118, 129, 135, 154, 161, 163
  self–sacrifice philosophy, 81
Japanese High Command, 70, 85
  secrecy, 52, 125–126
Japanese language, 47, 55
Japanese military code, 163, 205–206, 215
Japanese military police *see* Kenpeitai
Japanese Navy, 24, 33, 60–61, 70, 77, 270, 319
  14th Naval Base Force, 60–61, 63, 70, 74–76, 112, 194
  and Kavieng massacre, 111, 170
  structure and chain of command, 182–184, 191, 198
  83rd Naval Garrison Unit(NGU) Kavieng, 60–61, 74–78, 86, 111–112, 158
  and Kavieng massacre, 117–118, 170–171, 196, 226
  Land Defence Party, 98, 190, 195–196
  Sea Defence Party, 98, 195
  Security Detachment Hq., 98–99
  structure and chain of command, *164*, 182–184, 191, 275
  Headquarters South–East Area Naval Fleet, Rabaul, 60, 77, 111, 116, 170
  cover–up, 114, 158, 170–171, 226
  Kavieng investigations, 185
  Maizuru Special Naval Landing Force, 33
  ships
    aircraft carriers
      Akagi, 30, 52, 265
      Shokaku, 30, 52
      Soryu, 30, 52, 265
      Zuikaku, 30
    barges, 98, 102–106, *105*, *139*, 199, 275

    crews, 102, 104, 106, 184–191, 195–196, 226
  cargo vessel
    Choryu Maru, 74
    Kashi Maru, 72
    Nichiai Maru, 71
    No.1 Shinto Maru, 72
    No. 9 Tokuyama Maru, 74
    Sanko Maru, 72
    Shinkiku Maru, 72
    Taisyo Maru, 72
    Tatsugiko Maru, 74
  cargo/passenger vessel
    Kokai Maru, 72–73, 116–118, 155–156, 160, 163, 165–166, 169–173, 178, 182, 184, 272
    Kowa Maru, 72–73, 116–118, 135, 155–156, 158, 160, 163, 165–167, 169–173, 178, 182, 184, 197, 203, 223–224, 226, 272
    Naguara, 72, 73
  cruiser *Mikuma*, 52
  destroyer, *Akikaze*, 64–65, 118, 138, 156, 161, 168, 171, 177, 272
  minelayer, *Natsushima*, 74
  submarine chasers, 71–72, 74, 165
Japanese Navy proclamations, 47, 268
Japanese Navy records, 59, 128, 165, 182, 215, 276
Japanese Navy regulations, 214
Japanese on New Ireland, 47, 53, 59
  after US bombardment, 97
  military personnel, 33, 112
Japanese Prisoner of War Information Bureau, 270
Japanese prisoners of war, 281
  early release, 228
  identifying, 129, 215, 282
Japanese student–tourists, 11, 12
Java, 28
Jervis, CC, 257
Jitsukawa, Seaman K, 102, 184, 188–191, 198
Jones, KW, 282

Kabien (Japanese) *see* Kavieng
Kai, Lt Y, 168
Kairiru Island, 64, 138
Kalili Harbour, 42, 44, 243
Kalili Plantation, 42–44, 46, 49, 56, 244–245, 251–252, 268

Kambe, PO R, 102, 184, 195, 200
Kamiraba Plantation, 41, 243, 250
Kanam Plantation, 254
Kapsu Plantation, 41, 241
Karu Plantation, 41, 246, 251
Kasuka, Vice–Adm J, 118, 154, 155, 168
Katu Plantation, 41, 57, 247, 252
Kaut Harbour, 33, 38, 40, 257
Kavieng, 3–9, *11*, 156, 238
   evacuation, 29–30, 33
   Japanese air attacks on, 265
   Japanese air force withdrawal, 70
   Japanese garrison 83rd NGU, 60–61, 74–78, 86, 111–112
   repatriation, 161
   Japanese occupation, xv, 12, 30–33, *31*, 40, 42
   surrender, 216
   trading companies, 10
   US air raids, *72*, 73–76, *74*, *75*, 92–94
   US bombardment, 33, 73, 82, *88*, 89–90, *90*, 92, 94–98, 112, 177, 198–199, 216–217, 274, 282
   US isolation plans, 88
   US recapture plans, 68, 71, 85, 86
Kavieng airfields, 7, 30, 33, 69–70, 97
Kavieng Catholic Mission, 56, 248
Kavieng gaol, 55
Kavieng garage, 48, 56, 62
Kavieng harbour, xvv, 7, *9*, 12, 30, 68, 97, *99*
Kavieng Hospital, 9, 30, 44, 58
Kavieng Hotel, 62
Kavieng internment camps, 56, 59–65, 138, 267
   conditions, 62–64, 101, 116, 271
   deaths, 58
   guards, 60
   officer responsible, 77
   records, 59, 128, 215
   US bombardment, 97, 98
   see also Kulangit camp; Panapi camp; Panapi Plantation
Kavieng massacre, 102–107
   apologies, 231–232, 237–238
   arrest warrants, 191
   Australian official records, 238
   barge crews, 102, 104, 106, 184–185, 187–191, 195–196, 198
   blindfolding victims, 104
   conspiracy network, 172, 184, 196, 226
   date, 196, 198–199, 275
   deception of internees, 99–101, 104
   disposal of bodies, 98, *100*, 104, 106, 128, 214–215, 226
   execution party, 98–101, 106
   identification of victims, 215–216
   investigations, 161, 185, 225–226
   Japanese naval records, 165
   lies and cover–up, 99–100, 111, 113–119, 171–172, 190–191, 199, 211, 226
   Memorial plaque, viii
   murder, 98–99, 103–107, 183, 195–196
   'conducted humanely', 214
   possessions, disposal of, 106, 111, 128, 215
   presumed dead, 155–156, 175
   Tamura's secret orders, 78–81, 97–98, 100, 112, 114
   trial, 201–203, 207–214, 230
   not–guilty pleas, 212–214, 218
   sentences, 218–223, 229–230
victims
   Australian, 240–247
   German, 247–248
witnesses, 111, 117–118, 136–138, 142, 165–168, 176–178, 195–200
Kavieng Sports and Social Club, 9, 38
Kavieng Volunteer Rifles, 24–25, *25*, 57, 270
Kavieng wharves, 99, *99*, 101–106, *103*, 117, 177, 190, 199, 274
   murder scene, 183, 195
Kelly, ETC, 257
Kenpeitai, 54–55, 154–155, 188, 269
Kentish, Rev LN, 149, 162–163, 279
Kimadan Plantation, 40–42, 56, 246, 251
King, Adm. E, 67, 86
King, AJ, 257
Klestadt, Albert, *148*, 149, 227–228, 236, 238, 278
65th Aust. Infantry Btn, 151–153, *152*
Allied Occupation Forces, 151
Australian Army Intelligence Corps, 150
Australian War Crimes Section, 161
escape, 266
Far Eastern Liaison Office, 150–151, *151*
Germany, 143–146
interviews and interrogations, 188–191, 195–202, 270
Japan, 144–145
Kavieng case, 168–169, 171–172, 176, 182–184, 186–187, 224, 226
   prosecution witness, 208

Index

Kowa Maru, 167
  Philippines, 146–148
Kohlstette, Fr H, 55, 248
Koka Plantation, 43, 242, 251
Kokai Maru, 72–73, 116, 118, 155–156, 160, 163, 272
  conspiracy, 172–173, 178, 184
  survivors, 165–166, 169–171, 182
Kokoda campaign, 53, 54
Kokola Plantation, 46, 249
Kokopo, 22, 24
Koluba Plantation, 42, 48, 243, 250
Komalu, 55, 137, 248, 268
Konishiike, I, 208, 209, 214
Kowa Maru, 72–73, 116–118, 135, 155–156, 158, 160, 163, 203, 272
  conspiracy, 169–173, 178, 184, 197, 223–224, 226
  survivors/witnesses, 165–167, 169, 172, 182
Krutzenbichler, Fr J, 55, 248
Kulangit camp, 56–57, 60, 65, 76, 241–247, 270
  abandoned and deserted, 111, 176–177, 216–217, 275
  German missionaries, 58, 76, 97, 177, 247–248, 271, 273
  execution, 106, 174–175
Kurumut Plantation, 48, 49, 57, 244, 250
Kusonose, Col M, 265
Kutscher, Fr P, 55, 248
Kyle, AF 'Bill', 30, *36*, 37–38, 41, 266
  executed on Nago Island, 55, 138

Labor Party, xi, xii–xiii
Lae, 70
Lakaff, Fr J, 56, 248
Lakurafanga Plantation, 48, 56, 245
Lakuramau Mission, internment camp, 55, 135
Lamerika Plantation, 41, 241, 249
Lamussong Catholic Mission, 55, 249
Lamussong Plantation, 41, 243, 249
Lark Force *see* Australian Army Battalions, 2/22 Infantry Battalion
Lavongai Catholic Mission, 56, 248
League of Nations, 5
Lelet Plateau, 42
Lemakot Catholic Mission, 43, 55, 58, 244, 248, 270
  Australian soldiers at, 43–44
  Japanese army base, 43, 44, 112

Lemus Island, 26–27, 30, 48, 237, 243
Levy, PM 'Phil', 38, 40, 42, 48, 56, 106, 244, 251, 268
Lightbody, HL, 42–47, 49, 57–58, 64, 244, 249, 252, 270
Lihir Catholic Mission, 56, 248
Linggood, Rev WLI, 262
Livingstone, WJ 'Bill', 38, 258, 267
Lockhart, J, 258
Lossuk Bay, *137*
Lundin, J, 136
Lussick, A, 25, 267
Luzon Island, 54, 134, 146

MacArthur, Gen D, 67, 68, 84–86, *84*, 113, 129, 194, 207
McArthur, Rev LA, 262
McCheane, G, 258
McCullagh, Rev Fr D, 262
MacDonald J, *25*, 29, 37–38, *43*, 44
  correspondence carried by, 133
  hostility towards, 42, 44
  official report, 38
MacDonald–Murray escape party, 41–42, 44–46, 48, 266–267
McDougall, D, 258
McEvoy, JT, 258
Mackay, Maj A, 208, 214, 217, 224–226, 282
Mackellar, C 'Col', 35, 258
McLaren, TW, 258
Maclean, CHR, 258
McLeod, Maj N, *206*, 208, 209
Macpherson, R, 35, 258
Majuro Atoll, 89, 92, 95
Malalang, 35
Malendok Island, 47, 48, 244
malnutrition, 101
Mandated Territory of New Guinea, xii, 5, 18–19, 23, 66
  see also Papua and New Guinea
Mantle, FW, 258
Manus Island, 64, 127, 138, 247, 250
  Australian Military Court, 205
Maramakas plantation, 254
Marianas, 70
Maritsoan plantation, 259
Marshall Islands, 89, 92, 95
Martin, Fr K, 38, 55, 138
mass graves, 138, 156, 159, 171–173, 176, 279
Mater, CSP, 258

299

Matsumoto, Lt–Cdr. H, 116, 170–172, 197
Maye, Sr D, 30, 43–44, 267, 278
Melanesians, 7, 10, 26, 42, 61
  Christian workers, 271
  Japanese treatment of, 54–55
  on New Ireland, 30, 59, 96–97, 156, 171, 271
Melbourne Sun, 224, 282
Memorial plaque and roll of honour, Kavieng, viii
Menzies, Rt Hon R, xi–xiii
Mermin, TP *see* Mernin, TP
Mernin, TP, 247
Meteinge Plantation, 255
Methodist Missionaries, 7, 149, 261–262, 268
Midway Island, battle, 52, 53, 269
military courts *see* Australian Military Courts
Miller, ER 'Dusty', *25*, 38, 40, 57, 58, 177, 244–245, 249, 251
Millington, B, 258
missionaries, 5, 7, 9–10, 29–30, 38, 47, 64–65, 149, 261–262, 268
  missing, 253–262
  see also Akikaze; Catholic missionaries; German missionaries; Methodist missionaries; Seventh Day Adventist missionaries
Missionaries of the Most Sacred Heart of Jesus (MSC), 10, 55–56, 262, 269
Mitchell, EHF, 258
Mitchell, Maj Gen (US), *40*
Miyamoto, CPO H, 102, 184, 195, 200
Miyazaki, M, 169
Mochizuki, Lt, 98, 100, 195, 200, 218–223, 229
Mollison, Lt PJ, *137*, 142, 269
Moni, J, 282
Montevideo Maru, 52, 54, 115, *134*, 236, 261
  list of passengers, 133–134, 215, 253–262, 267, 277
Moore, RKP, 258
Morell, J, 261
Mori, CPO (Eng) Y, 102, 184
Mori, Lt K, 77, 79, 81–82, 97, 111, 112, 220
  arrest and release, 195, 229
  carried out the order, 196–197, 217
  cover–up, 117, 171–172, 190–191, 198, 274
  promoted, 117
  trial and sentence, 213, 218–223, 227–228
  witness statement, 199, 200
Moro people, 147–150
Moseley, AE, 41, 56–57, 63, 106, 245, 251, 270
MSC *see* Missionaries of the Most Sacred Heart of Jesus (MSC)
Muggleton, HA, 258
Mulligan, EWC, 258
Mulvey, N, 258
Muraoka, WO, 98–99, 103, 104
Murphy, Fr M, 38, 55, 138, 252
Murray, Capt HJ 'Harry', *25*, 37–40, *39*, *40*, 42, 44–46, 267
  letters carried by, 133
  search on NI post–war, 156
Murray escape *see* MacDonald–Murray escape party
Murray, GH, 258
Murray, M, 232, 284
Mussau Island, 35
MV *Induna Star*, 33, 257, 258, 259, 261
MV *Macdhui*, 9
MV *Navanora*, 29–30, 34
MV *Neptuna*, 34
MV *Shamrock*, 34, 35
MV *Zenda*, 34

Nadzab, 70
Nagaura submarine chaser, 165, 166, 169–170, 224, 272
Nago Island, 36, 54, 98–99, *100*, 106
  executions, 55, 136, 138, 142, 177
Nagumo, Vice–Adm, 24, 30, 50, 52, 265–266
Namatanai, 10, *11*, 30, 37, 49, 156, 259, 267
  89 Naval Garrison Unit, 111, 197, 216
  escape group, 41
  surrender and recapture, 86, 113, *115*, 216
Namatanai Catholic Mission, 55, 248
National Archives of Australia, 237, 253
National Security (Inquiries) Regulations, 126
National Security (War Deaths) Regulations, 156, 178, *179*, 180
Naughton, JF 'Jim', 43–44, 46, 56, 62, 106, 216, 245, 251, 270
Naulty, PG, 258
Neuhaus, Fr K, 248
'Neutral European Aliens', 56, 247–248, 273

Index

New Britain, 3, 12, 24, *27*, 30, 68, 243
   civilians missing, 175
   escapees, 35
   Japanese defeat, 70
   POWS & internees moved, 53–54
New Guinea *see* Papua and New Guinea
New Guinea Infantry Battalion, *155*
New Guinea Volunteer Rifles, 24, 57, 242–243, 246
New Guinea Women's Club, 132
New Hanover Island, 7, 38, 56, 71, 136, 142, 169, 177, 248, 255, 259
New Ireland, 3, *6*, 12, *27*
   Australians on, 8, 9, 30
   civilians left behind, 38, 133
   destruction, 156
   evacuation, 29–30, 38
   invasion and occupation, 30, 38, 40, 47, 54, 61–62, 267
   Japanese garrison, 59, 61, 176
   planters & missionaries moved, 54
   population, 7, 30, 59
   US air raids, 73–76, *74*, *75*, *78*, 92
   US invasion, 66, 68–69, 70, 85
   rumours, 100, 112
New Zealand servicemen, 69
Nimitz, Adm C, 86
Nissan Island, 257
Noble, Gen A, 89
NSW Public Trustee, 179
Numanne Island Plantation, 136
Nunan, AC, 258
nuns, 43, 55, 60, 135, 269
nurses, 29–30, 43–44, 267, 278
Nusa Channel, 26, *100*, 242
Nyman, Lt Col, 114

Oakes, Rev WD, 262
Oaten, FE, 258
O'Dwyer, N, 258
Okamura, Y, 169
Oosawa, R, 219
'Operation Forearm', 71, 85–86, 88–90, 93, 216
Ormond, JL, 259
Osaka Shosen Kaisha, 133
Ose, Toshio, 169–170
Ostrom, C 'Charlie', 48, 56, 106, 241
Ostrom, MJ 'Max', 48, 56, 106, 241
Otsu, Y, 166–168
Owen Stanley Ranges, 53
Oyabu, M, 280

Pacific Islands Monthly, 132–134, 252, 277
   list of missing civilians and next of kin, 132–134, 240, 247
Pacific Territories Association, 132
Page, C, 14, 38, 55, 138, 267
Page, HH, 259
Palau, 70, 72, 165–166
Panapai airfield, 33, 68, 97
Panapai camp, 56, 58, 65, 247–248, 270
Panapai Plantation, 56, 65, 177, 247–248, 260, 270
Panaras Plantation, 42, 48, 242, 254, 256
Papua and New Guinea, 4, 5–6, 150, 263–264
   Australian & US campaign, 53, 71
   Germany annexation, 5
   Japanese invasion, 33
Parliament *see* Australian Parliament
Parry, AR, 259
Patlangat Plantation, 254, 260
patrol officers, 37, 176, 256, 282
Paulus, 30
peace treaty, 228
Pearce, EW, 262
Pearl Harbour, 24, 29–30, 50, 86, 146, 268
Pearson, Rev HJ, 262
Peekel, Fr, 270
Penipol Plantation, 41, 241, 249, 255
Perrett, A, 259
Pickering, MB, 259
Pigibut Island, 258
Pinching, E, 259
Pines, CM 'Cedric', 35, 259
Pinikidu Methodist Mission, 268
Pinnock, LJ, 41, 106, 246, 251
planters, 7–9, 21, 38, 41, 237, 264
   imprisoned by Japanese, 48, 269
Plunkett, TM, 259
Poole, Rev JW, 262
Port Moresby, 5, 10, 12, 24, 30, 38, 53
   invasion postponed, 51
   surrender of Japanese, 113
press releases, Army, 223–224
Price, E, 27, 191, 227
Prisoner of War Information Bureau, Tokyo, 59
prisoners of Japanese, 28, 276
   allied bombing of, 115–116
   Australian service men and women, 28, 33
   conditions and treatment, 53, 70, 125, 271
   contingency preparations, 70

executed, 28, 54–55, 102–107, 118, 138
killed on Japanese ships, 115–116
repatriation, 113
secrecy, 125
Prisoners of War, Japanese, 129, 215, 228, 281, 282
Prisoners' Welfare Section list, 132, 240, 247, 252
proclamations on New Ireland, 47, 268
propaganda
  Allied, 129
  Japanese, 119, 120–121
psychological warfare, 120–121, 188–189
Psychological Warfare Branch (US), 120–121, 129
Pusi, 282
Put Plantation, 35, 48, 244, 250

Quang Wha, 37
Quebec Conference, 68

Rabaul, 5, 10, 12, 22, 24, 26, 30, 77–78
  invasion, 33
  Japanese air attacks, 265
  Japanese air forces withdrawal, 70
  Japanese garrison, 33, 79, 111
  US air raids, 77–78, 93–94
  US isolation plans, 88
  US plans for recapture, 68, 85
Rabaul internment camp, 33, 35, 44, 115, 117, 254
  internees moved north, 53–54
Rabaul Military Court, 127, 154–155, 158
Rabaul prison camp for Japanese, 114, 127, 138, 154–155, 267
Rabauru (Japanese) *see* Rabaul
Raff, GS, 259
Rand, D, 259
Rankin, DJ, 259
records, Japanese Navy, 59, 128, 165, 182, 215, 276
Reed, AR, 259
Reeson, M, viii–ix
relatives
  and Australian government, 132–133, 142, 155–156, 174, 232
  legal and financial issues, 156, 175
  letters from department, *157*, 178–180
  search on New Ireland, 156, 232–233
Renton, A, 259
reprisals by Japanese, 51, 142

Returned Sailors', Soldiers' and Airmens' Imperial League, 127–128
Reynolds, JA, 259
Ridges, J, viii, 247–248, 254, 267, 273, 280
Roberts, DL, 35, 259
Robertson, Maj–Gen HCH, 150, 153
Robinson, HE, 259
Robinson, W, 259
Rokyo Maru, 276
Rooty Hill NSW, 16
Royal Australian Air Force, 24
Ryan, WJ, 259

Sacred Heart Mission *see* Missionaries of the Most Sacred Heart of Jesus (MSC)
St George's Channel, 4, 35
St Matthias Group, 35
Sakanoto, Col, 112
Salamaua, 70
Sanagi, Capt S, 114, 116, 118, 154–155, 170, 197, 225–226, 276, 283
Santa Isabel, 85
Sato, Maj, 197
Saunders, FV 'Frank', *25*, 34–35, 48, 259–60, 266
  escape party, 255–256, 258–261
Saunders Wharf *see* Kavieng wharves
Savage, SK, 260
Sawkins, A, 260
Schleutter, Rev Fr K, 55, 248
Schmidt, A, 260
Scott, H, 260
seaplanes, 7, 33, 69
Sedgers, JC, 260
Selapiu Island Plantation, 256
Setchell, WP, 260
Seventh Day Adventist missionaries, 35, 261–262
Shebler, A, 260
Shelton, Rev HB, 262
shipping, 10, 113
signals intelligence codebreakers *see* codebreakers
Simpson Harbour, 33, 78, 115, 163, 165
Simpson, Rev TN, 262
Singapore, 28, 116, 128
slave labourers, 54, 116
Smith, D McD, 260
Smith, J, 260
Smith, JO, 260
Snook, S, 260
soldier–settlers, 7, 8, 264

Solomon, EE, 260
Solomon Islands, 12, 24, 33, 37, 53, 66–68, *67*, 70–71, 150, 264
   US campaign to retake, 83, 84
Solomons, RL, 260
Soubu plantation, 41, 241, 255
South Wharf *see* Kavieng wharves
Spanner, H, 141–142, 241–246, 255, 258–259, 278
Spensley, W, 253, 261
Squires, RT, 260
Staley, WG, 260
Stanfield, E, 25
Stanley Prison, Hong Kong, 201, 204, 222–223, 283
Steffen Straits, 7, 101, 256
Stephen, RJ, 260
Stevens, RH, 260
Stewart, J, 260
Strathearn, AJ, 260
Sugamo Peace Movement, 228
Sugamo Prison, 192, 194, 200, 203, 229–230, 280
suicide by Japanese, 83, 188, 271
Sumuna plantation, 257
surrender by Japanese, 112–*115*, 127, 129–130, 135, *137*, *141*, 150–*153*
Sutherland, Gen R, 86
Suzuki, Ens S, 60, 98–101, 103–104, 111, 172, 190–191, 270
   arrest and release, 195, 229
   cover-up, 196
   interrogation and statement, 20, 183, 198, 200
   trial and sentence, 213–214, 218–223, 282
Symes, HHC, 260

Tabar Island, 38, 48, 55, 138, 246, 251–252, 258
Takada, WO K, 99, 102–103, 106, 184, 223
   suicide, 188
Takata, PO J, 98, 102, 191, 195–196, 198
Takeda, Cdr K, 111, 197
Talmage, JS 'Jack', 38, 55, 138, 252, 267
Tamura, Rear-Adm. R, 78–81, *80*, *136*, 191
   advised of task completed, 111–112
   arrest, 195
   cover-up, 117, 156, 165, 168, 170, 197
   interrogation and testimony, 154–156, 163, 171–172, 178, 185–186, 200–201, 274
   interview by Backhouse, 158–159, 170, 279
   interview by Haviland, 138–140, 170, 277
   promoted, 113
   repatriated to Japan, 159, 165
   secret orders, 97–98, 112, 114, 186, 196–197, 217, 273
   surrender, 113, 118, 276
   trial and sentence, 209, 211–212, 218–223
Tanga Island Group, 48, 244
Tanga Islands Catholic Mission, 55, 248
Taskul Leprosy Centre, 259
Tatau Island, 252
Tereri Plantation, 48, 246
Theresa, 30
Thomas, C, 260
Thompson, LC, 260
Tichener, J, 260
Timor, 28
Tojo, Gen H, 24, 192–193, 211, 229, 281
Tokyo, 51, 69–70
   see also Australian War Crimes Section 2 Tokyo
Tol Plantation, 28, 265
Tomalabat Plantation, 252
Topal, DJ, 48, 56, 65, 106, 177–178, 216, 246, 251
Topal, HJI, 48, 56–57, 64, 106, 177–178, 246, 251, 270
Townsend, HO, 260
Trevitt, Rev JW, 262
Tritton, AJ, 260
tropical diseases, 101, 271
Truk, 163, 169
Tsaliui Island, 38, 58, 245, 251
Tulagi, 37
Tuppal Station, Tocumwal, 14–15
Turnbull, HF, 260
Tynan, J, 260

Ulapatur, 30, 38, 63
Ulul–Nono Plantation, 41, 246, 247, 251
Ungan Island plantation, 40, 242, 249
United Australia Party, xi
United States, 11, 273–274
   post-war occupation of Japan, 129–130, 192
US Army Air Force
   13th-Air Force, 92–93
   air raids, 51, 71–76, *74*, *75*, 78, 273
   Rabaul, 93–94

Kavieng attacks, 86, 92–95, 97, 198, 217
Kokai Maru, Kowa Maru, 165
US Army, Eighth Army, 192
US Joint Chiefs of Staff, 66, 86, 88–89
US Marine Corps, 66, 67
   1st Marine Div, 53, 67
   4th Marine Div, 89
US Navy, 71, 217
   Destroyer Squadron, 72–74
   Kavieng bombardment, 33, 82, 88–90, 95–97
   Naval Base Majuro Atoll, 89, 95
   Pacific Fleet, 50, 52, 85
     Enterprise, 50
     Idaho, 90, 93
     Lexington, 50
     Mississippi, 90
     New Mexico, 91, 92
     Saratoga, 50
     submarine *Sturgeon*, 54, *115*
     Tennessee, *94*, 95
US offensive, 66–76
US servicemen, South-west Pacific, 69
Usien Island, 106
Utsch, Fr F, 56, 248

Van Hertz Dutch Ship, 38
Voss, GHD, 260
Vunapope, New Britain, 30, 266

Waitavalo Plantation, 28, 265
Walker, T, 260
Wallace, TV, 261
Walsh, TR, 261
war crimes
   amnesty and early release, 154, 228–229
   Class A criminals, 131, 192–194, 228–230, 281
   death sentences, 127, 131, 229–230
   investigations, 125–129, 205–206, 228–229

   pressure to wind down, 129–131, 226, 277
   see also Australian War Crimes Section
Ward, Eddie MHR, xii–xv, 5, 156, 263
Warner–Shand, Capt F, 135, *136*, *137*
Washington, HJ, 261
Wat Wat Plantation, 22
Wayne, RN, 261
Webb, Sir W, 126, 206, 208
Wewak, 127, 150
Whitehead, BN, 41, 57, 106, 246, 251
Whiteman, AK, 261
Wilkin, WM 'Bill', 35, 261
Williams, LL, 41, 56, 106, 246, 251, 267
Williams, Maj H, 133–134, 152, 161, 163, 165–166, 171, 173, 187, 191, 215, 224, 270, 277
Wilmot, P, 261
Wilson, Maj, 38, 267
Witu Island, 26
Woodhouse, ESF, 41, 57, 63, 247, 252
Woolcott, LG 'Len', 42, 106, 247, 252
World War I
   ex–soldiers in Kavieng, 56–57, 242–247, 258
   Versailles treaty settlement, 5, 6, 7–8, 11

Yamamoto, Adm I, 50, 51, 52
Yamao, Ch Eng U, 102, 184
   witness to killings, 198–199
Yasukuni Shrine, 229
Yokohama Municipal Crematorium, 229
Yoshino, Cmdr. S, 77, 79–81, 98, 111–112, 114, 116, 191, 216
   arrest and amnesty, 195, 229
   cover–up, 117, 170–172, 196–198, 276
   trial and sentence, 212–213, 218–223
Youlden, R, 261
Young, Sec Lt F, 148–150, *148*

Zunkley, Br H, 56, 248